Pathological
and Normal
Language

Pathological and Normal Language

by Julius Laffal

Atherton Press
70 Fifth Avenue, New York, New York   1965

Pathological and Normal Language

Julius Laffal

Copyright © 1965 by Atherton Press

Copyright under Pan American and Universal Copyright Conventions

All rights reserved. No part of this book may be reproduced in any form, except for brief quotation in a review, without written permission from the publishers. All inquiries should be addressed to:

Atherton Press
70 Fifth Avenue
New York 10011

Library of Congress Catalog Card Number 65–10709
Printed in the United States of America

PSI/BO2420/653

**Atherton Press
Books in the
Behavioral Sciences**

*William E. Henry
General Editor*

Attraction and Hostility
  Albert Pepitone

Contemporary Approaches to
Creative Thinking
  *Howard E. Gruber,
  Glenn Terrell, and
  Michael Wertheimer*, Eds.

Ego & Milieu
  *John Cumming and
  Elaine Cumming*

Immigrants on the Threshold
  Judith T. Shuval

Pathological and
Normal Language
  Julius Laffal

Personality in Middle
and Late Life
  Bernice L. Neugarten

Processes of Aging
  *Richard H. Williams,
  Clark Tibbitts, and
  Wilma Donahue, Editors*

Psychiatric Rehabilitation
  *Denise Bystryn Kandel and
  Richard H. Williams*

Psychotherapy Through
the Group Process
  *Dorothy Stock Whitaker and
  Morton A. Lieberman*

Schizophrenic Women
  *Harold Sampson,
  Sheldon L. Messinger,
  and Robert D. Towne*

The Study of Lives
  Robert W. White, Editor

Taboo Topics
  Norman L. Farberow, Editor

Utopiates: The Use &
Users of LSD—25
  Richard Blum and Associates

Julius Laffal:
A Biographical Sketch

Since getting his Ph.D. in clinical psychology at the State University of Iowa in 1951, Julius Laffal has been actively engaged in clinical treatment and research with disturbed patients and in teaching psychology trainees and psychiatric residents in the Yale University program. His doctoral thesis was in the area of word association disturbances; and in his work with patients he has continued his interest in the nature of language disturbances and his attempts to include such phenomena in a more general psychological theory of language. This has led to a synthesis of ideas from linguistics, psychoanalysis, and experimental psychology. From linguistics Dr. Laffal has drawn on those aspects dealing with language as the basis of a world-view, and with methods of approximating the fundamental contents which underlie the vast diversity of words. With his background of training in psychoanalysis as a research candidate at The Western New England Institute for Psychoanalysis, Dr. Laffal has drawn from Freud's theory of language and from general psychoanalytic theory, to provide a psychodynamic rationale for the idea of language as a structure underlying experience. Experimental studies of association have provided the basic demonstration of the existence of clusters, groupings, and structure in language.

Dr. Laffal is Director of Research, Psychology Service, at the Veterans Administration Hospital in West Haven, Connecticut. He is also Associate Clinical Professor of Psychology (Psychiatry) at Yale University.

To my wife, Flo

An old gentleman in Charles Dickens' *Nicholas Nickleby,* climbing over a wall in order to make love to the neighboring lady, finds his ankles grasped by his keeper.

Preface

"It's you, is it?" said the old gentleman.

"Yes, it's me," replied a gruff voice.

"How's the Emperor of Tartary?" said the old gentleman.

"Oh! He's much the same as usual," was the reply. "No better and no worse."

"The young Prince of China," said the old gentleman, with much interest. "Is he reconciled to his father-in-law the great potato salesman?"

"No," answered the gruff voice; "and he says he never will be, that's more."

"If that's the case," observed the old gentleman, "perhaps I'd better come down."

"Well," said the man on the other side, "I think you had, perhaps."

The old man's responses to the crude fact of his attendant's grip refer only to the grand and the great: the Emperor of Tartary, the young Prince of China, the father-in-law who is a great potato salesman. A few select verbalizations cast a regal light over an unpalatable reality, and, with an "in that case" which implies a conclusive logic, the old man comes back to earth as airily as he ascended the wall.

The aim of the following pages is a psychological analysis of language. Often processes indistinct in normal language become accentuated and apparent in the language—such as that of the old man in Dickens' novel—of disturbed individuals, the study of which may thus prove a boon in the development of a scheme applicable to the whole range of meaningful verbal processes, normal as well as disturbed. We know that normal and abnormal are not discontinuous, and the underlying propositions of an account of normal language must be sufficiently encompassing to include disturbed language.

Contributions to a psychological understanding of language come from diverse sources. Some of the more important influences which have shaped the present discussion are: (1) associationistic principles, which have been prominent in recent years in word-association studies; (2) the work of the French linguist, Ferdinand de Saussure, and in particular his idea of *la langue;* (3) the work of linguists such as Leo Weisgerber, Walther von Wartburg, and Rudolf Hallig, who conceive of language as a *Zwischenwelt* between man and the world of experience, and who attempt to establish a conceptual framework of language which will faithfully reflect this *Zwischenwelt.* American psychologists know the *Zwischenwelt* idea largely in connection with the theories of B. L. Whorf (1956); (4) the ideas of Ernst Cassirer regarding the power of the word to infuse essences into experience; (5) the writings of Sigmund Freud on the nature of language. It is not widely realized that Freud had a great deal to say about the nature of language and that language figured centrally in his idea of the unconscious. Of great importance are his distinction between "word concept" and "thing concept," his idea of "primary process," and his stress on motivational aspects of language distortion.

The major themes around which this book is written are: (1) that verbal stimuli potentiate hierarchies of possible responses out of which the speaker draws the response to be uttered; (2) that there is an underlying structure in vocabulary which reflects fundamental experiential dimensions; (3) that motivation and psychological conflict play significant roles in shaping and distorting language responses.

The first chapter establishes the relationship between words and experiences, develops the idea of common experiences and communal language, and shows how the individual draws in his associations from the common language.

The second chapter presents the theoretical position that language does its work by evoking and joining associations. This is approached by considering the idea of meaning and by examining how various theories of language define meaning. This chapter further develops the importance of the association hierarchy.

The third chapter examines studies of word association in order to establish the relationship between group and individual associations and to demonstrate the role of structure in the association hierarchy. The fourth chapter establishes the links between word association and free speech and gives attention to the function of motivation in response selection and response distortion.

The fifth chapter develops the idea that the structure of language reflects the structure of experience and discusses the possibilities of developing a conceptual-category dictionary capable of displaying the underlying verbal-experiential content in language.

The sixth chapter illustrates the possibilities of application of category analysis to the language of schizophrenic patients. The reader may wish to examine Appendix I in connection with Chapter 5 and Chapter 6. Appendix I is a detailed presentation of a conceptual scheme for the categorization of words, with definitions and examples. This appendix is the foundation of a projected category dictionary which has as its objective the classification of all the common words of the English language.

Chapter 7, the final chapter, is based on Freud's theory of language and develops lines of connection between this theory and the ideas of *la langue* and of language as a structure linking man with his world. Illustrations are drawn from the language of an aphasic patient and a schizophrenic patient.

I wish to mention briefly two aspects of language (among numerous others) which have *not* been treated in this book. One is syntax and the other is "extralinguistic" phenomena in free speech.

In Chapter 2, which discusses meaning as a central problem in the psychology of language, the role of meaning is seen to be a very limited one in the methodology of structural linguistics. Despite this, many psychologists have become interested in psychological aspects of syntax, a central subject matter of structural linguistics (Miller, 1962; Mowrer, 1954; Osgood, 1963). The term "psycholinguistics" itself suggests such an interest (Laffal, 1964b). Words, it is worth noting, have only dubious status as linguistic forms (Greenberg, 1954) as compared, for example, with phonemes and morphemes, and psychologists have occasionally been accused of linguistic naiveté in treating words as if they had some inherent property as units of language (Olmsted & Moore, 1952). Yet few people would contest the assertion that meaning in language is basically carried by words. In the present work, syntax is not under consideration as such, but words are because of the view that the psychological essence of language lies in meaning which is largely in words. Insofar as syntax contributes to meaning by placing emphases, pointing directions of action and modification, establishing sequences and relationships, and otherwise *organizing* words, it becomes of importance psychologically. The study of its contribution in these respects is, however, not undertaken in the present work.

We know that much can be said about the personalities and the conflicts of speakers merely from listening to their voices, even if the actual words are not identified, and that people tend to respond with typical judgments to certain voice qualities (Allport & Cantril, 1934). Prosodic features such as pitch, accent and volume, pauses, and incidental sounds are not represented in the written codifications of speech content. But that a vast amount of information may be gathered by microscopic examination of such features has been demonstrated by Lorenz and Cobb (1953), Mahl (1956; 1959; 1961), Pittenger and Smith (1957), and McQuown (1957). It is also well established that gestures and body movements accompanying speech may reveal considerable information about the individual and also serve a communicative function; (Birdwhistell, 1952; Krout, 1931). I believe these "extralinguistic" phenomena (Mahl & Schulze, 1962) are best understood as potentially significant behavioral concomitants of a particular modality of language, namely spoken language, rather than as integral parts of *la langue,* the common language. An individual setting out to say something might use one kind of language in speaking and another in writing about the matter, but the spoken words could be put into writing, and the written words could be spoken without extreme change in their connection with *la langue.* The modality of language, written or spoken, is therefore of only secondary importance in the present work, and those features which are peculiar to only a particular modality, such as the "extralinguistic" phenomena, are not taken up.

The discussion in the following pages ranges over three main areas: (1) a general theory of language; (2) psychopathological language; (3) methodology for the investigation of language. Each one of these topics could be treated separately, but a comprehensive statement must include all three. I believe it is not possible to speak of disturbed language without some conception of how language functions ordinarily. By the same token, any account of normal language must contain within it the possibility of explaining disturbed language not merely as an afterthought, but as an integral part. Finally, with respect to methodology, I believe we have reached the point in psychology where an author who proposes a theory must also provide the practical means of exercising and testing it.

I have tried my best to be orderly and logical in the presentation. I think, however, that the subject often defies such strict control, and I plead this as excuse where I have strayed on to byways of the main argument.

I wish to acknowledge my obligations. I am grateful to the United States Public Health Service which, through grants over several years, and most recently with Grant M-6228, has supported much of my research. My indebtedness to the U.S. Veterans Administration, and in particular to the West Haven Veterans Administration Hospital, is very great indeed. They provided me the time, the freedom, and the opportunity to pursue my research. I owe gratitude to all of the psychology and psychiatry staff at the West Haven Hospital and to the psychology trainees and psychiatric residents there who have continuously afforded the kind of stimulating interaction which is the seed and soil of ideas. The research seminars in the Department of Psychiatry at Yale University have been a good testing place for many of my ideas relating to disturbed language and to methodology for the analysis of free-flowing language.

I acknowledge with pleasure my obligation to Professor Arthur L. Benton of the University of Iowa. Many years ago he supervised my thesis on word association, and the present volume has had the benefit of his criticism. Professor Stephen Ullmann of the University of Leeds provided a detailed critique of Appendix I, as well as of some of the research studies reported in the book. His contribution was invaluable and is gratefully recognized.

I owe a special debt to Mrs. Rae Bartozzi, who has assisted me in my work for over six years. Her unflagging efforts, devotion to the task at hand, versatility, and good spirits have played an important part in carrying forward the research effort of which this book is one outcome.

Julius Laffal

West Haven, Conn.

Contents

Julius Laffal:
    A Biographical Sketch   vii

Preface   ix

List of Figures and Tables   xvii

Quotation Acknowledg-
    ments   xix

1. The Psychological Study
    of Language   1

2. Meaning: How Lan-
    guage Does Its Work   19

3. The Word-Association
    Task and the Structure
    of Associations   47

4. Distortion and Structure
    in Free Speech   73

5. Language and the Struc-
    ture of Experience   97

6. Analyses of Psychotic
    Language   125

7. Language in Psycho-
    analytic Theory   157

Appendix I: A System of
    Categories   183

References   227

Index   241

List of Figures and Tables

Figure 1.   Diagram of Thought, Symbol, and Referent   2
Figure 2.   Diagram of the Speech Circuit   8
Figure 3.   Utterance of a Response to a Stimulus Word in
    Word Association with Two Psychological Sets Operating   76
Figure 4.   Schematic Representation of the Remark, *He
    worked in a bakery but quit because he was not rising*   80
Figure 5.   Schematic Representation of the Remark, *His
    battalion was swallowed in the Bulgium belch (Belgium
    Bulge)*   82

Table 1.   Associations to *table*   11
Table 2.   Word Associations of Adults in the Kent-Rosanoff
    Study and of Children in the Woodrow-Lowell Study to
    the Stimulus Word *table*   18
Table 3.   Associations to *black* and *spider*   43
Table 4.   Table Showing Distributions of Common, Indi-
    vidual, and Doubtful Associations of Normal and Psy-
    chotic Subjects   50
Table 5.   Table Showing Some of the Word Associations
    of Two Dementia Praecox Patients   51
Table 6.   Common, Individual, Doubtful, and Failure Re-
    sponses in Various Age Groups   53
Table 7.   Single Word Association, Overlap Coefficients of
    Category Profiles for 16 Stimulus Words   68

Table 8.   Continuous Word Association, Overlap Coefficients of Category Profiles for 16 Stimulus Words   69

Table 9.   Single Word Association, Rotated Factor Loadings of Overlap Coefficients of 16 Stimulus Words   70

Table 10.   Continuous Word Association, Rotated Factor
Loadings of Overlap Coefficients of 16 Stimulus Words   71

Table 11.   Responses from the Russell-Jenkins List (1954)
to the Stimulus Word *table*   74

Table 12.   Correlation Matrix of Free-Speech Profiles of 8
Stimulus Words and a Random Variable   92

Table 13.   Rotated Factor Loadings of Correlations of 8
Stimulus Words and a Random Variable in Free Speech   92

Table 14.   Entropy of Single Word Association, Continuous
Word Association, and Free Speech   95

Table 15.   Word Categories Used in the Contextual Analysis of Schreber's Language   150

Table 16.   Pearson Product-Moment Correlations Between
Context Profiles of Key Words   153

Table 17.   Average Correlations Ranked from Highest to
Lowest   155

Table 18.   Reliabilities and Intercorrelations of Category
Profiles from Patients A and B and Schreber's Autobiography   180

Table 19.   Correlations of Profiles of Categories Derived
from Early, Middle, and Late Interviews of Patient A
($N = 34$ Categories)   181

Table 20.   Information Scores of Early, Middle, and Late
Interviews of Patient A   181

Table 21.   Alphabetic Listing of Categories by Heading
Word   188

Table 22.   Category Profile of the Quoted Sample from
Swift's "Voyage to the Country of the Houyhnhnms,"
Showing Frequency of Occurrence of Each Category   224

Quotation Acknowledgments

It is with pleasure that acknowledgment is made of permissions given by editors, publishers, and authors for the various quotations which have been used in this book. I am indebted to Academic Press for permission to quote from the *Journal of Verbal Learning and Verbal Behavior;* to AMA Music Corp. for permission to quote a "boner" from Rivoli Records; to the *American Journal of Psychiatry* for permission to quote from the *American Journal of Insanity;* to the American Psychological Association for permission to quote from the *Journal of Abnormal and Social Psychology;* to Appleton-Century-Crofts for permission to quote from B. F. Skinner, *Verbal Behavior,* copyright © 1957 by Appleton-Century-Crofts, Inc.; to Basil Blackwell, Publisher, for permission to quote from S. Ullmann, *Semantics: An Introduction to the Science of Meaning;* to Kermit Schafer of Bloopers, Inc., for permission to quote from recorded collections by Kermit Schafer; to W. A. Bousfield, B. H. Cohen, and G. A. Whitmarsh for permission to quote from their *Technical Report No. 23,* University of Connecticut; to Cambridge University Press for permission to quote from Caroline Spurgeon's *Shakespeare's Imagery;* to Columbia University Press for permission to quote from *American Speech;* to Duke University Press, D. Dulany, Jr., and R. Schafer for permission to quote

from articles in the *Journal of Personality;* to Harcourt, Brace &
World, Inc., for permission to reproduce a figure and quote from C. K.
Ogden and I. A. Richards' *The Meaning of Meaning;* to Harper and
Row, Publishers, Inc., for permission to quote from E. Cassirer,
Language and Myth; to Humanities Press, Inc., for permission to quote
from J. Piaget, *The Child's Conception of Physical Causality;* to W. A.
Russell and J. J. Jenkins for permission to quote from *The Complete
Minnesota Norms for Responses to 100 Words from the Kent-Rosanoff
Word Association Test,* Technical Report No. 11, University of Min-
nesota; to the International Universities Press, Inc., and R. R. Holt
for permission to quote from an article in the *Journal of the American
Psychoanalytic Association;* to the Journal Press for permission to
quote from the *Journal of General Psychology;* to the Macmillan Company for permission to quote from Sir J. G. Frazer, *The Golden
Bough,* from M. C. Longerich and J. Bordeaux, *Aphasia Therapeutics,*
and from L. H. Gray, *Foundations of Language;* to the *New Haven
Register* for permission to quote from a news article of March 11,
1963; to The Library of Living Philosophers and The Open Court
Publishing Company, LaSalle, Illinois, for permission to quote from an
article by Susanne K. Langer in Paul Schilpp (Ed.), *The Philosophy
of Ernst Cassirer;* to the Philosophical Library for permission to reproduce a figure and quote from Ferdinand de Saussure, *Course in
General Linguistics;* to the *Philosophical Review* for permission to quote
from an article by A. Naess, "Synonymity as Revealed by Intuition";
to the *Psychoanalytic Quarterly* for permission to quote from articles
by William G. Niederland and Lawrence S. Kubie and also for permission to use material from an article of mine, "Freud's Theory of
Language," which first appeared in the *Psychoanalytic Quarterly;* to
Robert Bentley, Inc., for permission to quote from Ida Macalpine and
R. A. Hunter, *Daniel Paul Schreber: Memoirs of my Nervous Illness;*
to the editors of *Scientia* for permission to quote from that journal; to
the University of Chicago Press for permission to quote from H. Hoijer
(Ed.), *Language in Culture,* copyright 1954 by Robert Redfield and
from Z. S. Harris, *Methods in Structural Linguistics,* copyright 1951
by the University of Chicago Press; to John Wiley & Sons, Inc., for
permission to quote from L. Vygotsky, *Thought and Language;* to
Williams and Wilkins Company for permission to quote from C. G.
Jung, *The Psychology of Dementia Praecox;* to Yale University Press
for permission to quote from Grace A. de Laguna's *Speech, Its Function and Development.*

In addition, I wish to make the following acknowledgments. Quotations from *Dialogues of Alfred North Whitehead* by Lucien Price,

copyright 1954 by Lucien Price, are reprinted by permission of At-
lantic-Little, Brown and Company, Publishers. A quotation from "Over
Sir John's Hill," from *The Collected Poems of Dylan Thomas,* copyright 1953 by Dylan Thomas, 1957 by New Directions, is reprinted by
permission of New Directions, Publishers. Quotations from *Behaviorism,* by John B. Watson, copyright 1924, 1925 by The People's Institute Publishing Company, Inc., copyright 1930, Revised Edition,
W. W. Norton & Company, Inc., copyright 1952, 1953 by John B.
Watson, is reprinted by permission of W. W. Norton & Company, Inc.,
New York, New York. W. W. Norton & Company, Inc., has also given
permission to quote from S. Freud, *An Outline of Psychoanalysis.*

Hogarth Press, Ltd., and Basic Books, Inc., have given permission
to quote from *The Standard Edition of the Complete Psychological
Works of Sigmund Freud,* edited by James Strachey, as follows:
"On the Psychical Mechanism of Hysterical Phenomena," "Psychoanalytic Notes upon an Autobiographical Account of a Case of Paranoia," "The Unconscious," and "Negation." Basic Books, Inc., has
given permission to quote from Sigmund Freud's *The Origins of
Psycho-analysis,* and from *The Selected Papers of Sandor Ferenczi.*

1. The Psychological Study of Language

The study of language as a psychological phenomenon focuses upon the individual as stimulated by and as responding with language. Sometimes, in examining the language process, psychologists attempt to arrive at what is going on inside the individual, and sometimes they study the observable events occurring between individuals. In either case, what language does to the individual and what it does for him are the questions scrutinized. An old dichotomy, that between "word" and "thing," is a good place to begin our discussion of language as a psychological event. This will lead us to a consideration of language both as communal phenomenon and as behavior of individual speakers; to an analysis of verbal stimulation and verbal response; and to the idea of the association hierarchy, which is a cornerstone of the present work.

WORD AND THING

Discussions of words and things usually concern themselves with how words come to represent things, how this word *horse* comes to stand for or mean that object "horse." The implicit view is that there are two things outside the individual, the object "horse" and the word *horse,* the word being available to the individual whenever he wishes to refer to the object. The individual

himself is seen as no more than a sampler of words and things which
have a relationship of their own.

However, the idea that the word *horse* refers to or means the
object "horse" in some absolute way independent of the speaker is
deceptively and erroneously simple. For relationships between words
and things exist only by virtue of and within the minds of the people
who use the words and perform the acts of referring to and of meaning. The locus of meaning is inescapably within the individual user of
language; to picture the relation of word and thing without the user of
language is to miss completely the psychological nature of language.

Ogden and Richards (1923) have made this point by means of a
triangle, connecting symbol, referent, and thought, whose major features are reproduced below.

FIGURE 1

DIAGRAM OF THOUGHT, SYMBOL, AND REFERENT: OGDEN
AND RICHARDS (1923, P. 11)

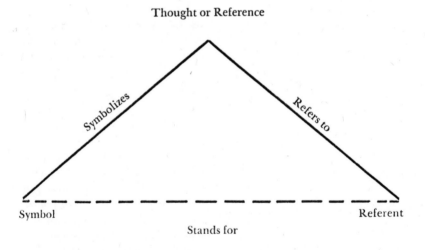

In describing the diagram, they say:

> Between a thought and a symbol causal relations hold.
> When we speak, the symbolism we employ is caused partly
> by the reference we are making and partly by social and
> psychological factors—the purpose for which we are mak-
> ing the reference, the proposed effect of our symbols on

other persons, and our own attitude. When we hear what is said, the symbols both cause us to perform an act of reference and to assume an attitude which will, according to circumstances, be more or less similar to the act and the attitude of the speaker.

Between the Thought and the Referent there is also a relation; more or less direct (as when we think about or attend to a coloured surface we see), or indirect (as when we "think of" or "refer to" Napoleon), in which case there may be a very long chain of sign-situations intervening between the act and its referent: word–historian–contemporary record–eye-witness–referent (Napoleon).

Between the symbol and the referent there is no relevant relation other than the indirect one, which consists in its being used by someone to stand for a referent. Symbol and Referent, that is to say, are not connected directly (and when, for grammatical reasons, we imply such a relation, it will merely be an imputed, as opposed to a real, relation) but only indirectly round the two sides of the triangle (p. 10).

In the present analysis, we must look more closely at what Ogden and Richards call the relation between thought and referent. The referent is a thing in the world outside of myself. The thought is my psychic representation of that thing. The word *horse*, as I use it, refers to my internal representation of "horse" rather than, as the oversimplified idea of word and thing would have it, directly to a real object "horse" which exists outside of me. When I use the word *horse* in speaking to another person, my word evokes his particular internal representation, and both of us would point to the object "horse" as the thing of which we have such representations. The fact that we would both point to the object "horse," if required to find among objects what it is we refer to when we use the word *horse*, shows that there is a degree of overlap in our representations and provides us with an incomparable advantage in communicating with each other. It is such facts that lend to language a superindividual, communal quality and that sometimes trick us into talking about language and its relations to things as if these relations were independent of people. For the individual speaker there is an apposition not between words and things, but between words and psychic representations of things. This is the basis of an important distinction made by Freud between "word concept" and "thing concept."

This distinction was used by Freud in his book *On Aphasia* (1891,

p. 78 ff.) in which he attempted to explain various types of aphasic disorders in terms of damage to areas of the brain contributing to "word" and "thing" functions. The distinction also played a crucial part in his theory of the unconscious and in his description of the efforts of schizophrenic patients to re-establish relations with the world (1915, p. 204; 1917, p. 229).[1]

The distinction may be illustrated from a hypothetical case of expressive aphasia. The patient is given a pencil. He smiles, takes it in his hand, and draws with it on the paper. When asked what it is he has in his hand, he is unable to name the object, although he again shows the examiner the uses to which it is put. The patient has an intuitive knowledge of, feeling for, and ability to respond to and with the object in a manner appropriate to the nature of the object. But he cannot muster the word associated with the object, which for other individuals would be a name implying all of the experiential qualities pertinent to the object. The handicap this places him under is tremendous. If he needs a pencil and must communicate this to someone, he has available only his feel for the object and some pantomime of its use. If his chain of thinking involves the use of a pencil, the summary sign (a word) of all the experiences involving the object is not available to him, and he must think kinesthetically, or with imagery, or even in some vaguer way about the object "pencil."

One cannot fail to be impressed by the fact that patients may lose their ability to call up or respond to language because of brain damage but retain much of their experiential familiarity with the world around them. The fact that the crucial function of language may be separated from the rest of experience in some disorders lends credence to the distinction between "word concept" and "thing concept" or "word representation" and "thing representation," as we shall refer to them.

The illustration of the aphasic patient is one in which the thing representation is present to the patient, but the word representation is not. Thing representation refers to an intuitive experiential response. Word representation refers to the verbalizations which accompany and shape this experiential response. There are brain-damaged patients who, when handed a pencil, will regard it with a kind of puzzlement, will hold it awkwardly, will make no effort to write with it, and will give every indication that it is for them a totally unfamiliar object. If the examiner offers the word *pencil* to them, they may repeat the word without any effect on their obvious absence of recognition. These agnostic patients have no inner response of familiarity to the common

---

[1] Chapter 7 discusses Freud's theories of language.

object. It comes to them as a new thing in their experience. In such instances not only is the word representation absent, but the thing representation is of an unfamiliar object.

Let us consider a situation in which a word representation is present, but where the thing representation is inconsistent with reality. When the psychotic old man in *Nicholas Nickleby* says, "How's the Emperor of Tartary?"[2] we assume that he knows no real person who is the Emperor of Tartary. However, we cannot assume that such a person does not exist in his fantasy. If the old man were asked to describe the Emperor of Tartary and to give some intimate details of his life, his doing so would be entirely plausible. Here then is a situation where the name, *Emperor of Tartary,* presumably evokes many familiar feelings within the subject who employs the name, but where there is no real object outside of the individual to which his use of the name would be appropriate. The patient has invested a name, *Emperor of Tartary,* with an idiosyncratic elaboration or has attached this name to a grandiose fantasy. Even if there were a real-life Emperor of Tartary, he would not fit the old man's construction. The name has become, for the patient, a reference to an experience of his (a thing representation) which does not accord with reality as those around him know it, but which is quite in accord with his own needs for esteem and recognition.

With respect to externally identifiable objects and events, it will be readily apparent where an individual's thing representation breaks with reality. Thus, the brain-damaged patient who gives every indication of wanting to write but tries to write with a key or a comb has a disjuncture between his thing representation for writing tool and what is available in reality for this purpose. However, where the reference of an individual's thing representation is less clearly identifiable in the external world, it is difficult to know to what extent his thing representation matches or fails to match reality. Thus, if I say of someone that he is angry, it might well be a matter of doubt whether he is in fact angry or whether the perception of anger is entirely my own, stemming from my particular way of perceiving emotions in others. Here the disjuncture between my experience of someone's being angry and the reality might be an extremely subtle and scarcely discernible one. When I say *He is angry,* the words are those associated with my internal experience, but my experiences may be erroneous with respect to reality because of needs and conflicts of my own. To the extent that reality and an individual's experiences do not match, it may be said that his word representations prevail over his

[2] See Preface.

thing representations and that he behaves as if a thing were so, when in reality it is not so. In more blatant reality disjunctures, such as in the case of the psychotic old man and the Emperor of Tartary, the distortions are readily perceived. Where the distortions are less severe, the break between the reality aspects of things and their presentations in experience will be much more difficult to identify.

These ideas of thing representation and word representation are fundamental and always implicit in discussions of language. It is all too easy to overlook the fact that, when we speak of the relation between language and things, we are speaking of language as bound to the experience of things rather than as bound to things themselves.

LA LANGUE AND LA PAROLE

The notion of a reality of which the thing representation is the psychic representative leads us into a problem of language with which linguists have struggled for some time. There may be a person who has the title Emperor of Tartary, but the old man's fantasy will in some way be discordant with the facts about this Emperor of Tartary. However, there is nothing absolute about such facts, and the old man might argue that, since all men perceive idiosyncratically, his perceptions are as valid as anyone else's. In one sense, this is literally true. If two judges differ about something, there is no way of knowing who is right. Such differences are usually resolved by resorting to other people's judgments. Where the judgment of one individual is inconsistent with that of several others, then it becomes more likely that he is wrong. However, he is wrong only in the sense that he differs with a consensus of others who, on the average, have normally functioning sensory and cognitive apparatus. Thus, if a dozen people making observations under given conditions judge that event A has taken place, but one individual making observations under the same conditions demurs, then that one individual is asserting something discordant with reality. The common judgment is a reliable one, and, where one individual differs with a reliable judgment, we consider him in error. If the old man speaks of the Emperor of Tartary, but others cannot discover such a figure or find him different from the figure described by the old man, then the old man has made an error. This is a long way of saying that his thing representation does not fit reality. But the important point is that reality is a matter determined by a consensus of individuals. It has a validity reflected by agreement of numbers of individuals; it is, in this sense, a social phenomenon.

The individual uses language, but language has a consensual quality. If in my language the utterance *gryx* refers to the object "horse," people will simply stare at me when I use *gryx* without responding in any way consistent with my thing representation of "horse." However, if I use the word *horse* and have a thing representation of the object "dog," people will also respond in a manner inconsistent with my thing representation and will begin to find that my usage of the word *horse* is a peculiar and idiosyncratic one. These are exaggerated examples, but they lead to the ideas put forward by the noted French linguist, Ferdinand de Saussure (1915), of *la langue* —a cumulative, consensually valid common language—and *la parole,* language as used by the individual.

The distinction made by Saussure between *la langue* and *la parole* is illustrated by a diagram of the speaking circuit between two speakers. In this circuit are included psychological and nonpsychological aspects of speech. The nonpsychological aspects have to do with the physiology of phonation and audition and with the physical means of transmission of sound by vibration. In the psychological segment of the speaking circuit, there is an active and a passive part. The active part is an executive function in which is included everything that goes from the associative centers of the speaker to phonation. The passive or receptive part is what goes from the ear of the listener to his associative centers. In the diagram, c (concept) $\rightarrow$ s (sound image) is active or executive, and s (sound image) $\rightarrow$ c (concept) is passive or receptive. The executive side of the speaking circuit is what Saussure calls *la parole.* The passive, receptive (and coordinating) side of the speaking circuit is the locus of *la langue,* which exists by virtue of the fact that "among all the individuals that are linked together by speech, some sort of average will be set up: all will reproduce—not exactly of course, but approximately—the same signs united with the same concepts" (p. 13).

Saussure distinguishes between the act of speaking on the part of the individual speaker and the phenomenon of language, a socially established set of conventions and possibilities from which the individual speaker draws in speaking.

> Through the functioning of the receptive and co-ordinating faculties, impressions that are perceptibly the same for all are made on the minds of speakers. How can that social product be pictured in such a way that language will stand apart from everything else? If we could embrace the sum of word-images stored in the minds of all individuals, we could identify the social bond that constitutes language. It is a storehouse filled by the members of a given community through their active use of speaking, a grammatical

FIGURE 2

DIAGRAM OF THE SPEECH CIRCUIT: SAUSSURE (1915, p. 12).

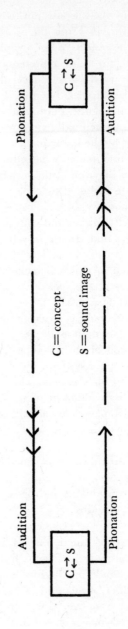

system that has a potential existence in each brain, or, more specifically, in the brains of a group of individuals. For language is not complete in any speaker; it exists perfectly only within a collectivity.

In separating language from speaking we are at the same time separating: (1) what is social from what is individual; and (2) what is essential from what is accessory and more or less accidental (p. 13).

The collective phenomenon which Saussure calls *la langue* is in itself not the subject matter of psychological study, but it is our subject of study insofar as the individual participates in it or shares it.

Linguists have introduced the idea of an "idiolect" (Hall, 1951; Ullmann, 1962, p. 22) as a middle term between *la langue* and *la parole,* referring to the totality of the speech habits of a single person at a given time. *La langue* is a composite of many idiolects, each of which may be known only through *la parole.* The concept of an idiolect does not in any way imply a language inconsistent with *la langue,* even though one individual's idiolect may contain only a portion of *la langue.* The individual whose language is inconsistent with *la langue* would have an idiolect sufficient unto itself, but even more, an idiolect which took its very character from the fact that it deviated from *la langue.* To the extent that the idiolect deviates from *la langue,* it will have broken with reality, with the consensually accepted order as established in *la langue.* It has already been shown that, when the individual's language diverges from the common language and when he does not use language in a consensually valid way, his thing representations will be radically different from those of his fellow users of the same words. Since the psychological study of language concerns itself with individuals as stimulated by and responding with language, the concept of idiolect is very relevant to such study.

In Saussure's description, language is a system which is not completely definable or describable, but which exists as a set of established facts and rules plus a set of potentials derived from the collection of individual phenomena. It may be pictured as a reference dictionary and grammar from which individuals may draw in their speaking or to which particular usages may be referred to determine their acceptability in the common language.

According to Saussure there are two distinct types of language relationships which reflect distinct types of mental activity. One of these is the syntagmatic, which has to do with the sequential arrangements and dependencies of words. "In the syntagm a term acquires its value only because it stands in opposition to everything that precedes or follows it, or to both" (p. 123). The other is the associative relation. Associative relations are not dependent on occurrences of sequences. "Whereas a syntagm immediately suggests an order of succession and a fixed number of elements, terms in an associative family occur neither in fixed numbers nor in a definite order" (p. 126). Expressions like *How are you? Good heavens!* and *If the weather is nice, we'll go for a walk* are all examples of syntagms. On the other hand, associations have no fixed sequential character, but may radiate in many directions, based on a variety of features in common between stimulus and response. As Saussure has characterized the associative relationship, "a particular word is like the center of a constellation; it is the point of convergence of an indefinite number of co-ordinated terms" (p. 125). This associative aspect of language shall concern us extensively.

Ideally, the word *horse* would evoke a universally common reference to a certain class of animals, and in addition would have a universally common set of associated words whose qualities and experiences involved such things as stables, wagons, riding, racing, fodder, and so on. This matrix of associations could be summarized by a set of words headed by the word *horse,* and including such words as *stable, wagon, ride, race, hay, mane, whinny, tail, farm, cow,* and the like.[3] Such an ideal set of verbal possibilities would be the reference dictionary against which each user could match his own particular associations and from which each user could learn more of the potential which other users might already have achieved. It would also, by exclusion, show unacceptable, that is, completely idiosyncratic, associations.

The platonic ideal of a collectively valid set of associations in *la langue,* may, in fact, be approximated by certain word-association experiments in which responses are drawn from a large number of individuals and combined to provide a group pattern.

VERBAL STIMULATION AND VERBAL RESPONSE

The idea of an actual word-association hierarchy, obtained by word-association techniques, representative of *la langue,* the collective

---

[3] Bally, a disciple of Saussure, introduced the term "associative fields" to describe such associative relationships. According to Bally, "The associative field is a halo which surrounds the sign and whose outer fringes merge into their environment. . . . The word *ox* makes one think (1) of *cow, bull, calf, horns, ruminating, bellowing,* etc.; (2) of *tilling, plough, yoke,* etc.; finally, (3) it can evoke and does evoke in French, ideas of strength, endurance, patient work, but also of slowness, heaviness and passivity" (Quoted in Ullmann, 1962, p. 238).

language, lends importance to a distinction between verbal stimulation and verbal response. In the typical word-association task, subjects are given a series of stimulus words, one at a time, and required to respond to each word with the first different word that comes to mind. The task may be oral or written. Table 1 gives the actual responses obtained from 1008 subjects to the stimulus word *table* in a study by Russell and Jenkins (1954) in which a written form of the test was used.

TABLE 1

ASSOCIATIONS TO *table*: RUSSELL AND JENKINS (1954)

TABLE ($N = 1008$)

840 chair	6 wood	1 four, spoon, lamp, bed,
41 food	3 dinner, tennis,	card, board, hard, huge,
21 desk	Mable	plate, pool, book, maple,
15 top	2 door, cup,	house, sink, stable, sable,
11 leg(s)	room, fork,	mesa, drink, leaf, set,
9 eat	round, floor,	black, meat, tablecloth,
8 cloth	silver	kitchen, flat, study,
7 dish(es)		company

The assumption may be made that, when a stimulus word such as *table* is presented to an individual, a set of verbal responses comparable to those obtained from the group is potentiated (made more likely to be uttered).[4] From among the many so potentiated, the individual selects one response for utterance. Verbal stimulation refers to this potentiation of a constellation of associations, representing, within the idiolect of the individual, the ideal constellation of associations in *la langue*. Saussure described this part of the speech cycle as the passive, receptive side. Verbal response refers to the selection and utterance of a response by the individual. This, as we have seen, was characterized by Saussure as the active, executive side of the speaking cycle, *la parole*. Where verbal stimulation is concerned, the focus is upon the verbal structure potentiated by the stimulus. Where verbal response is under study, matters of intention and motivation are of prime importance.

There is thus a parallelism between *la langue* and verbal stimulation, and between *la parole* and verbal response. Verbal stimulation of course involves a stimulated individual and an idiolect, whereas *la langue* is a conception which, although derived ultimately from the contributions of individual speakers, transcends them in proposing an

---

[4] Chapter 3 considers the evidence relevant to this assumption.

ideal linguistic possibility. For the individual, the stimulus serves to bring into play the relevant portions of *la langue* within his idiolect. *La parole* is the actual selection and utterance of a particular response from those available.

The hierarchy of responses potentiated by a verbal stimulus is the storehouse out of which the individual draws in responding. If no other variables were operating, the response selected for utterance would be determined simply by the relative strengths of the various choices. In such a situation, the dominant response for an individual would be the one given commonly by the group of which he is a member. Obviously, in many instances, this simple condition does not apply. Especially in the disturbed language of the psychotic patient, we see responses that, by our criteria of commonality and expectancy, are extremely strange and puzzling. We must therefore reason that factors other than communal response strength have contributed to the response choice. Under certain conditions normal subjects may also produce responses which cannot be found anywhere in the tabulations obtained from comparable subjects responding to the same stimulus word. Such conditions obtain in situations of extreme need or deprivation. In addition, the physical setting in which the task of association is presented, if there is something striking or unusual about it, may influence associations in the direction of unusual responses.

Taking the word-association task, in which a stimulus word is presented and a response word uttered, as a prototype, the variables which contribute to the production of a verbal response may be grouped under four headings:

1. The response hierarchy. This variable has to do with the verbal stimulation; it is the hierarchy of responses called into play by the stimulus word. The associative response hierarchy obtained from group responses is an approximation of the relevant associations in *la langue* from which the responding individual will draw.

2. Needs, conflicts, and psychic structure of the subject. This variable relates to the special needs, conflict conditions, and personality dynamics of the responding subject. Under ordinary circumstances, where no marked conflicts or unsatisfied needs are present, a highly common response will be uttered. However, where there is a psychological disturbance, an idiosyncratic or unusual response may be produced.

3. Reality demands. The presence of an experimenter as communicant functions as a social, reality-orienting influence and fosters implicitly a socially acceptable and pertinent response.

4. Intrusive stimuli. Physical aspects of the task situation may

foster unusual associations. Where such aspects are obtrusive, the response may be to them rather than to the stimulus word, or to both. Irrelevant stimuli may intrude not only because of their accidental accentuation, but also because the psychological state of the subject may foster a division of attention.

The response hierarchy which is tied to verbal stimulation, the needs, conflicts, and personality dynamics of the subject, the reality demands represented by the communicant, and intrusive stimuli are the broad classes of factors which interact in the production of a verbal response. Intrusive, irrelevant aspects of the communication situation are attended to ordinarily only by extremely disturbed individuals. The factors which usually bear most weight in the production of responses are the response hierarchy, the needs and conflicts of the individual, and the implicit demands represented by the communicant. Since the communicant's role is essentially to force the response toward a social norm, toward comprehensibility, appropriateness, and propriety, distorting influences may be attributed largely to the individual's special needs and conflicts. These lead to the hypervaluation of ordinarily subordinate or idiosyncratic associations, as is often seen in the language of disturbed individuals. Words are then used as if certain ordinarily weak meanings or associations were in fact dominant.

VERBAL STIMULATION AND DEVIANT VERBAL RESPONSE

The distinction between verbal stimulation and verbal response is especially helpful in the study of disturbed language, in which verbal stimuli often evoke unanticipated effects in the patient, and in which the patient's utterances can often be understood only in terms of the unusual conditions which contributed to their production.

The stimulus aspect of language may be illustrated in the case of a psychotic patient who responded violently on several occasions, to the surprise of everyone present. On one of these occasions his father was visiting him in the hospital and offered him "a nice piece of fruit." The patient responded by punching his father. At another time, on Washington's Birthday, the patients were eating a dessert of cherry cake. An individual seated beside the patient mentioned the word *fruit*, and the patient became agitated. The nurse noted this and attempted to placate him by asking if he was enjoying his dessert. In response to this, he assaulted the nurse. According to the patient's therapist, who knew him intimately, the precipitating cause in both incidents was the evocation of homosexual concerns upon hearing the word *fruit*. Ordinarily our associations to *fruit* have to do with edibles, especially if the context maximizes such responses. For the patient, however, the stimulus word *fruit* evoked powerful associations in the area of homosexuality, even though the circumstances favored associations related to food.

It is worthy of note that the homosexual meaning is well known to us, and in this sense is part of *la langue,* but also that it is pertinent as a meaning only in highly specific contexts considerably unlike the one in which the patient responded so explosively. To the extent that the patient's behavior in response to the verbal stimulus evoked surprise and puzzlement on the part of individuals around him, it may be said that his associations were inconsistent with those experienced by the others in his presence and, by the same token, with *la langue.*

Response aspects of distorted language may be illustrated by the following aphorism produced by a schizophrenic patient during a psychotherapeutic session: *Genius has no place in a newspaper; it belongs in the boudoir.* Perhaps no one would contest this assertion in principle. Newspapers being for the most part routine operations, it is not difficult to understand why geniuses do not belong there. That they belong in boudoirs may be taken as a reflection of the patient's biases about the due and right of intelligence with respect to sex.

The two sides of the aphorism, that genius does not belong in a newspaper and that it does belong in the boudoir, seem in themselves to be straightforward and legitimate. But why did the patient present them together as an associated opposition? If the reader will pause for a moment and explore in his own mind possible ways in which the two statements might be related, he might gain an insight into what is happening when a patient produces an unusual verbalization.

The patient's explanation of the aphorism was that *genius,* the English word, is derived from Latin *genus,* which means to reproduce, rather than to mass produce; hence genius is more appropriate to the boudoir (reproduction) than to the newspaper (mass production). We respond to the verbalizations of the patient with associations which have a high likelihood of occurring among other normal individuals exposed to the same stimuli. For the patient, however, associations which are relatively weak by our standards are for the moment preeminent. The odd linkage of intellectual, journalistic, and procreative functions in the aphorism is a prime example of the heavy burden of personal values which verbalizations may carry. High intelligence and creative writing were often expressed desiderata of the patient, whereas sexual problems were avoided in his talk. The aphorism may have reflected a resolution on the part of the patient that a man of genius like himself should not be wasting his time in noncreative writing for newspapers (a small piece of his had once appeared in a local newspaper, and he had written for the hospital newspaper) but should give some attention to creation in the sexual area. The patient's account of his aphorism does not make a good one of it. Nevertheless, this particular production, like those of many other patients, is, in its use of ordinarily weak associations, not far removed in kind from creative language.

We have an inkling of the role that some of the patient's personal needs played in utilizing remote associations for shaping his aphorism. But why did the patient utter it, and why did he address it to his communicant, his psychotherapist? What was the interpersonal function for him of this communication? The answer to such questions would require detailed documentation, which shall not be attempted at this point, of the patient's personality and of the relationship between the patient and his therapist.

We encounter daily instances of nonpathological language behavior in which a socially motivated and appropriate response is mingled with a highly personal motivation. Let us take one such example from normal language behavior, to which the reader will surely find parallels in his own experience. Two young brothers were shown a baseball bat and a ball, and each was asked to choose which one he would rather have. The older boy immediately responded, *I want the bat*. The young one thereupon said, *I want the bat*. After some demurrals, the older boy relinquished his choice and accepted the ball, which was what he had wanted from the very beginning. The verbal behavior of the older boy was designed to meet a complex situation in which his wish to have the ball was threatened. A choice was demanded of the boys; the younger brother—as the older boy knew from past frustrations—stood ready to contest whatever choice the older boy made; the older boy wanted the ball. The response *I want the bat,* whereas in reality the older boy did not want the bat, although manifestly the opposite of what he wanted to say, was actually designed to cope with a situation which would interfere with his getting what he wanted should he affirm his desire directly. The older boy's verbal response was inappropriate to his wish for the ball, but it was not only a response to this wish. It also dealt with a conflict between himself and the younger boy. The fact that a single piece of verbal behavior effectively met the requirement to state a choice, expressly denied the wish, averted a conflict, and ultimately achieved the wish reflects the remarkable interaction of motivations which participate in the language response.

In a later chapter we shall examine the language behavior of a schizophrenic patient who, when he wished to affirm something, would use the negative and, when he wished to deny something, would use the affirmative. In the case of the patient there was no such conscious design as appeared in the behavior of the older boy in the example, and, therefore, the verbal response could be more justifiably labeled distorted. However, the example of the boys gives us a glimmer of the kind of complex situations in which choice of verbalizations serves multiple purposes, some of them consistent with the apparent social situation and some of them pertinent to the individual's unique perception of the situation or to his own needs. These are some of the complexities which must be taken into account when verbalizations are considered from the response side.

THE ACQUISITION AND NATURE OF ASSOCIATION HIERARCHIES

Associative hierarchies within the idiolect of the individual speaker are the products of a long history of learning, in which reinforcement, imitation, and the individual's inherent psychological capacities and structures have played significant roles. The child utters an approximate sound pertinent to an object whose name is being learned, and this response is reinforced by parental approval and other practical consequences. The reinforcement increases the likelihood of further similar efforts in the presence of the object or when the object is needed. In addition, the reinforcement is applied selectively to the child's utterance so that ultimately he produces a correct sound. With respect to the object "table," the child hears the word *table* repeatedly: *Come to the table, Hold on to the table, Put the toy on the table, Sit at the table*. In turn, the child is given lavish approval when he approximates the word *table* in the presence of "tables." Gradually a strong association between the object "table" and the word *table* is built up for the child. This thing-word association of "table" and *table* also takes place with great frequency in the presence of other objects and activities associated with "tables," for example, "chairs" and "food." Furthermore, throughout the life of the individual, "chairs," "tables," and "food" constantly occur together, so that the association between the objects "table," "chair," and "food" will also be very strong. Concurrently, the words *chair* and *eat* (and their variants) will be strongly associated with word *table*. The child, of course, soon learns that object "table" has a special relationship to word *table*, a relationship which is called naming. He discriminates, in this sense, between "tables" and "chairs." If asked to show what he is talking about when he says *table*, he will point to the object "table," and not to "chair" or "food." That he can do so in no way negates the fact that he has associations like *chair* and *eat* to the word *table*. In all of this the child is an active participant, fitting his idea of "table" into some world view, applying his idea to parts of the world around him, and organizing some small segment of his world under the rubric *table*. At some point in his learning it would be appropriate to say not only that he is discovering what things may be labeled *table,* but also that his idea of "table" is in some manner influencing his perception of things. This model of word-and-association learning is, of course, highly oversimplified.

Many significant events in the lives of children and adults take place around the object "table," events relating to family, to frustrations, to gratifications. Although, in a statistical sense, an object like "chair" and an activity like "eating" are much more consistently associated with "table" than are less easily identified family and need conditions, it would be an error to assume that such other associations are either absent or even weak. Many responses which range into vital need areas may be firmly related to the stimulus word *table*. The fact that, out of a group of 1008 normal adult subjects, 840 give the response *chair* to *table* and 41 give the response *food* tells us what to expect from normal adult subjects in this task under ordinary conditions. But we should be well aware that the events that accompany learning, not only externally visible and identifiable events, but those within the learner as well, are manifold and that the process of association knows no biases.

Freud made this fact a central feature in his studies of dreams, in which he demonstrated that the most unlikely detail may be a bridge from the trivial to the essential. In his account of symbolism in dreams, Freud maintains that "table" is a symbol for the woman. He says that the relationship of eating to woman as the original source of nourishment, as well as the one who presides over the kitchen, is not to be overlooked. Woodrow and Lowell (1916) secured associations of 1000 children between the ages of nine and eleven to 90 of the Kent-Rosanoff stimulus words. Below is the tabulation of the most frequent responses to *table* for these children and for the 1000 adults from the original Kent-Rosanoff list: [5]

---

[5] The original Kent-Rosanoff response frequencies differ from those in the Russell-Jenkins list, which gives *chair* as occurring 840 times in a population of 1008 subjects. This is perhaps in part accounted for by the differences in populations and in data-collecting procedure. The Kent-Rosanoff associations were obtained from an extremely heterogeneous population of hospital workers, visitors, and others, and the test was given orally. The Russell-Jenkins norms were obtained from students in beginning psychology courses at the University of Minnesota, and the test was administered in writing.

It may be seen from Table 2 that for children the emphasis is on the word *eat* and for adults it is on *chair*. *Eat* is a response with many psychological overtones; *chair* is comparatively innocuous. Apparently a shift takes place as the child grows older, and *eat* associations become less frequent compared with *chair* in response to the stimulus word

TABLE 2

WORD ASSOCIATIONS OF ADULTS IN THE KENT-ROSANOFF STUDY AND OF CHILDREN IN THE WOODROW-LOWELL STUDY TO THE STIMULUS WORD *table*: WOODROW AND LOWELL (1916, p. 93)

Response Word	*Frequencies*	
	adults	children
chair	267	16
wood	76	21
furniture	75	0
eat	63	358
dishes	40	126
legs	10	70

table. Brown and Berko (1960) have attempted to account for such shifts in terms of a tendency, increasing with age, to associate words within a syntactic part of speech. According to their view, the child's associations are without regard to syntactic homogeneity. He gives a verb response to a noun stimulus. But he learns gradually to organize his vocabulary into syntactic classes, and so, as an adult, he gives a noun response to the noun stimulus *table*. However, their theory does not satisfactorily account for why *eat* should be replaced in preeminence by *chair*, which occurs 16 times in the children's responses, rather than, for example, by *dishes*, which occurs 126 times, or by *dish*, which occurs 33 times. It seems not unlikely that significant needs that were prominent and readily expressed in the child by such words as *eat* are submerged, controlled, and less readily revealed in the adult. Here we find the suggestion that, even in the case of a normal adult and a common association, an intricate interplay of psychological needs and defenses is just below the surface. The words in our crudely obtained associative hierarchies are the summarizing notations of complex experiences; at the same time they have powerful motivating and evocative force. We will, in what follows, attempt to deepen our understanding of association hierarchies, and to see more clearly what role they play in the psychology of language.

2. Meaning:
How Language Does
Its Work

Since the idea of the response hierarchy—a constellation of associations brought into play by verbal stimulation—is a central one in the present analysis of the psychology of language, it must accordingly enter into our definition of meaning. But the idea of meaning itself is of fundamental importance in the psychological study of language and has a way of haunting psychologists and philosophers who believe they have laid that problem to rest. It must therefore be understood in its own right.

Although some authors maintain that there is no problem of meaning (Humphrey, 1951) and some that the term is better dropped because it is encrusted with imprecise connotations (Morris, 1946; Skinner, 1957), others continue to use it and puzzle and write about it. Ultimately, whoever writes about language defines something which is essentially an idea of meaning, and it does no good to banish the term as if it were the culprit. Indeed, in order to find out on what major principle an interpretation of language is constructed, one need only examine how the problem of meaning is dealt with. Here are to be found the crux of theories of language and the key to programs of language research and study.

We are accustomed to thinking that meaning is a phenomenon, a fact of life, and we believe that it is up to the linguist, the psychologist, and the philosopher to specify where it is located and how it functions. However, anyone who undertakes such an investigation of meaning will only discover what he has already assumed. This is so because meaning is essentially *a theory* applied to a set of data—utterances or acts—which defines some point of view about the relation of these phenomena to their users.

But if meaning is a matter of definition, and if definitions abound as do definers, then does it not make good sense to drop the term altogether? No matter how we try, we will not be able to escape the idea of meaning; meaning has to do with basic theory on how language works for its users. Whoever has such a theory has, by that fact, defined meaning in some way.

MEANING IN LINGUISTICS, SEMIOTIC, AND POETRY

It is possible, of course, to deal with aspects of language in which the psychological role of the user is irrelevant or limited, and, to the extent that this is the case, definitions of meaning may be dispensed with. Studies of the physical properties of sounds produced by the vocal apparatus may exclude the functional relationship of such sounds to the users. Studies of the physiology of speech production and audition may also exclude concern with meaning, since they deal only with certain physical properties of the sounds and with certain mechanical features of human language production and audition. Linguists have sought to introduce the kind of scientific rigor found in physical and physiological sciences into their own studies by severely limiting the role of meaning, that is, by excluding as far as possible any reference to the user of language.

Such efforts to increase the rigorousness of linguistics as a science at the cost of exclusion of meaning are well illustrated in the following discussion between a philosopher, Abraham Kaplan, and two linguists, Charles F. Hockett and Joseph H. Greenberg (Hoijer, 1954).

> HOCKETT: I said that we may have to use semantic evidence in order to figure out what the linguistic system of a language is, but that the system does not include the semantics. The system is abstract, it is a signaling system, and as soon as we study semantics we are no longer studying language but the semantic system associated with language (p. 152).
>
> KAPLAN: I have several times this afternoon and on

previous occasions heard what sounds to me like the following statement: that beginning with an analysis which does not take any explicit account of meanings it is possible to arrive at something that would be identified as such by whoever would use that language. I would like to have that statement either corrected or explained, since it seems to me to be plainly false (p. 152).

GREENBERG: . . . There is no doubt that any language system has a structure side and a semantic side, and it is possible to state them separately. I think that is all that is involved—the difference between making a dictionary and stating the meanings and writing the grammar (p. 156).

KAPLAN: It is disappointing, I may say, since a philosopher is so very concerned with problems of semantics and expects that the linguist will help him with them, to find that the linguist does not want to touch them either (p. 157).

The minimal way in which these linguists take meaning into account has been made explicit by Harris (1951):

It is empirically discoverable that in all languages which have been described we can find some part of one utterance which will be similar to a part of some other utterance. "Similar" here means not physically identical but substitutable without obtaining a change in response from native speakers who hear the utterance before and after the substitution: *e.g.* the last of *He's in.* is substitutable for the last part of *That's my pin.* In accepting this criterion of hearer's response, we approach the reliance on "meaning" usually required by linguists. Something of this order seems inescapable, at least in the present stage of linguistics: in addition to the data concerning sounds we require data about the hearer's response (p. 20).

There is a lively dispute among linguists (Ullmann, 1959) regarding the advantages of limiting definitions of meaning to informant "same" and "different" responses, as against dealing with meaning in a richer sense affording the user or informant a greater role. American structural linguists seem generally to attempt to limit their use of meaning to the simple one described by Harris above, and in effect to have specified that language users will enter into their accounts only insofar as such users may be required to judge similarity or difference. Although these linguists recognize a broader meaning outside their science, as defined, for example, in terms of social context (Harris, 1951, p. 187), they explicitly limit the meaning with which they work to the user response indicating "same" or "different."

A tripartite division of semiotic, the science of language, proposed by Morris (1938; 1946) and by Carnap (1942), separates roughly some of the areas of interest in language and bears on the idea of meaning. According to Morris, there are three aspects of the science of language: the syntactic, the semantic, and the pragmatic. The syntactic area has to do with the formal relations of signs to each other. The semantic area has to do with the relations between signs and the objects to which the signs are applicable. The pragmatic area has to do with the relations between signs and users of signs.

Linguistics would be classed under syntactics, since it devotes itself to the descriptive study of formal characteristics of language, excluding to a large extent any concern with matters relating to meaning and the user of the language (Bloomfield, 1933; Bloch & Trager, 1942; Joos, 1950; Harris, 1951). Some linguists must, of course, by the very nature of their work, deal with content and reference in language. Such, for example, are the lexicologists, and their work is accordingly in the semantic area. Many anthropological studies would be classified under the semantic aspect of language, since they attempt to define systematically the *designata* of sets of language forms (Conklin, 1955; Goodenough, 1956; Lounsbury, 1956). Psychologists clearly group near the pragmatic side of this tripartite division, since the individual users of language are of critical interest to them. However, the middle term, semantics, poses some problems.

Its definition in terms of signs and their *designata* (Carnap, 1942) or in terms of "the signification of signs in all modes of signifying" (Morris, 1946, p. 219) contains a paradox. The definition suggests that only a relationship between a sign and a significate or a *designatum* is under consideration, and *not* the user of signs. But Morris has clearly shown that signification is an activity in relation to people, and obviously the user of the language is the locus in which a sign is related to a *designatum*. The attempt to define an area called semantics which deals strictly with signs and significates or *designata* also leaves unaccounted for that vast no man's land that has been called connotation. If connotation is accepted as a legitimate aspect of the relationship between signs and things, then it too ought to be included in semantics. If so, semantics then becomes merged openly with pragmatics, since connotation is often distinguished as that component of meaning which varies with individuals, as opposed to denotation, which is the conventional or common meaning. On the other hand, any attempt to relegate connotation to the area of pragmatics and to separate it from semantics would narrow semantics to an extremely limited applicability.

The referential relationship, although of prime importance, is *primus inter pares* in language. Associative relationships other than of a naming, referring type bear important weight in filling out the meaning of a verbal stimulus. It is only when we take into account the cloud of associations—the connotations—which trail every verbalization, the evocative as well as the referential qualities of language, that we can fully appreciate the functioning of language. That this is so is abundantly clear when we examine disturbed language or those creative forms of language which seek to convey subtleties of experience having no name of their own.

It is no accident, for example, that the disturbed language of the psychotic patient will often strike the listener as having poetic qualities. Poetry calls upon the audience for responses other than the ordinarily dominant ones, and it is in this area of relatively remote or weak associations that the disturbed patient operates. The following lines from Dylan Thomas's poem, "Over Sir John's Hill," illustrate well a kind of nonreferential communication.

> Over Sir John's Hill
> The hawk on fire hangs still;
> In a hoisted cloud, at drop of dusk, he pulls to his claws,
> And gallows, up the rays of his eyes the small birds of the bay
> And the shrill child's play
> Wars of the sparrows and such who swansing, dusk, in wrangling
>   hedges.

The hawk on fire obviously does not refer to a burning hawk, nor does *wrangling hedges* refer to arguing and fighting hedges. These are examples of metaphor and metonymy, but the suggestion in such special terms of a process somehow different from that which takes place in ordinary discourse is erroneous. Metaphor and metonymy are terms which tell us that responses originally appropriate to one verbal stimulus or one situation are now being utilized for another verbal stimulus or situation. They also indicate that ordinarily weak responses among the associations to the stimuli are being solicited. The word *fire* in our experience is primarily associated with burning, but it is also associated with bright colors, passion, anger, and so on, and it is these latter qualities which are to be understood in *hawk on fire,* while in *wrangling hedges* we may hear the frantic chatter of birds among the bushes. These are the kinds of responses that are subsumed under the connotative aspect of a stimulus and that may, at any moment, and especially in literature, assume greater importance than the denotative or referential aspects.

William Empson (1955), in a brilliant analysis of ambiguity in poetry, has shown what a wealth of meaning may be found in words if we shift our focus away from their ordinary references to some of the attendant associations. The appreciation of poetry helps give proper emphasis to nonreferential and even remote associations in verbal responding and shows us the difficulties in distinguishing semantics from pragmatics. On the basis of our discussion, we must reject that distinction.

Everyday use of the term *meaning* involves implicitly a theory about how language serves us. The theory is that language creates meaning either by an act of referring to something (by or for a user) or suggesting something (by or for a user). That language both refers and suggests is abundantly clear, but, at the same time, it is a complication which has been virtually insuperable in developing a unitary definition of meaning.

Part of the difficulty stems from the habit we have of thinking of words and things as if they were directly related, independently of speakers. We have already seen how the idea of semantics as a distinct area separate from pragmatics fosters such a notion. In suggesting a divorce between language and its individual users, this viewpoint suggests that meanings may exist independently of users of the language as relationships between signs and things.

In broadest terms, meaning in language has to do with how language does work for its users. We may take this as a preliminary statement of the nature of meaning. The elaboration of this statement will be crucial in any psychological theory of language. But before considering the *how* in the present framework, which will take us back again to the association hierarchy, let us look at some of the work which language performs for its users.

THE WORK OF LANGUAGE: RATIONAL FUNCTIONS

Views of the rational function of language tend to group around three positions: (1) that language is the means by which the user reveals or expresses his ideas; (2) that language is an instrument of interpersonal behavior and that its function is to elicit desired responses from other individuals; and (3) that language is essentially a means of incorporating the individual into an existing cultural matrix and of guaranteeing his contribution to the needs and aspirations of the culture. This last view has achieved considerable prominence in recent years through the wider publication of the writings of Benjamin L. Whorf (1956). Since it deals with language from the aspect of the culture rather than from that of the individual user of language, its discussion will be deferred for the moment and taken up again in Chapter 5.

The first approach has been called the mentalistic view of language (Kantor, 1936). Language from the mentalistic standpoint is regarded as the expression, or symbolization, of mental contents. Thus Gray (1939) says: "In its broadest and most general sense, language may be said to be any means of expressing emotional or mental concepts by any living being or beings whatsoever, and of communicating them to, or receiving them from, other living beings" (p. 13). Within this tradition is the work of Ogden and Richards (1956): "A symbol as we have defined it symbolizes an act of reference. . . . Thus a language transaction or a communication may be defined as a use of symbols in such a way that acts of reference occur in a hearer which are similar in all relevant respects to those which are symbolized by them in the speaker" (p. 20).

However, Ogden and Richards also recognize another usage of language: "But besides this referential use which for all reflective, intellectual use of language should be paramount, words have other functions which may be grouped together as emotive" (p. 10). "The difference between the two uses may be more exactly characterized as follows: in symbolic speech the essential considerations are the correctness of the symbolization and the truth of the references. In evocative speech the essential consideration is the character of the attitude aroused" (p. 239). The evocative use of language occurs most characteristically in poetry, in which sounds, articulatory movements, associations, and rhythm play important roles. The rational use of language, according to Ogden and Richards, involves the symbolization of an act of reference on the part of the speaker. This idea is essentially a crystallization of the mentalistic tradition. The further postulation of an evocative function in language, which acts differently, is an attempt to deal with that recurrent problem in the psychology of language, the connotative aspects of language. The word *tree,* for example, in the Ogden and Richards view, might symbolize an act of reference to the object "tree." However, to describe the act of reference only leaves out the many other attendant features which might be evoked in a hearer, such as the feeling that a tree is beautiful and good, that it is associated with nature, and so on, all of which are important but nonreferential responses to the word.

It may be seen from Gray's and from Ogden and Richards's definitions that the so-called mentalistic tradition does not, as it has been sometimes taken to task for doing, exclude notions of communication between individuals, nor does it exclude affective, emotive communication. It does, however, focus on the function of language in the psychic economy of the single individual, and it regards language as a device for making manifest his mental contents and for garnering such contents from others, as well as for emotive expression and for emotive manipulation of others. The mentalistic tradition stresses the work of making open and known to others the mental or psychical events within the individual, the expression of emotion, and the evocation of attitudes and emotions in others.

The second view, that of language as an interpersonal phenomenon, has often been contrasted with the mentalistic view, undoubtedly to make the point of a marked difference in emphasis, but sometimes with the implication that the mentalist view is erroneous. Thus De Laguna (1927) says:

> What is primarily needed for the successful study of the psychology of speech is a deliberate setting aside, if not abandonment, of the metaphysical dualism which can conceive speech only as an external physical manifestation of inner psychical processes. Once we deliberately ask the question:—*What does speech do? What objective function does it perform in human life?*—the answer is not far to seek. Speech is the great medium through which human cooperation is brought about. It is the means by which the diverse activities of men are coordinated and correlated with each other for the attainment of common and reciprocal ends. Men do not speak simply to relieve their feelings or to air their views, but to awaken a response in their fellows and to influence their attitudes and acts (p. 19).

Kantor (1936), Pronko (1946), and more recently Skinner (1957) are adherents of this view, which says that the work which language performs is to bring another person into action for the satisfaction of the individual's needs or their mutual needs. Actually, although there is a difference of emphasis as compared with the mentalist view of language, there is no irreconcilable contradiction between the two positions.

THE WORK OF LANGUAGE: MAGIC AND SCHIZOPHRENIC DISTORTION

It is clear that language serves the rational purposes of man—communication, organizing experience according to well-established classes, reasoning, keeping records. However, in the same way as we noted a vaguer, more global, connotative aspect of language alongside the sharper, more limited denotative aspect, so we must note that there are irrational uses of language alongside the rational. In these uses language is employed as if it were a direct manipulation of things, or as if it were effective directly and without further mediation in controlling events. Children often utter, in play or in seriousness, incantations designed to ward off the unpleasant or to bring victory over an enemy (*Rain, rain go away! Everything you say flies off me and sticks on you!*).

Cassirer (1946) traces the evolution of language and myth to a common source which lends the word its magical force.

> At this point, the word which denotes that thought content is not a mere conventional symbol, but is merged with its object in an indissoluble unity. The conscious experience is not merely wedded to the word, but is consumed by it. Whatever has been fixed by a name, henceforth is not only real, but is Reality. The potential between "symbol" and "meaning" is resolved; in place of a more or less adequate "expression," we find a relation of identity, of complete congruence between "image" and "object," between the name and the thing (p. 58).

The attitude of magic stems, according to Freud (1913), from the narcissism belonging to early stages of childhood in which there is a tremendous overvaluation by the individual of his own thoughts and fantasies. Piaget (1930) has characterized the young child's construction of reality in the following manner:

> From the point of view of logic, it is pure *autism*, or thought akin to dreams or daydreams, thought in which truth is confused with desire. To every desire corresponds

immediately an image or illusion which transforms this desire into reality, thanks to a sort of pseudo-hallucination
or play. No objective observation or reasoning is possible:
there is only perpetual play which transforms perceptions
and creates situations in accordance with the subject's
pleasure. From the ontological viewpoint, what corresponds
to this manner of thinking is primitive *psychological causality,* probably in a form that implies *magic* proper: the
belief that any desire whatsoever can influence objects, the
belief in the obedience of external things. Magic and autism are therefore two different sides of one and the same
phenomenon—that confusion between the self and the
world which destroys both logical truth and objective existence (p. 302 ff.).

At a certain level of generality there is a parallelism between the
magical attitude and use of language in children and the schizophrenic
use of language. Werner and Kaplan, for example, describe a "thing-
like handling of linguistic forms" (1963, p. 258) which is the same in
young children and schizophrenic patients. However, there are vast
differences between schizophrenic language and child language which
vitiate any efforts to ascribe the same dynamics to both. The child,
depending upon his age and level of development, finds himself at
some stage of mastery of the communal language of his adult mentors
while he is beginning to abandon or internalize his egocentric language
(Piaget, 1962; Vygotsky, 1934). He will not, until well into adolescence, master the conceptual apparatus available to the adults of his
community, so that at any point he may be seen as operating with a
relatively incomplete set of tools, whose incompleteness will become
especially manifest if he is required to do some of the logical tasks
which come easily to his elders. His efforts to stretch what he has
available to cope with problems beyond his capacity are characterized
as "syncretism," or "magical" behavior. It is this aspect of his behavior which finds its parallels in schizophrenic language, and also
in the language of peoples we call primitive by our own standards of
cultural development. But the schizophrenic patient, unlike the child,
has already mastered the language of his community, and what we
witness in his distortions of language is a *change of function* from
communal use to idiosyncratic use induced by the upsurge of powerful
needs and conflicts. What he cannot achieve realistically, the patient
attempts to achieve magically with his language. His efforts are like

those of the child only to the extent that both may be using language in a noncommunal, unrealistic way.

The descriptions by Cassirer of magical thought and by Piaget of syncretic thought give statements relating childish and schizophrenic language their necessary depth. It is not to be inferred that, when the schizophrenic patient uses words as if he were manipulating reality, he believes and acts upon the idea that "the word is the thing." But words have become for him the magical incantations for thing representations which his fantasy has uniquely constructed, without regard to reality and communal usage, to fit his own needs.

One of the peculiar difficulties in understanding schizophrenic speech has to do with the fact that it has changed in some way from the familiar, rational function, while its form and structure have remained basically the same as that of everyone else's speech. Freud, in his study, "The Unconscious" (1915), notes that in schizophrenic language words are subjected to primary-process distortion comparable to the distortion of dream images and that a single word, if suitable because of its many associative connections, may contain the condensation of a whole train of thought.

Freud points out that language in schizophrenia is a means by which the patient attempts to recover a world from which his libidinal investments have been withdrawn. The first attempts in this direction appear in his language, which becomes a highly personal effort to re-establish contact with the world around him. He treats words magically, as if they were both the things to which they refer and the things which they suggest, and by means of language he seeks to promote a liaison with objects. But language is a double-edged sword. In the same way that he employs it in an effort to make contact with lost objects, so he must fear the disastrous consequences of verbal missteps and dread its effects upon himself. The vast powers and inherent dangers of language for the disturbed patient may best be brought home by a detailed illustration.

Frazer (1922, p. 13) tells of a Malay charm: If one would kill an enemy, one transfixes an image of him with a needle, enshrouds it as a corpse, prays over it as if one were praying over the dead, then buries it in the path where the victim is likely to step over it. In order that the victim's blood will not be on one's head, one then says:

> It is not I who am burying him,
> It is Gabriel who is burying him.

In this way the archangel Gabriel bears the responsibility.

A comparable use of language may be illustrated in the case of a psychotic patient reported by Laffal, Lenkoski, and Ameen (1956) and Laffal and Ameen (1959) which at the same time gives us an inkling of the tremendous task of reshaping the world borne by language in severe mental disturbance. They described a syndrome in a young schizophrenic patient which they called "opposite speech." The syndrome consisted in the use of *yes* by the patient when he clearly meant *no* by communal standards, and vice versa. Besides interchanging *yes* and *no*, the opposite speech included interchanging *right* and *wrong, do* and *don't,* and occasionally *something* and *nothing* and *like* and *hate.* The syndrome was both receptive and expressive, bearing on the patient's understanding of what was said to him as well as on his own use of language, and it included written and spoken language.

The patient was a twenty-four-year-old single man who first exhibited psychotic behavior while serving as a gunner with a rifle company in combat in Korea. At the time of admission to the field hospital he was mute, and subsequently he neither ate nor talked for three days. Information accompanying him to the field hospital revealed that he had been hearing voices telling him he was dirty, that he spread disease, that he was an s.o.b. and a pervert. He was transferred to the United States one month later. At that time he ate very little because he felt that his food contained chopped up people and worms. He equated worms with penises. After a total of forty-five electric shock treatments without sustained improvement, he was transferred to a Veterans Administration Hospital. There he was better oriented and in fair contact, and, during the next few months, he was given several passes and leaves of absence and was finally placed on trial visit approximately fourteen months after his initial breakdown on the battlefield. Three months after the beginning of his trial visit, he became quite agitated, telling his mother that one of the girls in the neighborhood was calling his name and would not leave him alone.[1] He began to pound on the wall and shout that he wanted the name-calling to stop. It was at this point that the patient was brought again to the hospital.

The patient was an only child, an older brother having died at birth. His parents were frugal lower-middle-class people who apparently were always able to provide their son with things other boys had. They described him as having been shy and introverted but always a good boy. He was an average student, and graduated from high

[1] This aspect of the patient's language is illustrated by verbatim quotations in Chapter 5.

school at the age of eighteen. Being of slender physique, he sometimes worked with weights to build himself up. He was too bashful to go out with girls, and, as far as could be ascertained, he had had no hetero-sexual relations. Following graduation from high school, he worked in a carpentry shop until drafted into the Army. The family matrix included an exceedingly protective, indulgent, and yet controlling mother, and a relatively ineffectual father.

In asking the patient routine questions at admission, the resident psychiatrist was struck by the confusing answers that he received. The patient appeared to substitute *yes* for *no* and *always* for *never*. The patient's parents first noted this type of reversal on the day prior to his admission, when the patient said at lunchtime, *I'm hungry*. His mother prepared a sandwich, but when she offered it to him, he re-jected it. In his behavior on the ward, the patient was withdrawn, un-communicative, but compliant and well-behaved despite some agitated periods when he hallucinated a marriage and the presence of his "wife" in the hospital, and when he hallucinated the presence of his mother on the ward. The hallucinatory and delusional content was mainly sexual and religious in nature.

Psychological tests reflected the clinically patent thought disorder. Eight responses were given to the Rorschach, all of which were whole animal responses. The Wechsler-Bellevue IQ was 71, with verbal IQ 89 and performance IQ 56. The breakdown in intellectual functioning was clearly due to the intrusion of psychotic material, and, in light of the patient's scholastic record as a high-school graduate, his intellectual potential was judged to be higher than shown by the tests. Word-association and sentence-completion tests demonstrated the opposite speech syndrome in some of the responses. Thus, to the stimulus *limp* he responded, *limping around, able to walk*. To *disgust*, he responded, *disgusted, when you're feeling good, happy and contented*. To *stam-mer,* he responded, *stutter, when the words come out easier and you have trouble*. On the sentence-completion test, some of the oral com-pletions were as follows: "What makes me angry is" *if things go right, the weather is good, if I'm feeling good, and mad at myself;* "When people make fun of me" *I feel good, I get very nervous inside, I start to like;* "Home" *There's any place like home. Home is the best cure;* "I feel like cursing when" *things go good, or if I have any hard luck, get in trouble in any way. Well, if things go right, if I have some plans and things come up to break it, don't come up to break it;* "I dream" *of, sometimes of things that are, things that seem real, but they are real, but they don't seem real, could be true, yet not fictitious. You dream you're a doctor when you are a doctor, when you're just an ordinary person;* "She disliked him when he" *was with her, against her, not against her, making her happy, comfortable;* "I feel like smashing things when" *I'm calm.*

In explaining proverbs, the patient's opposite speech was apparent, and it was evident as well that the reversals were not always consistent. Thus, when asked to explain the saying, "When the cat is away the mice will play," the patient responded, *If the mice are in the presence of the cat they won't play. If the cat isn't present while the mice aren't there, of course the mice can't play.* To "Don't cross your bridges until you come to them," the patient responded, *Why worry about your bridges. In other words, when you're in front of something, worry about it. Before you meet it* (patient pauses, examiner encourages him). *If I got to meet somebody that's my enemy, well, suppose I didn't know it and I don't meet him, what in heaven's name am I going to do about it? Just confront him even if I didn't know I was going to meet him.* To "Don't look a gift horse in the mouth," the patient responded, *I know what the hell a gift horse is.*

The following is a portion of a recorded interview with the patient during the administration of the Wechsler-Bellevue Intelligence Test.

DR. Who invented the airplane?

PT. I do know.

DR. You mean, you don't know.

PT. I do know.

DR. You do know.

PT. Yes, I do.

DR. If you do know, can you tell me?

PT. If I do know, how can I tell you? I could.

DR. You could tell me.

PT. Yes, because I do know, I do know, I do know, ah, who invented the airplane.

DR. Okay. If you do know who invented the airplane, tell me who invented the airplane.

PT. I can.

DR. You can.

PT. I sure could.

DR. You sure could. Okay. Can you tell me now who invented the airplane?

PT. I do know.

DR. You do know.

PT. Yes, I know.

Dr. That means that you have the answer. You have the answer to that question.

Pt. Yes.

Dr. Yes. All right, now can you tell me what the answer is?

Pt. Who invented the airplane, I do know.

Dr. What you mean to say is that you don't know.

Pt. I do know. If I don't know, I, I, I, I wouldn't be able to tell you.

Dr. You're not able to tell me, though, are you?

Pt. Yes I am, for I do know.

In an effort to determine the extent of the patient's conscious control of the opposite speech, he was interviewed under amytal. The following transcript shows how firmly entrenched the syndrome was. Note that there were two doctors present, one identified as Dr. J. and the other as Dr. L.

Dr. J. Joseph, I want to ask you something. I'm holding a pipe here in my hand. Do you see this pipe?

Pt. No.

Dr. J. Doctor L., do you see this pipe?

Dr. L. Yes, I see the pipe.

Dr. J. Joseph, how is it when I show you the pipe, you say no you don't see it, and Doctor L. says yes, he does see it? How is it he says yes and you say no?

Pt. Well. The doctor says he don't see it?

Dr. L. I do see it.

Pt. You do see it?

Dr. J. What do you say, Joseph?

Pt. I do see the pipe.

Dr. J. You do see the pipe?

Pt. Uhuh.

Dr. J. Now, wait. You tell me. I've got the pipe here in my hand. Do you see the pipe?

Pt. Nope, I don't see it.

Dr. J. Doctor L., do you see this pipe?

Dr. L. Yes, I do.

Dr. J. Joseph, how is it that Doctor L. says yes and you say no, and I ask you both the same question. How is that? Can you explain that?

Pt. Well. What was that?

Dr. J. How is it when I show you and Doctor L. the pipe

> and I say do you see the pipe, you say no, I don't
> see it, and Doctor L. says yes, I do see it? You're
> both looking at it and you both give different an-
> swers. How is that?
>
> Pt. Probably in his eyes he sees it some way different.
> Dr. L. What's in his hand, Joseph?
> Pt. A pipe.
> Dr. L. What color is it?
> Pt. It's brown.
> Dr. L. Do you think it's brown?
> Pt. No.

Freud (1925, p. 235) has described negation as "a way of taking account of what is repressed, indeed, it is actually a removal of the repression, though not, of course, an acceptance of what is repressed." In this patient the speech reversal may have served as a way of dealing with ideas which were unacceptable. The pressure to give utterance to the pertinent language was strong in the patient, yet words reflecting his own impulses were unacceptable. The speech reversal extended to the whole of his language, and this ensured an immediate denial or negation whenever the feared impulses were verbalized. It was hypothesized that the patient was terrified of, and had to deny, his own aggressive impulses.

One of the features of this patient's personality, remarked upon by all who came into contact with him, was his extreme passivity. On only one occasion during his hospitalization did the patient become overtly aggressive. This was when his mother, who had been visiting regularly, appeared one day at a time when he was desperately requesting release from the hospital. Seeing her, he began to pound on the door with his fists and to accuse her of keeping him locked up. He calmed down in a few minutes and had a very quiet visit with his mother a short time later. On several occasions he was attacked by other patients, perhaps because of the very fact that he presented such a passive exterior, and in each case he accepted the attack without attempting to fight back. There was a notable lack of either aggressive fantasy or aggressive behavior in situations where it seemed to be pertinent.

The interpretation of the patient's opposite speech as a way of dealing with unacceptable aggressive impulses received strong support in the subsequent course of treatment.[2] During a trial visit at home,

---

[2] Kaplan (1957) has suggested an interpretation of opposite speech in terms of Werner's theory of the dedifferentiation of language in schizophrenia

the patient became extremely hostile and threatening toward his parents. Fearing for their lives, they called the police and returned the patient to the hospital. It was at this time that the opposite speech was first noted to be absent, and it was shortly after his return to the hospital that the patient's psychosis cleared up. Psychotherapeutic treatment of the patient continued on an outpatient basis, and it was here that the patient finally brought up an anxiety-ridden, obsessive fantasy of being unexpectedly seized and subjected to electric-shock treatment. After almost two years the outpatient treatment was ended by mutual agreement between patient and therapist. The patient had returned to work and, shortly after the end of treatment, married.

The opposite speech of this schizophrenic patient shows the fantastic ways in which language may be turned to irrational uses when the individual must cope with intolerable impulses. It is worthy of note that the patient's language remained formally correct even though the introduction of the opposite speech produced a bizarre distortion.

HOW LANGUAGE DOES ITS WORK: MEANING

Whatever the work of language, whether to act magically upon the self and the world, whether to express, to symbolize, to evoke, or to enlist the cooperation of another, we have still to explore the questions posed in this chapter: How does language do this work? What is the modality of operation of language? What is meaning?

Three psychological views of meaning have gained prominence in recent years. One of these views is that meaning involves the specification of the conditions of learning and reinforcement of a particular stimulus-response association (Miller, 1951; Skinner, 1957). A second is the mediational theory proposed by Osgood, Suci, and Tannenbaum (1957), in which meaning is seen as a mediating process within the individual. In this view similarity of meaning is defined as the situation in which similar mediational processes are evoked by different stimuli. A third approach defines meaning in terms of the verbal associations evoked by a stimulus, and similarity of meaning in terms of overlap of such associations. The work of Noble (1952), of Bousfield, Cohen, and Whitmarsh (1958a), and of Deese (1959; 1962) is based on this idea.

The position taken by Skinner, in rejecting traditional lay notions of meaning, is that, "technically, meanings are to be found among the independent variables in a functional account, rather than as properties of the dependent variable. When someone says that he can see

---

(see Werner, 1940; Werner & Kaplan, 1963). Staats (1957) suggested an anxiety theory to account for the reversal. These suggested interpretations are analyzed in an article by Laffal and Ameen (1959).

the meaning of a response, he means that he can infer some of the variables of which the response is usually a function" (p. 14). The special property of verbal behavior is that it is behavior which is reinforced by the mediation of another person who has been conditioned precisely in order to reinforce the behavior of the speaker. The meaning of a verbalization thus involves (1) the presence of a motivation in the speaker which brings certain operant responses into play; and (2) the conditions of reinforcement of the response through the mediation of another person. In some instances, the self may serve in the role of another person. The process of language-learning in children follows this model: in the child the response appropriate to his motivation and to his situation—that is, the one most likely to evoke the mediating reinforcement—is gradually shaped and discriminated from other responses through selective reinforcement by the parents.

The delineation of language as a process in which there is an other-person reinforcer, and the definition of meaning in terms of the variables involved in the reinforcement situation, has stimulated considerable research in verbal reinforcement (Krasner, 1958; Salzinger, 1959). A verbal choice situation is usually presented to the subject, and one class of verbal responses is positively (or negatively) reinforced by some generalized verbal reinforcer, such as *right, wrong, mm hm,* or *uh uh* on the part of the experimenter, with the subsequent finding that the frequency of the class of reinforced responses is influenced by the experimenter's response. Some studies have shown a response change in subjects as a consequence of the sounding of a buzzer or flashing of a light when certain classes of responses were issued. Some studies have shown differences among personality types in their apparent susceptibility to influence by the reinforcing response. A significant question which has been raised in the course of these studies has to do with the role of awareness, on the part of the subject, of the experimenter's reinforcement. The issue interests us here because it shows the bearing of the meaning definition upon a language research program.

When an experimenter reinforces a subject's issuance of plural nouns by saying *mm hm* or *good,* plural nouns increase in frequency. Is this because the subject has been aware of the examiner's approval each time he produced a plural noun and makes a further effort to produce the desired response? Or is it due simply to a fact requiring no reference to internal states of the subject, namely, that people behave in that way which has the greatest likelihood of producing reinforcement? The concern of experimenters with the problem of awareness in the verbal-reinforcement experiment appears to stem from the question whether the paradigm of the subject responding as a function of the experimenter's reinforcement is applicable when such an intra-individual process as awareness intervenes between the reinforcement and the subject's response.

A detailed critique of awareness in verbal reinforcement has come from Dulany (1961; 1962). In a series of studies he examined changes in the subject's verbal responses in verbal-conditioning situations as a function of the subject's reinforcement hypotheses (hypotheses about the significance of the reinforcement), his behavioral hypotheses (ideas of what he ought to do in response to the reinforcing event), and his behavioral intention (self-instruction to respond in a certain way). He found that the reinforcement as such was far less significant in influencing responses than the hypotheses and intentions which were revealed by the subject's report or which were induced by instruction. Dulany (1961) concluded:

> In the research summarized here we repeatedly find no evidence of verbal operant conditioning without awareness —using report of a correct or correlated hypothesis as the indicator of awareness and a tone, "Umhmm," "good," or avoidance of shock as the consequence. Certainly it is possible that with somewhat different conditions—perhaps longer series of trials, more potent reinforcers, or less figural response classes—we would have found it. But if this kind of learning or conditioning without awareness is to have the social generality commonly imputed to it (as by Dollard and Miller, 1950, for example) it seems likely that we would have found it in some of these experiments. Set against this is the repeated finding that subjects who report certain forms of awareness, or are informed in terms cognate with these forms, differ significantly—and usually dramatically—from controls (p. 126).

When a complex intrapsychic process such as awareness intervenes between the experimenter's reinforcement and the subject's response, the model of verbal behavior as behavior reinforced by the mediation of another individual requires considerable elaboration. Some experimenters have attempted to preserve the model by eliminating from their studies subjects who indicated awareness of the reinforcement. As soon as intrapsychic processes of the subject are in evidence, the investigator finds that he has left the area of applicability of the other-person reinforcer model of language, which excludes considerations of internal psychical processes except insofar as they may be defined in terms of an observable situation in which there is an other-person reinforcer.

A second approach to meaning puts the operation of this construct squarely inside the individual. This is the approach which treats meaning as a mediational process occurring in the subject. Osgood, Suci, and Tannenbaum (1957) had subjects rate a number of words and concepts on a variety of scales consisting of adjectives in opposition, such as *good-bad, harmonious-dissonant, meaningful-meaningless, healthy-sick, strong-weak, serious-humorous, masculine-feminine, active-passive, fast-slow,* and so on. The original scales were constructed from adjectives used by college students in responding to the Kent-Rosanoff stimulus words. Subsequently, in an effort to obtain a more exhaustive sampling of semantic dimensions, Roget's thesaurus was used as a source. From each paired category in the thesaurus a pair of polar adjectives was selected. The available adjective pairs were then reduced to a set of 76 such pairs by various procedures designed to eliminate essentially similar pairs. In various studies other approaches have been employed to develop sets of adjectival scales upon which subjects could rate concepts which were to be judged. Factor analyses of the ratings by large numbers of subjects have repeatedly shown three major factors plus a number of subordinate factors. The major factors have been given the names evaluation, potency, and activity. The evaluation factor is well represented by the *good-bad* scale; the potency factor by the *hard-soft* and *strong-weak* scales; the activity factor by the *active-passive* scale. Cross-cultural studies have also shown the presence of the same factors in other languages, and have thus provided additional support for the universality of the original dimensions.

Since the factors do not have referential specificity, Osgood, Suci, and Tannenbaum have noted that the meaning they refer to is connotative rather than denotative. The meaning measured by "the semantic differential" (a set of scales of polar adjectives) is a multidimensional space in which any given concept is located according to the strengths of the three major factors demonstrated by the subject's scaling of the concepts.

Mowrer (1954) has given a refined theoretical account of how learning of meaning takes place, basing his discussion on the mediational theory of meaning. The basic *modus operandi* of language, according to Mowrer, is seen in the paradigm of predication. A grammatical subject is related to a predicate, as in the statement, *Tom is a thief,* and the hearer then responds as follows. There is a mediating response to the stimulus word *Tom,* which is some portion of the total complex of the reaction to the person "Tom." This mediating response gets associated with the meaning (mediational) response evoked by the stimulus word *thief.* Temporal juxtaposition of the two mediating reactions results in conditioning of the meaning reaction for *thief* to the meaning reaction and the stimulus for *Tom.* The actual nature of the complex mediational response and that portion of it which is considered the meaning response are left unspecified, although it is suggested that the response is basically some neural or physiological one. Osgood's factor analysis of scales, from which the semantic differential is derived, represents an effort to find some measures related to these mediating processes and, hence, representative of meaning. The consistency of the appearance of the three basic factors, potency, evaluation, and activity, in various factor analytic studies has led to considerable confidence in the idea that the specific scales from which the factors are constructed do, in fact, tap the meanings in the mediational process.

The approach developed by Osgood and his group seems especially suited for the systematic exploration of what Ogden and Richards called the evocative function of language. However, the whole area of reference or denotation remains untouched by it. Evaluation, potency, and activity indeed seem to be ever present in our responses, and clearly some words would be as well described by measurements along these dimensions as by any other conceivable means. Thus the words *fine, disgusting, win, leader, rest, run,* and so on appear highly suitable for this type of analysis. However, words like *green, fifty, time, apart, move, place* and so on do not. The dimensions of the semantic space undoubtedly pervade human judgmental activity: Is it good or bad; is it strong or weak; is it active or passive? Judgments along these dimensions may be readily applied by subjects to almost any stimulus upon demand. However, the availability of such judgments appears more to reflect their universality rather than their special relevance to the particular stimulus being judged. The fact that a stimulus concept or word may be located in the various dimensions of semantic space reflected in the semantic differential scales does not of necessity mean that these dimensions play important roles in the meaning of the stimulus under consideration.

Perhaps a basic failing in the semantic differential approach to meaning, in its present form, is the small number of dimensions actually utilized. This limits the meaning space in which a word or concept may be located, and words which hardly seem to fit together by

our common usage often find themselves neighbors (Weinreich, 1958).
Nevertheless, the approach has had impressive results within a limited
area, and if expanded might well provide a base for the analysis of a
much broader range of words and concepts. Other dimensions, such
as *up-down, past-present, begin-end, in-out, open-shut,* might evolve
from the testing of other scales than those on which the semantic differential was originally constructed. Osgood (1962) has recognized
this:

> From the standpoint of the practice of semantic measure-
> ment, . . . there is no such entity as "The Semantic Dif-
> ferential," with a rigidly defined set of factors—except
> perhaps in the sense of a common denominator from which
> more specific instruments are to be derived. For significant
> concept classes we will therefore want to develop specific
> instruments, and for the important class of personality
> concepts we have already done some work (p. 24).

The increase of available dimensions for measuring meaning in Osgood's sense might well lead to a system in which both denotative
and connotative meaning were handled adequately. Such an expansion
of the factor-analytic approach would probably ultimately require that
the idea of a physiological or neural mediational process be dropped.
Whether this would involve a radical change in theoretical under-
pinnings of the system, in the light of Mowrer's description of the
process of predication, and whether a strictly psychological mediational process might then replace the current notion are not clear.

Meaning, in the third view to be discussed, has been defined by
Bousfield, Cohen, and Whitmarsh (1958a) as a matrix of associations.

> Suppose, for example, the word *BLACK* is presented
> to a typical subject. It appears reasonable to suppose that
> his first response is an implicit one which may be described
> as the saying of *BLACK*. By so reacting he makes a dis-
> tinctive verbal representative response, R_{vr}. The subject
> then reacts by making a group of implicit verbal associa-
> tive responses, *e.g., WHITE, DARK, CAT*, etc. These re-
> sponses may be said to comprise the associative response
> composite, $R_{va}comp$. Under appropriate conditions the
> subject may produce the R_{vr} and the $R_{va}comp$ explicitly
> by saying or writing them. Though a definition of meaning

is perhaps gratuitous in this discussion, we believe it is useful to identify meaning with the $R_{va}comp$ (p. 1).

This view is an extension of a definition originally proposed by Noble (1952), in which meaningfulness was defined as the average number of different associations given to a stimulus word by a large number of subjects in a specified time. The index which Bousfield and his group employed was also used by Jenkins and Cofer (1957), without identifying it as a measure of meaning, to examine the associative overlap of stimulus words presented individually and in pairs.

A number of studies by Bousfield and his group support the thesis that learning of paired associates entails the association of the associated verbal composite of the stimulus with the learned responses. Bousfield, Whitmarsh, and Danick (1958) have demonstrated that the amount of generalization of learned response X to stimulus word B, where X has been learned in response to stimulus word A, may be predicted from the partial response identities of the associated responses of word A and word B.

Deese (1962) has made the associative definition of meaning more central in some of his studies. According to Deese, two stimuli may be said to resemble one another in associative meaning to the extent that they have the same distribution of associates. Deese has also factor-analyzed distributions of associations for the purpose of finding common factors which bind different associative structures together. About associative meaning, Deese says, "Associative meaning, in general, should predict the words that will occur in the verbal environment of a particular word. . . . The words may appear in the same environment in two ways: (*a*) as substitutes for one another, or (*b*) as part of one another's environment" (p. 172).

The definition of meaning which is basic to the present work is consistent with the material of Noble, Bousfield, and Deese. The meaning of a word is defined as the hierarchy of responses, including the stimulus itself as the primary word, brought into play when a person is stimulated by a word. The reader must bear in mind here the discussion of "word representation" and "thing representation" in Chapter 1. When we speak of words or of verbal associations, we refer not to words in isolation, but as welded to "thing representations." Language does its work by evoking experiential associations which are suggested by the pertinent words or, to put it a little differently, by rearranging the relative strengths and likelihoods of occurrence of groups of word-thing responses. The evoked hierarchy of associations, the meaning, reflects a fundamental behavioral and attitudinal shift in the listener in response to the stimulus. Meaning refers to the stimulus side of language, that portion of *la langue* within each speaker which is activated upon the occurrence of a stimulus.

If a number of subjects are asked to respond with the first word that comes to mind to the word *table,* most of them will respond with *chair.* The definition which has been offered would assert that, in addition to the aspect of meaning represented by *table* itself, a significant aspect is that represented by *chair.* In the same way, when the stimulus word is *black,* the two primary experiential complexes have to do with *black,* the stimulus word, and *white,* the most frequent response; when the stimulus word is *man,* the primary associated response beside *man* is *woman* (see Russell & Jenkins, 1954).

When verbal meaning is defined as the hierarchy of associated verbal responses, it must be understood that the traditional notion of reference in which the meaning of a word is taken either as the thing to which it refers, or as the act of referring to a thing, has been for the most part abandoned. This may be made more clear if one asks for associations to words like *democracy* and *threat.* Here the actual thing-reference may be quite obscure, but the associations will be consistent with our anticipations and will define the realms of experience in which such words have application. The distorted language of the schizophrenic patient is understood best if one looks beyond denotation and even beyond common dominant associations to remote and idiosyncratic associations. Semanticists (Chase, 1938; Hayakawa, 1941; Korzybski, 1933) might shudder at the introduction of such diffuseness into meaning. Nevertheless, its practical value is great.

In an intriguing epilogue, entitled "No Black Scorpion," to his book on verbal behavior, Skinner (1957) offers a guess at explaining a challenging repartee made by Alfred North Whitehead in the course of a conversation. The conversation, according to Skinner, took place in 1934 at a dinner at the Harvard Society of Fellows. Skinner at the time was thirty years old, and Whitehead was seventy-three. Seeking, as he says, to strike a blow for the cause of behaviorism, Skinner was maintaining that science could account for all of human behavior, but Whitehead would only agree that science might be successful in accounting for human behavior providing one made an exception of verbal behavior, and challenged Skinner to "account for my behavior as I sit here saying 'No black scorpion is falling upon this table' " (p. 457). Since it is precisely to such puzzling and apparently incomprehensible remarks that a good portion of the present book is devoted, it is not out of place to consider this matter further.

Years later Skinner attempted to account for Professor White-head's behavior as follows: "Perhaps there was a stimulus which evoked the response *black scorpion falling upon this table,* which in turn led to the autoclitic *No.* The stimulus may not have been much, but in a determined system it must have been something. Just as the physicist may suggest various explanations of the drop in temperature in order to show that it could be explained in lawful terms, so it is not entirely beside the point to make a guess here. I suggest, then, that *black scorpion* was a metaphorical response to the topic under discussion. The black scorpion was behaviorism" (p. 459).

This interpretation, of course, makes the point which Skinner wishes to clinch, namely, that verbal behavior is a function of operant stimuli and reinforcing agents. The operant stimulus—a complex one —would be the somewhat jarring ideas of the young behaviorist, and the reinforcement, that is, the desired outcome, would be the discomfiture of this enthusiast. Presumably the function of Whitehead's remark would be to rout the claims of the behaviorist.

The account nicely fits the theory of operant behavior, since stimulus and reinforcement are identified in the objective current setting. But why *black scorpion,* as Skinner asks, rather than *autumn leaf* or *snowflake?* The answer, I suggest, has to do with the current concerns of the philosopher which were as surely present at the dinner table as was the philosopher himself. What sort of concerns? The very verbalizations suggest them. For this, we may turn to associations. *Black* and *table* are words in the Kent-Rosanoff stimulus list, and, without extreme distortion, *spider,* which is also in the Kent-Rosanoff list, may be taken as close enough to *scorpion* to suggest the kinds of associations which *scorpion* might produce. The associations to *table* taken from the Russell-Jenkins study (1954) are given in Table 1. Below are the associations to *black* and *spider* from the same study.

TABLE 3

ASSOCIATIONS TO *black* AND *spider*:

RUSSELL AND JENKINS (1954)

Black (N = 1008)

751 white	3 coal, bottom,	1 dirt, cap, dismal, green,
54 dark	paper, car,	casket, big, shiny, nice,
26 cat	shoe	pitch, Sam, dirty, death,
22 light	2 horse, board,	hole, velvet, suit, spade,
20 night	coat, wool,	eat, stove, ebony, chair,

Black $(N = 1008)$—(Cont'd)

11 sheep	button, cold,	singe, magic, eye, dead,
10 color	brown, dress,	pants, witch, jack, telephone,
9 red	gray,	murder, afraid, ink, book,
6 blue, dog	blackboard	stocking, darkness, cave,
5 cloth		kitten, midnight, rake, wagon,
		depth, satin, good, marble,
		moon, whittle, hair, Negro,
		whiten, pit, body, blouse

Spider $(N = 1008)$

454	web	3	ish, widow,	1	mouse, mites, small,
152	insect		fright,		feelers, interesting,
97	bug(s)		arachnoid,		ladybug, insect, beetle,
50	leg(s)		net, dog,		shiver, cockroach,
37	fly		eight (8)		orthoptera, alarm,
34	black	2	wall,		avoid, gray, spider web,
18	crawl		tarantula,		cat, corner, distaste,
16	animal		dark, crawling,		spinning, ugh, morbid,
12	ant		run, zoology,		awful, horrible, rat,
9	black widow		(Miss) Muffet,		claw, boy, jump, fur,
6	fear, poison		creepy, icky,		scream, unbeneficial,
5	afraid, worm		snake, horrid,		pan, room, evil, turn,
4	bite, spin,		scared, cob-		furry, unpleasant,
	ugly		webs, bird,		squirm, chills, sit,
			poisonous		life science, arm,
					shape, thin, man

Perhaps thoughts of death were in Whitehead's mind, since both *black* and *scorpion* are associated with such matters. Skinner himself recognizes this at the end of the anecdote when he in effect reassures the reader that behaviorism is not a black scorpion (unpleasant thing). At any rate, Whitehead responded with piercing aptness to a disturbing challenge. But he was responding not only to behaviorism, but to the fact that it was being presented by a young man, and to the fact that he himself was in his waning years. The *no,* in this sense, may have been a warding off operation, a denial, and a reassurance directed to the self. The interpretation can be of course labored endlessly, and, after all, the point which is being made here is merely slanted to illustrate a difference in approach from that of Skinner. Skinner drew his inferences from the immediately present and observable data. However, part of these immediate data, although not readily observable, were certain facts about Whitehead's life. In a book by Lucien Price, *Dialogues of Alfred North Whitehead* (1954), there are two detailed accounts of dinners with the Whitehead family on April 6, 1934, and April 22, 1934. The opening paragraph of the report of the April 6 meeting is as follows:

> Seventeenth anniversary of the United States' entrance into the first world war. The declaration of war came on a Good Friday, an historic irony which no one seemed to notice at the time. This had occupied us at editorial conference and was still in my thoughts as I went out to Canton to dine with the Whiteheads. Their youngest son, Eric, an aviator, had been killed in the war. (p. 21).

One could surmise that, if Skinner's contact with Whitehead were also around this time, some of the sad recollections of his son's death may have been in the philosopher's thoughts. Further in the report, we discover that the Whiteheads' daughter had had an accident while skiing on Mt. Washington some time before, and that for weeks her life had been in danger. When this crisis ended, Mrs. Whitehead had had a heart attack and at the time was invalided. The second visit, which took place on April 22, has a most pertinent sequence. The conversation turned to the possibility of poets being administrative heads of government. Whitehead playfully suggested that he himself would like to be the head of a great department store. Someone commented that he might like to compete with Selfridge's in London. Whitehead's reply was, "Not necessarily. Mr. Selfridge might be considerate enough to die and leave me to manage the store" (p. 40). It was then maintained by someone that Selfridge had already died. Whitehead's reply was one of doubt; he then went off to get *Who's Who* to find out if Selfridge had died, and returned shortly, triumphantly reading, "He's still alive. Here he is, 'Gordon Selfridge' " (p.40).

Puzzling verbal responses are sometimes elucidated by considering the stimulus aspects (the hierarchy of associations) of the utterance, as in the case of *black scorpion*. Where the verbalization seems inconsistent with the context in which it is uttered, or irrelevant, the possibility arises that it is based on remote associations to what would be a more direct and relevant utterance. Since group associations to *black* and *scorpion* reveal many dysphoric elements, including words relating to death, so it may be reasoned that the speaker was talking about such concerns, probably without any clear awareness on his own part that he was doing so. Such examples, I believe, bring home the significance of an associative definition of meaning.

3. The Word-Association Task and the Structure of Associations

We have seen that the associative constellation evoked in verbal stimulation may play an important role in word meaning. Let us examine the constellation of associations more closely, with an eye both to the ideal—*la langue* —and the idiolect, the potential within the individual. The word-association task, in all its variations, is an important technique for approximating the associations pertinent to a stimulus word both in *la langue* and in the idiolects of individuals. For there are striking similarities in word associations obtained from a group of individuals when each one responds with a single word to a stimulus word, and the extended responses of any single individual responding at length to the same stimulus word. The distribution of word associations obtained from a group is in fact often taken as the best approximation of the responses available to a single individual (Deese, 1959; 1962; Rosen & Russell, 1957; Schlosberg & Heineman, 1950). The assumption involved in this equation is an important one, since it implies the possibility of elucidating the associative processes of the individual by reference to the associations of the group.

Aside from the empirical evidence which favors it, the idea has its justification in the following considerations, in which the reader will again recognize the foundations of the concept of *la langue.* Because of the essential similarity of basic experiences in growth and daily life for all individuals in a culture, and because of the intimate mingling of language with all activities, much verbal material has been learned and overlearned in certain typical combinations. When one individual speaks, his listener responds with associations which are culturally dominant and readily available, presumably the same associations which are present in the hierarchies from which the speaker selected his words. The chances are thus good that there will be a considerable matching between speaker's and listener's associations.

Dominant associations like *chair* to the stimulus word *table* reflect frequent and consistent experiences by members of the group in which the word *table* and the object "table" and the word *chair* and object "chair" have occurred together. Responses in the case of the stimulus *table,* like *four* or *company,* which are given by only single individuals in the group tap components of experience of particular individuals which are not necessarily shared by all members of the group. Individual differences in otherwise common experiences are inevitable, and it is to be expected that there will be numerous subordinate associations to any stimulus word which will differ from individual to individual. In addition, although certain experiences like those connecting *table* and *chair* have a clear pre-eminence for most members of the group, the same might not be true for a few members of the group for numerous possible reasons. Such members of the group would respond to the stimulus word *table* in ways which might be considered atypical, perhaps idiosyncratic.

Let us review briefly some of the studies which have provided important insights about word associations of the group and their relationship to word associations of the individual.

Interest in the word-association task since the end of the nineteenth century has followed two main courses: concern with the normative or group uniformities in response, and concern with the clinical and diagnostic significance of individual responses. Both of these lines of investigation have produced findings relevant to our discussion.

ASSOCIATION NORMS, PSYCHOTIC ASSOCIATIONS, AND CHILDREN'S ASSOCIATIONS

Thumb and Marbe, according to Woodworth (1938, p. 340 ff.), were among the first to point out that the frequency with which a response is given in word association by a group of subjects is related to the speed with which that same response is given by the individuals in the group. Woodworth has summarized the findings of several authors with respect to this phenomenon, which has come to be known as Marbe's Law. The law states, in effect, that responses given more frequently by the group are given more rapidly by the individual members of the group. Subsequent studies repeatedly confirmed Marbe's Law (Esper, 1918), and Schlosberg and Heineman (1950) advanced the idea that both latency of response of the individual and frequency of a response in a group were measures of response strength of a response *within* the individual. Using 204 subjects and 25 monosyllabic words from the Kent-Rosanoff (1910) association list, they were able to show that high communality responses were given with great rapidity and low communality responses less rapidly. Communality of a response was defined as the percentage of the total sample of 204 subjects who gave that particular response.

Bousfield and Barclay (1950) had subjects write associations, with instructions to list the names of as many of a class of items, such as birds, as possible. They then examined the relationship between order of occurrence of the associations for individuals, and frequency of occurrence of the associations for the group as a whole. They found a marked tendency for associations of high frequency in the group to occur early in the associations of the individuals and for those of lower frequencies to occur later.

Laffal (1955) used a word-association task in which the stimulus words were equated with respect to frequency in the written language at large by being selected from among those in the Thorndike-Lorge *Teacher's Word Book of 30,000 Words* (1944) which occurred between 10 and 25 times per million in the written language. These stimulus words were administered to 80 college undergraduates individually in oral testing sessions, with care being taken to record reaction times as well as response disturbances typically utilized in clinical application of the word-association test (Jung, 1910; Rapaport, Gill & Schafer, 1946). It was found that response faults, defined as reaction times over 2.6 seconds, or failure to recall the original responses when the stimulus list was presented a second time tended to occur on responses which were given rarely by the group, whereas responses which were given with great frequency in the group were seldom accompanied by response faults.

Studies such as these have been repeated in various forms by other experimenters. They show that communality of response in the group, as measured by frequency of occurrence of a response, is highly related to such characteristics of the individual's response as order of occurrence of the response in a sequence of responses, latency of response, and response faults of the kind utilized in clinical applications of the test.

Further light is thrown on the relation of group and individual associations by studies of word association in individuals whose language behavior is disturbed. The earliest large-scale study of word association was designed to explore how the verbal associations of psychotic individuals differed from those of normal individuals. Kent and Rosanoff (1910) compared the word associations of 1000 normal individuals of various ages, from various walks of life, with the associations of 247 psychotic patients. In this study a common reaction was defined as a response which appeared more than once in the protocols of the 1000 normal subjects and an individual reaction was defined as one which did not appear more than once in the normal protocols. A response which could not be found in the normal protocol in its identical form, but which was a grammatical variant of a word found there, was classified as doubtful. Table 4 shows the distribution of responses.

TABLE 4

TABLE SHOWING DISTRIBUTIONS OF COMMON, INDIVIDUAL, AND
DOUBTFUL ASSOCIATIONS OF NORMAL AND PSYCHOTIC
SUBJECTS: KENT AND ROSANOFF (1910, p. 317)

	Common Reaction	Individual Reaction	Doubtful Reaction
1000 Normal Subjects	91.7%	6.8%	1.5%
247 Insane Subjects	70.7%	26.8%	2.5%

The findings of Kent and Rosanoff are especially interesting in their revelation that the verbal associations of psychotic individuals are characterized by many individual or idiosyncratic responses. This conforms with our idea that the psychotic individual differs in his language from socially common and accepted usage. However, clinical experience with psychotic patients would suggest that only the more severely disturbed patients show such marked differences from normal associative tendencies, whereas the less disturbed psychotic patients tend to approximate the normal individual in their associations. Kent and Rosanoff recognized this and pointed out that, not infrequently, dementia praecox patients gave test records that could not be dis-

tinguished from normal records. Examples of the protocols of two of
the dementia praecox patients, shown in Table 5, do in fact suggest

TABLE 5

TABLE SHOWING SOME OF THE WORD ASSOCIATIONS
OF TWO DEMENTIA PRAECOX PATIENTS:
KENT AND ROSANOFF (1910, p. 332)

Stimulus Word	Case No. 4752	Case No. 5183
table	meadow	muss
dark	black	gone
music	sweet	caffa
sickness	dead	monk
man	mansion	boy
deep	near	lesson
soft	sooner	ness
eating	formble	pie
mountain	gair	Gus
house	temble	muss
black	benched	court
mutton	ranched	beef
comfort	bumble	ness
hand	semble	koy
short	simber	ness
fruit	narrow	dalb
butterfly	Ben	flack
smooth	gum	mess
command	bramble	cork
chair	low	ness
sweet	temper	Bess
whistle	bensid	toy
woman	hummery	girl
cold	gunst	cork
slow	bemper	mass
wish	tip	vell
river	gumper	mouth
white	Andes	cast
beautiful	gimper	ness
window	hummer	crow
rough	geep	ratter
citizen	humper	zide
foot	zuper	malloy
spider	gumper	straw
needle	himper	cast
red	gumper	Roman

Stimulus Word	Case No. 4752	Case No. 5183
sleep	moop	scack
anger	rumble	gois
carpet	slamper	noise
girl	hinker	call
high	humper	hort
working	gumpip	Kaffir
sour	imper	romerscotters
earth	gumper	bell
trouble	humper	tramine
soldier	guipper	gas
cabbage	phar	cor
hard	her	kalbas

that most idiosyncratic reactions in the Kent-Rosanoff psychotic population came from relatively few patients. Nonsense words, perseverations, and irrelevant responses predominate over pertinent associations in these examples. It is almost impossible to escape the impression that, although the patients complied with the examiner's request for verbal associations, they worked hard at giving worthless responses.

A study by Murphy (1923) provided some clarifying evaluations of the associations of psychotic patients of various diagnostic groups. He compared a manic depressive group, a dementia praecox group, and a normal group on the Kent-Rosanoff word-association test, and found that the manic depressive group closely paralleled the normal group in proportions of common responses, whereas the dementia praecox group showed markedly fewer common reactions.

Murphy also made interesting comparisons between the word associations of the various psychotic groups, the normal group, and a children's group, using the Woodrow-Lowell (1916) tables for the children's response frequencies. In these comparisons, the dementia praecox group showed a reduction in common responses, not only by comparison with the adult tables, but also by comparison with the children's table. Murphy concluded that the associations of the dementia praecox patients were decidedly more like the associations of the normal adults than like the associations of children, despite the tendency to low-frequency responses.

Using the original Kent-Rosanoff tables as criteria of common and individual responses, Rosanoff and Rosanoff (1913), in a study of the responses of 300 children from the ages of four to fifteen, found that there was a steady decrease in idiosyncratic, individual responses as the age of the subjects increased. Their findings with respect to common and individual responses are presented below in Table 6.

Several points were noted by Rosanoff and Rosanoff in connection with their study. For one thing the high incidence of individual responses in younger children was found to be in part a function of a tendency of these children to perseverate in giving the same response to succeeding stimulus words. Another point was that the fifteen-year-old group members were of lower mental status than other pupils, since they were still in grammar school where average students of that age were already in high school. Lower intelligence, the authors felt, accounted for the lower percentage of common reactions in this group.

TABLE 6

COMMON, INDIVIDUAL, DOUBTFUL, AND FAILURE RESPONSES IN
VARIOUS AGE GROUPS: ROSANOFF AND ROSANOFF (1913)

Age	Common Reactions (%)	Individual Reactions (%)	Doubtful and Failure Reactions (%)
4	41.5	25.3	33.2
5	57.1	21.4	21.5
6	64.9	18.6	15.5
7	68.9	20.0	11.1
8	74.2	18.0	7.8
9	80.6	14.2	5.2
10	81.3	14.3	4.4
11	89.1	8.6	2.3
12	90.4	7.6	2.0
13	89.5	8.5	2.0
14	90.4	7.7	1.9
15	86.3	10.8	2.9
adults	91.7	6.8	1.5

Examination of Table 6 reveals a rather striking shift in percentage of common and individual responses around the age of eleven. A study by Horan (1956) of the word associations of mentally retarded children also found that in the tenth and twelfth years retarded children seemed to show a significant increase in similarity of favored responses to those of adults. The evidence suggests that this early adolescent period may be one of crucial integration of the verbal processes. Werner and Kaplan (1950a; 1950b) have made the same point as a result of their studies of how children develop word meanings.

The study by Rosanoff and Rosanoff was criticized by Woodrow and Lowell (1916) on the ground that use of adult tables as criteria of common and individual responses from the children was arbitrary. For example, such use required that several of the responses given with a frequency of more than 10 by the children in their study be classified as individual responses since the adults did not give these responses at all. Woodrow and Lowell studied 1000 normal children between the ages of nine and twelve, using 90 of the Kent-Rosanoff stimulus words. They treated this age range as a single group, since breakdown by years showed that the three most frequently given responses for each stimulus were almost the same in all cases. In comparing the children's with the adults' word associations, they defined individual responses as those responses which appeared no more than once among the children, rather than using the Kent-Rosanoff tables as Rosanoff and Rosanoff had done. They found that their 1000 children gave an average of 52 individual responses per stimulus word compared with an average of 80 individual responses to the same words by the adults. On the average, the 1000 children gave 102 different associations to each stimulus word, whereas the 1000 adults gave an average of 143 associations. Woodrow and Lowell concluded that the adult responses differed from the children's not so much in the disappearance of the children's responses, as in the occurrence of additional responses which had not been available to the children.

Wheat (1931) tested 1,323 children in the fourth through eighth grades with a word-association technique using some Kent-Rosanoff words as well as some other highly frequent words. Wheat's criterion of communality was any response which appeared more than 10 times in 1000. This criterion was more stringent than the Kent-Rosanoff criterion (which defined as a common response any response appearing more than once among the responses of the 1000 normal subjects). Bearing in mind this difference, which resulted in lower percentages of common responses for Wheat's sample, the findings roughly paralleled those of Rosanoff and Rosanoff (1913). Thus the fourth grade, nine-year-old group gave 45.5 per cent common, and 28.3 per cent uncommon responses; the fifth grade, ten-year-old group gave 54.3 per cent common and 21.1 per cent uncommon responses; the sixth grade, eleven-year-old group gave 63.0 per cent common and 16.5 per cent uncommon responses; the seventh grade, twelve-year-old group gave 59.4 per cent common and 16.8 per cent uncommon responses; and the eighth grade, thirteen-year-old group gave 61.2 per cent common and 14.6 per cent uncommon responses. Here again, there appeared to be a striking change in the eleven-year-old group toward what seemed to be a stable proportion of common and uncommon associations.

These normative studies convey an orderliness and structure in word association which may be traced through the relationship between individual and group associations, through the idiosyncrasies in association of mentally disturbed individuals, and through the development of associations in children.

DIAGNOSTIC ASPECTS OF WORD ASSOCIATION

After Galton initiated word-association experiments on himself in 1879 as a way of exploring memory and thought processes, the method was taken up in Wundt's laboratory. There association studies were designed to elucidate the structure of mind, and interest was focused on speed of responding and the logical and grammatical relations of response word to stimulus word. Introspective reports taken from subjects in the studies of Aschaffenburg, Cattell, and others (see Woodworth, 1938, p. 362) indicated that reaction time was a function of a number of factors, some of which were related to pleasant and unpleasant emotions. Sometimes the subject reported that two or more responses struggled for utterance, interfering with each other, and sometimes he would be reminded of an interesting experience which momentarily occupied him to the neglect of the task of responding. A pleasant or unpleasant emotion might delay the response, and the subject occasionally reported a blank in which no response seemed to be available.

The interference phenomenon in word association was used effectively for the purpose of detecting guilt. This procedure was first introduced by Wertheimer in 1905. Typical lie-detection tests employ certain physiological measures along with the word-association task (Crosland, 1929). In the word-association task, key words relating to the criminal event are interspersed among words unrelated to the crime. Individuals for whom the critical words have significance will show interference effects and response faults of various types, whereas innocent subjects will not show any special sensitivity to the critical words.

The diagnostic application of the word-association method as an individualized technique for discovering areas of psychological conflict in patients is due to Jung (1910; 1918). Jung felt that the word-association task afforded a rapid, controlled way of getting at the psychological "complexes" of the subject, in the same way that Freud's method of free association did. Disturbances in the word-association task were regarded as "resistances" by Jung and attributed to the same mechanisms of repression and censorship which operate in dreams and in hysterical symptoms. His description of response disturbances in the association task is a good example of a clinically derived hypothesis about such disturbances (Jung, 1909):

> Whenever there is a diminution of attention there is an increase in the superficial associations and their value diminishes. Therefore, if during an association experiment without any artificial distraction there suddenly appear striking superficial associations, one is justified in supposing that a momentary diminution of attention has taken place. The cause of this is to be sought in an internal distraction. According to instructions the subject is supposed to fix his attention on the experiment. If his attention decreases, that is, if without any external reason the attention is turned away from the meaning of the stimulus word there must be an internal cause for this distractibility. We find this mostly in the antecedent or in the same reaction. There appears a strongly emotional idea, a complex, which on account of its strong feeling tone, assumes great distinction in consciousness, or when repressed sends an inhibition into consciousness, and in this way either suspends for a short time the effect of the directing idea (attention to the stimulus word) or simply diminishes it. The correctness of this supposition can usually be proven without any difficulty by analysis. The phenomenon described is therefore of practical value as a complex-indicator. From the repression it can send an inhibition into consciousness, thus disturbing the attention; in other words, it can check the intellectual functioning of consciousness (prolongation of reaction time), or can make it impossible (errors), or can diminish its value (sound associations) (p. 50).

The ideas of Jung regarding the significance of "complexes" in producing disturbances in word association were at first generally accepted, and a number of studies were devoted to determining the relative merits of various complex indicators (Hull & Lugoff, 1921; Kohs, 1914). An effort was also made to explore the functioning of unconscious conflicts by suggesting conflicts under hypnosis, and employing word association to examine the influence of the unconscious (suggested) conflicts on physiological responses as well as on intellectual processes in the posthypnotic state (Huston, Shakow, & Erickson, 1934; Luria, 1932). Diven (1937) gave his subjects word lists in which the words *red barn* were repeated several times, with a stop signal and electric shock occurring after *barn*. He found that physiological disturbances spread from the critical word to precritical and postcritical words, and to other words with rural connotations. He also found that for those subjects who were unaware of the relation between the stimulus word and the shock, compared to those who were aware of the connection, the physiological responses tended to be more marked and to increase with incubation over time. These studies tended to affirm the significance of unconscious psychological conflicts or complexes in producing interference effects on word association.

Some findings, however, tended to throw doubt on the simple notion of a direct relationship between word disturbance and psychological complex. Thus Kephart and Houtchens (1937) studied the responses of 50 boys from twelve to eighteen years of age to the Jung association list and the Kent-Rosanoff list, with the hypothesis that, since the Jung list was by design oriented toward exploring "complexes," whereas the Kent-Rosanoff list was composed of "neutral" words, responses to the Jung words ought to show more disturbances. They found, on the contrary, that there were no differences in number of disturbances evoked by the two lists. They therefore concluded that disturbances in the process of association represented a sample of the amount of mental disturbance rather than a specific conflict situation suggested by a specific stimulus word.

On the other hand, Rapaport, Gill, and Schafer (1946) and Schafer (1945) have given a detailed formulation of disturbances in word association which interprets disturbances over a whole record in the manner suggested by Kephart and Houtchens but also takes account of disturbances on specific stimulus words. These investigators came to the view that "disturbances of the associative process may be thought of as occurring in two settings: they may be precipitated by encountering an idea which is emotionally disturbing or they may be merely manifestations of a more or less generalized disorganization of thinking" (Schafer, 1945, p. 218).

Clinical studies of word association have naturally focused on the psychological structure of the individual and upon the way in which his unique needs, conflicts, and psychological integration affect his production of verbal responses. There have been a number of experimental attempts to study the role of needs and motivation on the associative response process, some of which we may now consider.

EXPERIMENTAL STUDIES OF NEEDS AND
WORD ASSOCIATION

Hunger, as a need which may be readily induced and which may be described objectively in terms of hours of deprivation, has quite naturally been the need employed most often in experimental studies of association. The earliest such studies were by Sanford (1936; 1937) who examined the effects of hunger on various perceptual and verbal tasks, including a word-association task. In the first experiment Sanford had 10 children between ages of seven and eleven respond to stimulus words and ambiguous pictures shortly before a regular meal and immediately after a regular meal. He tabulated and compared the food responses under the two conditions and found that subjects tested before a regular meal gave significantly more food responses than they gave after a regular meal. In a further, more extensive experiment, he examined how food responses varied during the total normal eating cycle (eating-abstinence-eating) and how such responses changed after a twenty-four-hour fast. In this experiment 27 college students fasted for the twenty-four-hour period and 37 subjects were tested at various times in the eating cycle. Various tests were used, among which were word association, chained associations, and completions of words, and the criterion measure was the number of food responses. The results in this study showed that food responses increased with time during the normal eating cycle and over the twenty-four-hour period of fasting. However, the increase in food responses of the fasters was not in direct proportion to the increase in time since last eating. At the end of the twenty-four-hour fast, the average food response of the fasters was only slightly greater than that of the subjects who were examined near the close of the normal eating cycle.

Sanford reasoned that two factors were operating to produce change in the numbers of food responses. The first was a habitual tendency toward eating related to time cycles, and the second was an actual food need independent of the habitual eating cycle. Where testing of the subjects occurred in a "latent" phase of the eating cycle—that is, where food need under normal circumstances was minimal—food responses were relatively low despite the fact that the subjects were fasting. When testing occurred at a time when maximal habitual food tension and food deprivation were operating jointly, the greatest number of food responses was given.

However, Sanford raised the further possibility that the increase in food responses after twenty-four hours of fasting might have been even greater if it were not for the operation of what he called a process of suppression which tended to inhibit the giving of food responses in order to avoid aggravation of the need. This hypothesis echoes some of the clinical ideas about interference effects in word association.

What happens to food responses in extreme hunger was explored by Brozek, Guetzkow, Baldwin, and Cranston (1951) in a study of perception and association in experimental starvation. The subjects were 34 conscientious objectors in World War II who volunteered to serve as subjects in the experiment. There were three main periods in the experiment: a control period of twelve weeks, a period of semistarvation lasting twenty-four weeks, and a controlled rehabilitation period lasting twelve weeks. During the semistarvation period the caloric intake of the group averaged 1,570 calories, as compared with the intake of about 3,500 calories during the control period. The average body weight of the subjects at the end of the semistarvation period was 52.6 kilograms as compared with 69.4 kilograms at the end of the control period. The intensity of the food drive throughout the experiment was defined in terms of ratings obtained on the basis of interviews with and observations of the subjects. With reference to the food drive, the subjects were asked directly such questions as: To what extent do topics related to food enter your thinking, reading, and conversation? Are food and eating important to you? Do you think of the good old days when you could get as much food as you wanted? Do you often think of your old favorite dishes? To what extent are you conscious of your need for food?

On a scale from 0 (normal) to 5 (extreme), the mean ratings for appetite, defined as the "desire for food," rose to 2.7 after twelve weeks of semistarvation and to 3.1 after twenty-four weeks of semistarvation, declining to 1.6 after twelve weeks of rehabilitation. Five sources of data were used to evaluate the effects of heightened food drive. These were the word-association test, a restricted-associations test, dream content, the Rorschach test, and Rosenzweig's Picture Frustration Study.

Only the word-association test showed statistically significant change under the semistarvation condition. One hundred stimulus words were used, 50 of them having been selected from the original Kent-Rosanoff list. The additional 50 words were included for possible significance in evaluating psychodynamic factors in the subjects. The test was administered in standard fashion, the stimulus words being presented one at a time and the subjects being required to respond with the first word that came to mind. The responses were recorded and timed. After the first presentation, the subjects were asked to recall as many as possible of the stimulus words together with the responses they had given. The test was given only once, toward the end of the semistarvation period, and 31 conscientious objectors who participated in other projects carried out in the laboratory served as the control group for the evaluation of the responses of the 34 experimental subjects.

Interestingly enough there was practically no difference in the number of food responses of the experimental and control groups. In the experimental group 5.9 per cent of the responses related to food or eating, and, in the control group, 5.8 per cent fell in this category. However, a major finding was that the experimental group showed an increase in idiosyncratic responses, particularly to stimulus words referring to food and eating.

In this analysis, only the 50 words taken from the Kent-Rosanoff list were used, and O'Connor's (1928) norms were applied to determine which responses were idiosyncratic. Idiosyncratic responses were defined as those not appearing in O'Connor's list of words. O'Connor listed words which occurred at least 10 times either in the Kent-Rosanoff tables or in his own study of 1,000 subjects. Idiosyncratic words in the Brozek *et al.* study were thus words given less than 1 per cent of the time by both samples of 1000 subjects. The percentage of idiosyncratic responses given to all of the 50 Kent-Rosanoff words was slightly but not significantly higher for the experimental group, but, when only the 8 Kent-Rosanoff food words (*eating, bitter, fruit, sweet, hungry, sour, thirsty, cabbage*) were considered, it was found that the 34 experimental subjects gave on the average 27.2 per cent idiosyncratic responses to these words, whereas the control group gave on the average 15.7 per cent idiosyncratic responses to such words. This difference was significant by *t* test beyond the .02 level of confidence.

Another result of some interest was that, in the first 10 words recalled by the two groups of subjects, 26 per cent of the experimental group recalled the word *hungry,* whereas none of the control group did.

The findings in this study appear to fall into line with the hypothesis offered by Sanford (1937) that with prolonged fasting a tendency to suppress food responses comes into play as a way of preventing aggravation of the need. This would account for the paradoxical result that the experimental subjects showed no increase in food responses. The fact that there was an increase in idiosyncratic responses to food stimulus words may be explained as follows. The food need was a significant need, but there was also a striving to avoid further aggravation of this need. Food need ordinarily calls for food-related responses. The striving to suppress such responses where they might lead to exacerbation of a painful condition demands nonfood responses. Especially in the case of food-related stimulus words, the avoidance striving would have to contest the tendency toward high-communality food-related responses. The results obtained in the study indicated that the avoidance striving was successful and that many uncommon or idiosyncratic responses were produced by the hungry subjects.

One other study, by Wispé (1954), is pertinent to this discussion of the relationship between need and association. Wispé's subjects were 50 male and female college students, who were divided into 3 groups with different levels of food and water deprivation: a zero-to-two-hour deprivation or control group, a ten-hour deprivation group, and a twenty-four-hour deprivation group. Stimulus words were presented to individual subjects, who were instructed to give the first words which came to mind, and to continue associating until told to stop. The first 19 associations to each stimulus word were recorded. Forty-eight stimulus words were used, of which half were need-relevant and half neutral. Of the 24 need words, half were related to water and half to food; the need words were further divided into act words (referring to the taking of need satisfiers, as *eat, drink*) and object words (naming hunger and thirst satisfiers, as *pie, milk*). Wispé's findings were that increased deprivation selectively influenced the number and kind of need-related associations. While the numbers of act and object responses were not significantly different from each other in the three deprivation periods, the numbers of instrumental responses (names of objects and processes instrumental to need satisfaction, but not themselves satisfiers, as *restaurant, cook*) and affective responses (adjectival responses referring to hunger and thirst satisfiers as *delicious, sour*) varied significantly. Instrumental responses were lowest in the ten-hour deprivation group and highest in the twenty-four-hour deprivation group. Affective responses were highest in the ten-hour deprivation group and lowest in the twenty-four-hour group. As in Sanford's studies there was a shift in the group which was longest deprived away from words related directly to need satisfiers. In Wispé's study the shift was toward words related to the instrumental activities required to overcome the deprivation.

These studies suggest that changes in a need like hunger result in changes in associative responses. The most interesting situation occurs where the need runs into some conflicting tendency. This apparently occurred in all of the studies considered. In Sanford's experiments, a need to suppress was postulated to account for the reduced need-related responses in the most extremely deprived group. In the experiment of Brozek and his group, the dominant responses to the food stimulus words were interfered with, and idiosyncratic responses appeared. In Wispé's results, the longest deprived group of subjects showed a shift away from responses affectively related to the satisfying qualities of food and toward instrumental words relating to the means of procuring satisfaction. These experiments, which show the influence of hunger on word association, are supported by studies dealing with the effects of hunger on more involved verbal behavior (Atkinson & McClelland, 1948) as well as by studies of the influence of more complicated need systems on verbal behavior, such as the need for achievement (McClelland, Clark, Roby, & Atkinson, 1949) and sexual motivation (Clark, 1952). There is thus substantial evidence that needs influence verbal behavior, although the process is not always the simple one of increasing the need-related responses, and that alterations of the conditions of the association task may change the whole hierarchical structure, placing otherwise weak responses in a dominant position and ordinarily dominant responses in a subordinate position. Apparently the stability of the association ladder obtained from a group is guaranteed only by strict adherence to a standard procedure which attempts to evoke associations under conditions of absence of strong needs or stresses, absence of distractions, and absence of any directing or orienting instructions other than to respond with the first word that comes to mind.

Changes in instructions (for example, to respond like most college students) have also been shown to change the dominant responses (Jenkins, 1959). Placing subjects under stress by emphasizing speed of response may alter the relative frequency of responses (Siipola, Walker, & Kolb, 1955). It has even been demonstrated that responses may be affected when incidental, presumably irrelevant features of the task obtrude upon the subject's attention. Thus, Bentley (1939) had subjects sip from a beaker of colored water after each association and also gave the association test to subjects who had a bandage tightly around one arm. The study, which was directed against the thesis of Gellhorn and Kraines (1936) that decrease in oxygen supply results in increase of idiosyncratic and decrease of common associations, established that idiosyncratic responses increased markedly in the word association as a result of the kind of intrusive instrumentation employed by Gellhorn and Kraines to reduce oxygen supply.

The possibility of changing the hierarchical structure of associations by changing the conditions of association suggests that one or another of a large number of possible dimensions of association may be brought into prominence at any particular moment, depending on many factors, and reminds us once more of Saussure's idea of a constellation of associations ramifying in many different directions: "A particular word is like the center of a constellation; it is the point of convergence of an indefinite number of co-ordinated terms" (1915, p. 126). Thus, although we have referred to a hierarchy of associations, with its implication of a single hierarchical continuum, our analysis of the structure of associations must also take into account this multiplicity of lines of association to any particular stimulus.

THE STRUCTURE OF ASSOCIATIONS

A number of studies show that responses in associative tasks are in a major way determined by clustering tendencies among words, that is, by pre-existing organizing bonds or structures relating some of the words to each other. Bousfield and his group have done basic work in this area (Bousfield & Cohen, 1955a; 1955b). The model of these studies is simple. Lists of words subsumable under separate categories are prepared and organized into random sequence for presentation to the subjects. In one study there were 15 words each from the 4 categories: animals, names, professions, and vegetables. The words were equated for frequency of occurrence in the language at large by reference to the Thorndike-Lorge tables (1944). Lists were presented to subjects in a classroom by means of projector and screen, and subjects were then required to write down all the words they could recall. All sequences of two or more words in the same category, including intrusions (words not originally presented) which were clearly within any of the categories, were bracketed as clusters. It was found that the number of words in the same category occurring in clusters was significantly higher than would have been expected by chance.

Bousfield and Cohen attempted to put the verbal clustering phenomenon into a broad theoretical framework based on Hebb's theory of superordinate functions:

> To account for the phenomena of clustering, it appears necessary to go beyond the building up of habit strengths of isolated word-habits. Such habit strengths should be distributed randomly with respect to the categories. As shown in our earlier work it was necessary to postulate higher order mediating processes capable of adding to the strength possessed by the individual word-habits. To develop this conception we have relied heavily on Hebb's interpretation

of the development of superordinate perceptions. In essence, Hebb proposes that the repeated arousal of a group of related subordinate perceptions has as one of its major consequences the development of a superordinate structure whose activity constitutes the perception of the *whole*. As a result of such learning the occurrence of a single subordinate perception may activate the superordinate structure, which in turn will facilitate the responses of its subordinates. Transferring this notion to our experimental situation, we would regard the perceptions of the words as subordinate perceptions. The categories of our words correspond to superordinate structures. Thus, for example, the occurrence of the word *leopard* in recall results in the activation of its superordinate, namely, that corresponding to *animal*. This in turn facilitates its subordinates, and increases the likelihood of the subjects naming other animals (1955b, pp. 92–93).

Is clustering a function only of superordinate categories? Deese (1959) found that intrusions of words as items recalled in an associative learning task, when the intrusions did not occur at all as items learned in the task, could be traced to the associative connection of the intrusions with the learned words. This would suggest that clustering is also influenced by associative factors independently of the superordinate categories, and in a way such an idea is implicit in the word-association task. Gonzales and Cofer (1959), in a study of the effects of various modifiers on the clustering of nouns, suggested that, although the superordinate category ("coding") might affect the grouping of responses in recall, there was also a response strength factor which determined which of the available responses were recalled and an interword associative factor which could also lead to clustering. To apply this to a constellation of associations such as might be available for the stimulus *table,* we could say: (1) that there are distinct category groupings within the associations; (2) these categories may be strongly or weakly associated with each other in their own right; (3) within each category grouping, the various words have differing response strengths and accordingly are more or less likely to be uttered whenever the context invites use of that category. Such ideas have contributed to the study of the structure of associations and to the comparison of separate stimulus words in terms of associative structures.

Bousfield, Whitmarsh, and Danick (1958) developed what they

called an "index of generalization" of stimulus words based on the oc-currence of the same associations for separate stimulus words. The index of generalization is the sum of the frequencies of associations held in common by one stimulus word with another, divided by the total number of responses to the stimulus word. The index was shown to be related to generalization in a paired associates task in which a number was learned to a stimulus word and in which the subject was then required to respond with a number to other test words. Where the test word had a high index of generalization to the stimulus word, the number appropriate to the stimulus word was more likely to occur. Thus associative similarity predicted response generalization from the original stimulus to another stimulus.

Deese (1962) carried this approach further and developed what he called an "overlap coefficient" as a measure of the commonness of associative meaning. For any pair of stimuli, the overlap is the ratio of the sum of the overlapping frequencies of the various responses to the maximum possible sum. The maximum possible sum is twice the actual number of responses, since, in accordance with Bousfield, Whitmarsh, and Danick's procedure, each stimulus is regarded as being given im-plicitly as a response by the subject before he utters the overt re-sponses. If there are 50 subjects responding to the stimulus words *moth* and *insect,* and they respond with *fly* 10 times to *moth* and 9 times to *insect,* the overlap for this response is 9/100.

Deese obtained single word associations from 50 subjects to a series of words which appeared in the Russell-Jenkins (1954) list as responses to various stimulus words. One set of words, for example, consisted of such responses to *butterfly* as: *moth, insect, wing, bird, fly,* and so on. The 50 subjects gave single word associations to these words and overlap coefficients were computed for each pair of stim-ulus words. These overlap coefficients were entered into a matrix as if they were correlation coefficients, with communality scores of 100 (perfect overlap). The matrix was then factor analyzed in order to discover the structure which underlay the responses to the stimulus words.

What emerged from Deese's studies was what Bousfield had dis-covered in clustering, namely, that there were superordinate categories which clearly pertained to groups of stimulus words and which in-fluenced the associations given to these stimulus words. Deese suggests that such categories reflect an intrinsic feature of mind:

> The highly organized economy of associative meaning has impressed the author, however, and it was a belief that

the human mind derived associations from categories of its own that sent him on the search for a technique by which to study associative meaning. Thus, the least that can be offered is the suggestion that associations derive in whole or part from the structures or categories of the human mind (p. 174).

The single-word-association method obtains one response for each stimulus word from a large number of subjects. Another method for obtaining associations is the continuous-word-association method. In this method the subject is given a stimulus word and told to respond with as many associations as he can think of, returning after each association to the stimulus word. If there are inherent structures in vocabulary, these structures ought to manifest themselves both in the single-word-association method and in the continuous-word-association method. In a study by Laffal and Feldman (1962), continuous word associations were obtained from 20 subjects to certain stimulus words from the Russell-Jenkins (1954) list. The associations were obtained in individual sessions lasting a little more than an hour. Each subject was allowed 25 seconds in which to give as many responses as he could to each stimulus word, and he was allowed to repeat associations at will if they recurred to him in the course of associating. Stimulus words were presented by exposing three-by-five cards on which the words were printed. A total of 24 stimulus words were presented to each subject. Of these, 13 were intended as buffers to reduce a possible cumulating tendency in response to critical words of the same class. The critical words were animal, human, and color words. All 20 subjects had the words *red, yellow, black, lion, man,* and *priest* in their lists, but 10 subjects had the words *light, green, white, blue,* and *dark,* and 10 subjects had the words *spider, butterfly, eagle, woman,* and *sheep.* The responses were tape recorded and transcribed. The subjects averaged a little over 30 responses to each stimulus word, and, since some stimulus words were responded to by 10 subjects and some by all 20 subjects, the number of responses to the various stimulus words ranged from 326 to 954.

The continuous word associations of the subjects to the 16 key words enumerated above, as well as the single word responses to the same words by the 1008 subjects in the Russell-Jenkins list, were categorized into superordinate categories by a procedure described more fully in Appendix I. The percentages of agreement of three separate scorers in categorizing response words were 90 per cent, 83 per cent, and 82 per cent. Pearson product-moment correlations of the frequency profiles of categories obtained by separate scorers on the same protocol were .994, .976, and .970, showing that the categorizing procedure was highly reliable.

Following the categorization of the responses, a distribution of the frequencies of occurrence of the various categories for each stimulus word was prepared for the single word and for the continuous word associations. Overlap coefficients were then developed for the profiles of responses within the set of single word associations and within the set of continuous word associations. Overlap coefficients followed the procedure described by Bousfield, Whitmarsh, and Danick (1958) and Deese (1962) in comparing word-association profiles.

These total overlap scores for single word and for continuous word associations were then entered into separate sixteen-by-sixteen matrices, as if they were correlation coefficients, and factor analyzed, using the principal axes method (Harmon, 1960). The overlap matrices for single word and continuous word associations are shown in Tables 7 and 8. Communalities were given an overlap coefficient of 1.00.

The results of the two factor analyses are shown in Tables 9 and 10. Five factors accounted for 75 per cent of the variance for single word association, and six factors accounted for 73 per cent of the variance for continuous word association.

For both matrices, the first factor was a color factor, the highest loadings on it being among the words *blue, dark, light, white, black, red,* and *yellow. Green* was high on this factor for single word association, but not high on it in continuous word association.

Lion, sheep, and *spider* loaded high in both matrices on a second factor which may be identified as an animal factor.

A third factor for both matrices had clear relevance only to the words *man* and *woman.*

A fourth factor for both matrices included only the word *priest.*

A fifth factor common to both matrices had high negative loadings in the two words relating to flying creatures, *butterfly* and *eagle.*

The continuous-word-association factor analysis revealed one factor which was not apparent in the single word association. *Green* had highest loading on this factor, and other words which had moderate loadings on it were *yellow, red, sheep,* and *white.* This combination of words with *green* predominating might suggest such a factor as "nature" or "colored, edible vegetation."

The major conclusion to be drawn from these results is that the word-category structure obtained by the single-word-association method is substantially similar to that obtained by the continuous-word-asso-

TABLE 7

SINGLE WORD ASSOCIATION, OVERLAP COEFFICIENTS OF CATEGORY PROFILES FOR 16 STIMULUS WORDS: LAFFAL AND FELDMAN (1962, p. 58)

Words	black	red	dark	yellow	light	white	green	blue	butterfly	sheep	eagle	spider	lion	priest	woman	man
black	100															
red	79	100														
dark	86	72	100													
yellow	71	74	62	100												
light	70	72	69	68	100											
white	67	69	69	69	66	100										
green	57	62	64	66	56	57	100									
blue	56	59	53	63	56	58	57	100								
butterfly	16	17	52	27	15	14	15	30	100							
sheep	12	14	12	21	6	8	11	12	38	100						
eagle	9	13	4	16	7	9	11	25	73	43	100					
spider	11	10	4	18	7	10	8	11	46	56	46	100				
lion	9	13	8	18	5	8	10	11	44	64	46	64	100			
priest	5	7	6	6	4	8	9	9	5	7	3	24	13	100		
woman	5	8	3	6	3	5	5	10	5	17	5	4	10	8	100	
man	6	5	2	7	2	5	6	9	6	6	8	6	12	6	34	100

TABLE 8

CONTINUOUS WORD ASSOCIATION, OVERLAP COEFFICIENTS OF CATEGORY PROFILES FOR 16 STIMULUS WORDS: LAFFAL AND FELDMAN (1962, p. 59)

Words	black	red	dark	yellow	light	white	green	blue	butterfly	sheep	eagle	spider	lion	priest	woman	man
black	100															
red	62	100														
dark	59	54	100													
yellow	54	71	52	100												
light	46	51	57	55	100											
white	54	59	47	53	45	100										
green	44	53	40	56	39	47	100									
blue	50	55	56	56	45	49	47	100								
butterfly	36	43	42	53	39	34	41	39	100							
sheep	35	38	22	43	20	35	36	29	39	100						
eagle	31	34	33	35	25	27	30	38	48	41	100					
spider	40	39	41	40	26	31	30	34	48	42	45	100				
lion	32	42	26	38	22	30	35	31	43	50	48	57	100			
priest	29	29	21	23	20	33	24	23	17	26	23	23	34	100		
woman	26	34	17	28	20	30	28	22	24	30	25	25	28	32	100	
man	35	37	25	29	23	35	28	27	25	34	33	26	34	37	57	100

ciation method. This would indicate that data developed by single word associations from a group may be taken as paradigmatic of associations developed by other methods, if one has reference to the underlying configurations of the associations.

However, certain differences emerged in this study, and these seemed to be a function of the association method employed. The

TABLE 9

SINGLE WORD ASSOCIATION, ROTATED FACTOR LOADINGS OF OVERLAP
COEFFICIENTS OF 16 STIMULUS WORDS:
LAFFAL AND FELDMAN (1962, p. 60)

Words	Factors					
	I	II	III	IV	V	h^2
black	89	9	1	— 1	3	80
red	88	8	4	0	— 4	78
dark	85	5	— 3	3	7	73
yellow	85	13	4	— 1	—13	76
light	85	0	— 2	0	— 2	72
white	83	2	2	5	— 4	69
green	75	3	4	1	— 8	57
blue	71	— 7	12	9	—38	68
butterfly	13	31	0	1	—85	84
sheep	7	84	17	— 8	—15	77
eagle	5	35	3	— 2	—85	85
spider	6	79	— 5	24	—26	76
lion	6	85	6	4	—21	78
priest	5	11	6	98	1	98
woman	4	6	81	5	— 1	66
man	3	8	81	0	— 3	66
% total variance	34	15	9	6	11	75

factor loadings were more sharply separated into high and low for single word than for continuous word association. This undoubtedly stems from the fact that in single word association each subject may respond with only one word, with the result that there tends to be a much greater concentration of responses in a limited number of categories. Although in the continuous-word-association task described above, the subjects were allowed to repeat associations, there was nowhere near the heavy favoring of the so-called high communality responses which is found in the single word method. In effect, single word association screens out all but the most prominent categories of association, whereas in continuous word association there is greater co-occurrence of different categories. In a factor analysis, one therefore finds that the factors are much more distinct and sharply defined in single word than in continuous word association.

The factor in continuous word association which included the words *green, yellow, red, sheep,* and *white* shows this tendency of

TABLE 10

CONTINUOUS WORD ASSOCIATION, ROTATED FACTOR LOADINGS
OF OVERLAP COEFFICIENTS OF 16 STIMULUS WORDS:
LAFFAL AND FELDMAN (1962, p. 60)

Words	Factors						
	I	II	III	IV	V	VI	h^2
black	75	34	18	7	12	7	73
red	63	27	21	6	44	− 6	71
dark	83	11	4	4	− 1	−25	77
yellow	56	22	11	− 2	57	−22	75
light	70	−11	9	5	21	−28	64
white	58	20	20	20	41	9	63
green	32	10	12	12	73	−20	71
blue	63	9	7	12	28	−27	58
butterfly	29	27	8	− 7	31	−68	73
sheep	5	69	22	2	43	− 9	72
eagle	16	34	18	13	5	−72	71
spider	35	72	8	2	− 9	−31	75
lion	11	71	12	25	17	−32	72
priest	15	15	22	92	9	− 5	95
woman	9	10	86	7	16	−10	80
man	20	17	82	17	4	−11	78
% total variance	22	13	11	6	11	10	73

continuous-word-association responses most clearly. Single word association has *green* firmly joined with other color words, and *sheep* separately fixed among animal words. However, where secondary associations come into play in continuous association the words *green* and *sheep* begin to have something in common.

The fundamental similarity of five of six factors in single word and continuous word association lends support to the thesis—advanced by studies of association (Deese, 1962), by studies of clustering in recall (Bousfield & Cohen, 1955a; 1955b), and by linguistic field theories (Basilius, 1952; Hallig & Wartburg, 1952; 1963; Öhman, 1953; Trier,

1934)—that there is a basic category structure in vocabulary and that associations reflect this structure.

A simplified model of word association which emerges from this material may be described as follows. A stimulus word, which is itself representative of one or more superordinate categories, activates its own category as well as associated categories in the responding individual. In the same way as responses have been described as competing with each other for utterance, so the evoked categories compete. The factors determining which category prevails may include special needs at that moment active in the individual or more habitually operative idiosyncratic tendencies, as well as incidental and ordinarily irrelevant features of the test setting. That category which achieves dominance then becomes a determinant of the response which is uttered. The word which is actually uttered is that response which is strongest within the category. This analysis makes it a little easier to see how it is possible that in response to the stimulus *table,* some individuals uttered responses like *four, pool,* and *mesa* (see Table 1) in the face of the vastly prepotent group strength of a response like *chair.* Presumably for these individuals the category "furniture" (or some such equivalent) was either not aroused or was in a less dominant position than, for example, the category "mathematics" or "recreation" or "flatness." It was therefore not a question of all responses competing with each other, but only of responses within the momentarily dominant category competing with each other. One may assume that, if the group were instructed to respond to *table* in terms of "mathematics," "recreation," or "flatness," such ordinarily infrequent responses would occur with great frequency. The problem in understanding why some of the individuals responded with *four* or *pool* thus becomes one of understanding why the stimulus word *table* brought the categories from which these responses were drawn to the fore rather than arousing the "furniture" or "food" categories, as in most subjects. This is a problem which invites detailed clinical study.

4. Distortion and Structure in Free Speech

In the typical word-association test the subject is instructed to respond with the first word that comes to mind when he hears or sees the stimulus word. We have seen that a given stimulus word will tend to increase for any individual the likelihood of occurrence of a hierarchy of word categories and, within these categories, a hierarchy of words varying in response strength. Such a hierarchy may be illustrated by the Russell-Jenkins (1954) associations to the word *table,* which have already served us so well. In Table 11, the responses of the 1008 subjects are grouped into a number of categories showing which are more likely to precede and which to follow in a sequence of responses. On the right, responses are ranked in each category according to their frequencies and relative likelihoods of occurring.

Other factors being equal—that is, barring the presence of unusual conditions and unique psychological sets—the response uttered will be drawn from the dominant category and will be the same response as that given most often by the population at large tested with the same stimulus word. Thus, most subjects will give *chair* in response to the stimulus word *table,* since the fur-

niture category is the dominant one for the group, and the word
chair is the primary response within this category.

However, in the presence of unusual psychological sets (stemming from special aims of the individual, from states of accentuated
drive or psychological conflict, or from obtruding features of the task),

TABLE 11

RESPONSES FROM THE RUSSELL-JENKINS LIST (1954)
TO THE STIMULUS WORD *table*

Categories	Responses
864 furniture	840 chair, 21 desk, 1 lamp, 1 bed, 1 tablecloth
71 eating	41 food, 9 eat, 7 dish, 3 dinner, 2 cup, 2 fork, 2 silver, 1 spoon, 1 plate, 1 drink, 1 meat, 1 kitchen
19 flatness	15 top, 2 floor, 1 mesa, 1 flat
19 material	8 cloth, 6 wood, 2 silver, 1 board, 1 maple, 1 tablecloth
12 part (of furniture)	11 legs, 1 leaf
10 container	7 dish, 2 cup, 1 plate
9 vegetation	6 wood, 1 maple, 1 board, 1 leaf
4 rooms	1 room, 1 stable, 1 house, 1 kitchen
4 color	2 silver, 1 black, 1 sable
3 recreation	1 tennis, 1 card, 1 pool
3 learning	1 book, 1 study, 1 desk
2 shape	1 round, 1 flat
2 up-down	1 top, 1 floor
1 open-shut	1 door
1 size	1 huge
1 quality	1 hard
1 number	1 four
1 people	1 company

the response of the individual may be drawn not from the category
dominant for the group, but from another category of responses.

Very often, in word association, the subject will set himself to
respond in terms of common uses of the referent of the stimulus word,
in terms of definition of the stimulus word, or in terms of opposites.
If the subject does set himself in this manner, the response may be generated by a conscious intention other than the one provided by the
examiner whose instructions are to respond with the first word that
comes to mind. Thus, the subject who sets himself to respond with

synonyms, may give *timid, meek,* or *shy* to the stimulus *tame,* where the dominant response among a population at large, responding without any other intention than that evoked in the instruction, is *wild.* In free speech too, the speaker's special intention may generate responses which are different from those which the population at large might make at that particular point.

This is illustrated in the case of a mischievous boy learning morse code who prevailed upon his father to decode a message which he would send from the next room. The message got as far as *Greetings fathe,* when the parent said, *I've got it!* The key kept clicking and in a moment he had the full message, which read, *Greetings fathead.*

On a less consciously intentional level, if a subject were hungry while taking the association test, his response might be drawn from the food category. The most likely response to *table* from this category would be the word *food.* Some of the studies reviewed in Chapter 3 suggest, however, that the situation may become even more complicated. Thus, Brozek and his group (1951) found that increase in a unique psychological set (extreme hunger) led to idiosyncratic responses in the word-association task but without clear relevance to food and eating. The analysis of word association by Rapaport, Schafer, and Gill (1946) would also suggest that in such cases there may be "close" associations which would not necessarily bear the imprint of specific psychological conflicts, but would reflect instead a general disruption of functioning. So-called "clang" associations, as *Mable* in response to *table,* are of this nature. The subject associates to some irrelevant feature of the stimulus such as its sound. However, one cannot escape the possibility that even such a clang response as *Mable* may reveal an underlying psychological motivation—in this case, relating to women.

Although the subject may give a superficial association, he is still complying with the instructions of the task, namely, to respond. In this sense, the motivation stemming from the experimenter's instructions is still operative and must be taken into account as a determining variable. Whatever disrupts the giving of the ordinarily dominant response must be seen as interacting with the basic task motivation which continues to function.

Thus, it may be said that unusual (low frequency in the group) responses reflect the set of the individual to comply with the instructions, but also reveal the operation of a unique set which selectively interferes with the utterance of the ordinarily dominant response. The following figure illustrates this situation.

FIGURE 3

UTTERANCE OF A RESPONSE TO A STIMULUS WORD IN WORD
ASSOCIATION WITH TWO PSYCHOLOGICAL SETS OPERATING

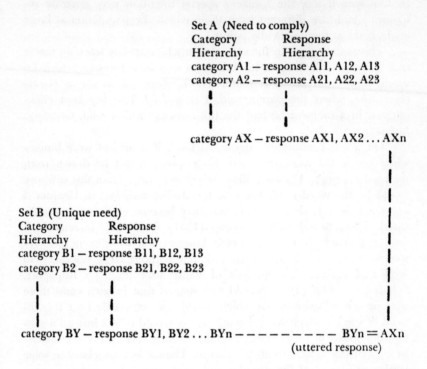

Set A (Need to comply)
Category   Response
Hierarchy   Hierarchy
category A1 — response A11, A12, A13
category A2 — response A21, A22, A23

category AX — response AX1, AX2 ... AXn

Set B (Unique need)
Category   Response
Hierarchy   Hierarchy
category B1 — response B11, B12, B13
category B2 — response B21, B22, B23

category BY — response BY1, BY2 ... BYn — — — — — — — — — BYn = AXn
                                                       (uttered response)

There are two psychological sets, Set A (the need to comply with
the instructions to respond with the first word that comes to mind)
and Set B (a unique need, such as hunger). Hypothetically, for each
one of these sets separately, a hierarchy of categories is called into play
when the given stimulus word is presented. Each category within these
hierarchies has its own internal hierarchy of responses. If both psychological sets were equally strong, the category ordinarily dominant for
each psychological set separately (Category A1 for Set A and Category
B1 for Set B) would no longer be dominant. Instead subordinate
categories which shared a common response (Category BY for Set B
and Category AX for Set A) would achieve dominance, and this
shared common response would ultimately be uttered—Response BYn
= AXn in the figure.

As one psychological set became markedly stronger than the other,
the response would become more like the common response of the

population at large for that stimulus and the stronger set. More than two psychological sets might be present and this would complicate the design. However, the basic principles would still hold.

An interesting possibility is that in which the strength of the second psychological set is a function of the response appropriate to the first psychological set. A case of this sort might be one in which the first psychological set is to respond as instructed or as demanded by the social context, but where utterance of the dominant response would fly in the face of a prohibition. In these circumstances, the individual might find some response which complied with the requirement to respond, but which avoided aggravation of the conflicting motivation.

This type of situation may be seen most clearly where the utterance of what would be an appropriate response for a given stimulus and a given motivation would create anxiety in the individual. Social prohibitions may, for example, forbid the utterance of an aggressive response which is momentarily dominant for the individual. Fearing the consequence of saying what he wants to say, the individual may consciously inhibit his response and utter instead a response which avoids the retribution and is socially acceptable. Such a response may bear only the faintest spore of the forbidden motivation.

PSYCHOLOGICAL CENSORSHIP, PRIMARY PROCESS, AND SYMBOLS

But the prohibition may go further than a social one and extend even to conscious awareness of the response. Awareness of an aggressive response in the self may be enough to create intense anxiety. The awareness must then be avoided in the same way that in the socially prohibiting context the utterance of the response must be avoided. In this state of affairs some response would ultimately appear which meets the need to respond, but which avoids exacerbation of the unacceptable need. Such a response, also, may show little evidence of the conflicting need.

These ideas relating to psychological sets and responses touch closely on what psychoanalysts have called "censorship." The main lines of the psychoanalytic interpretation of censored responses were laid down by Freud in *The Interpretation of Dreams* (1900), and the paradigm was extended by him to the interpretation of wit (Freud, 1905), to parapraxes in speech, and to instances of forgetting and other faults in daily behavior (Freud, 1901).

According to Freud, dreams serve a wish-fulfilling function. However, the censorship—which represents the conscious unacceptability of these wishes—makes it necessary for the nature of the wish to be hidden, denied, or otherwise distorted in the dream. The distortions take place by means of the psychological mechanisms of condensation and displacement. Condensation refers to the fact that a great deal of latent content—that is, associatively related unconscious content—is compressed into specific elements of the dream. Displacement refers to the fact that the psychical interest or intensities in the latent content of the dream are either absent in the manifest content or centered upon objects in the manifest content different from those on which the interest was focused in the latent content. The consequence is that, in their manifest content, dreams often appear confused and incomprehensible but may be analyzed into their latent content by a process of association to the various elements of the manifest content. The latent content reveals the unacceptable wish and the manner in which the dream has fulfilled it in disguised form. According to Freud, the latent content, in its deepest layers, goes back to early infantile wishes and fantasies which must be denied consciously.

The peculiar psychological process in dream distortion, which seems so alien to our normal way of thinking, was called by Freud "primary process" (Freud, 1900, p. 601) and contrasted by him with more rational thinking which he called "secondary process." There are certain implications in these terms having also to do with modalities of wish gratification—direct hallucinatory wish fulfillment in the primary process, and delay of gratification in the secondary process—which are beyond the scope of the present discussion. Some of the characteristics of primary process are that: (1) intensities of affect associated with individual ideas may pass over to each other so that certain ideas are formed endowed with great intensity. Condensation is the focusing of such intensities on a single idea; (2) because of the lability with which these affects may be transferred from idea to idea, certain compromise formations, as may be seen in slips of the tongue, readily occur; (3) the associative pathways over which affect and intensity are transferred may be of the loosest kind and may be based on verbal puns, on homonyms, and on verbal similarities; (4) logically contradictory ideas may persist side by side and actually form condensations as if there were no contradiction between them.

Responses which are related in a censored way to the pertinent need or wish have sometimes been called symbols. Psychoanalytic definitions of symbol generally stress a relationship like that between latent and manifest content as outlined by Freud in the analysis of dreams, but also the universality of the relationship among all individuals. Although various writers differ in detail (Jones, 1923; Rapaport, 1951, pp. 208–233; Silberer, 1912) the elements of a psychoanalytic definition of a symbol appear to be (1) the presence of a conflicted motivating need or wish; (2) the appearance of a response which is not obviously related to the wish, which indeed disguises the relationship; and (3) universality of the relationship between wish and response. Some definitions also stress the concreteness and the pictorial quality of the symbol, but this does not seem to be crucial.

In the verbal-association task, a censored response would be one which has appeared because a more direct and appropriate response would be unacceptable to the responding individual. If the verbal associative structure obtained from a group may be taken as representative of what is available to the individual, then an idiosyncratic association may under some circumstances be a censored response. The need to exclude certain wishes, impulses, or complexes from awareness is satisfied only if the response has little similarity to the ordinarily dominant, expected response. This analysis does not, however, exclude the possibility that a symbol, since it has certain universal features, may actually manifest itself as a highly common and expected response, but one whose relation to the unacceptable wish is obscured by the censorship.

Let us go on now to expand this discussion of motivational conflict, censorship, and symbols into a consideration of disturbances and distortions of free speech.

DISTURBANCES AND DISTORTIONS IN FREE SPEECH

Two types of faults in free speech are of special interest in providing illustrations of the application of word-association models to free speech. The first is the facilitation of an unusual response by some immediately precedent response, and the second is the tongue slip. The notable feature of the response in these situations is that, despite an intention generated by the speaker, stimuli irrelevant to that intention influence the response in question. The response then, although appropriate to the generating intention, is also the product of another, incidental, stimulus. Consider the remark made by the speaker in discussing an acquaintance:

He worked in a bakery but quit because he was not rising.

Rising here is clearly a choice related to the stimulus *bakery*. In our conception of the course of events, the word *bakery* serves as an incidental and irrelevant (irrelevant to the intention) stimulus for subsequent responses and increases the likelihood of occurrence of related responses, leading in one instance to the word *rising*, which is pertinent to *bakery* but at the same time not inconsistent with the controlling intention.

Let us assume that the speaker had a conscious intention to tell what the person worked at, the fact that he left the job, and why. Three distinct units are involved in this communication about the person: (1) type of work; (2) leaving; (3) lack of success. This is illustrated in the figure below. If we assume that only a single

FIGURE 4

SCHEMATIC REPRESENTATION OF THE REMARK,

He worked in a bakery but quit because he was not rising

Set: the conscious intention to tell what he worked at, the fact that he left the job, and why.	Stimulus 1: What he worked at	Stimulus 2: His leaving	Stimulus 3: Why he left

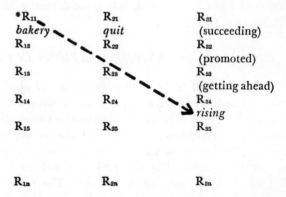

	$*R_{11}$ *bakery*	R_{21} *quit*	R_{31} (succeeding)
	R_{12}	R_{22}	R_{32} (promoted)
	R_{13}	R_{23}	R_{33} (getting ahead)
	R_{14}	R_{24}	R_{34} *rising*
	R_{15}	R_{25}	R_{35}
	R_{1n}	R_{2n}	R_{3n}

$*R_{a} \rightarrow R_{b}$ indicates that response R_{a} influences response R_{b}. Words in parentheses are hypothetical, possible responses. Italicized words are those actually uttered.

psychological set, the conscious intention to communicate certain information to someone else, is operating, then the example may be broken down into three simple stimulus sequences, the first having to do with type of work, the second with leaving, and the third with lack of success. Each stimulus (At what did he work? What happened? Why?) evokes a hierarchy of categories and, within each category, a hierarchy of specific responses. *Bakery* is drawn from a category of responses which might include a variety of occupations and more specifically those pertinent to baking. *Quit* is drawn from a category of responses which might include words like *leave, go, depart, separate, resign.* The word *rising* is especially interesting. It is drawn from a category of responses which might include such words as *succeed, promotion, ahead, up,* and it seems slightly incongruous. The reason, of course, is that it is also related to the previous word *bakery,* in something like a pun. Since he, the worker, was not doing what the dough was doing, namely, rising, he quit. We may regard the choice of *rising* as a kind of accidental result of the fact that the use of *bakery* had increased the response likelihood of responses related to baking and that, since a word like *rising* was needed to explain why he left the job, the choice fell to it. We have assumed that only the psychological set to communicate certain information was operating in the speaker. It is also possible that some intruding set may have been effective at the time the sentence was spoken and that the category which included *succeed, promote, ahead, rising, up* was in some way related to this intruding set. The intrusion then presumably interfered with the selection of the ordinarily dominant response (let us say, *succeeding*), and the result was an ordinarily weaker response (*rising*), which had been given an increment of strength by the prior stimulus *bakery.*

In the case of the tongue slip, the intruding set is much more in evidence. Take this example quoted by Simonini (1956, p. 255) from a collection of such boners and slips:

> *His battalion was swallowed in the Bulgium belch (Belgium Bulge).*

This remark may be conceptualized as in Figure 5. The speaker, intending to tell of the destruction of the unit at the Battle of the Bulge, and at the same time preoccupied with alimentary needs, utters a word (*swallow*) appropriate both to his rational intention and to his digestive need. This reinforces related alimentary responses, and the conflicting rational intention and bodily need eventuate in a tongue slip (*Bulgium belch*) whose constituents are more appropriate to the alimentary preoccupation than to the rational intention. If the whole speaking event is extended to include the conscious intention which preceded the utterance, then it is possible that the word *swallow* was

FIGURE 5

SCHEMATIC REPRESENTATION OF THE REMARK,
His battalion was swallowed in the Bulgium belch
(Belgium Bulge) : LAFFAL (1963, p. 55)

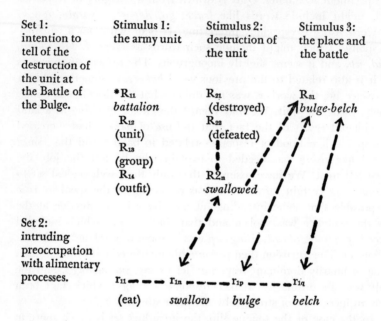

Set 1: intention to tell of the destruction of the unit at the Battle of the Bulge.	Stimulus 1: the army unit	Stimulus 2: destruction of the unit	Stimulus 3: the place and the battle
	*R_{11} *battalion*	R_{21} (destroyed)	R_{31} *bulge-belch*
	R_{12} (unit)	R_{22} (defeated)	
	R_{13} (group)		
	R_{14} (outfit)	$R2_n$ *swallowed*	

Set 2: intruding preoccupation with alimentary processes.

r_{11} — — r_{1n} — — — r_{1p} — — — r_{1q}

(eat)   *swallow*   *bulge*   *belch*

*$R_a \rightarrow R_b$ indicates that response R_a influences response R_b. $\longleftrightarrow$ indicates equivalent responses in separate response hierarchies. Words in parentheses are hypothetical, possible responses. Italicized words are those actually uttered.

at the outset influenced by the presence of the word *Bulge* in the intention. This is a nice instance of the manner in which all the responses of an utterance may be seen to interact with each other when the conscious intention as well as the utterance itself is taken into account. A conscious intention to tell of the destruction of the army unit at the Battle of the Bulge included a word *(Bulge)* which, as stimulus, provided an increment of strength to responses pertinent to an ongoing alimentary need. This led to the word *swallow* in the actual utterance, which further reinforced alimentary responses to the point where such responses became intrusive and interfered with the conscious intention.

These examples of interferences in normal speech provide a link with language distortions in schizophrenia. However, to understand language distortions in schizophrenia, it is not enough to recognize that conflicting needs may disrupt the conscious intention, produce faults, and make unusual responses momentarily dominant; one must also take into account the surprising ways in which the conflicting needs may influence verbal forms while remaining hidden both to the patient and the observer.

Remarks like that of the patient who said, *Genius has no place in a newspaper; it belongs in the boudoir* are sometimes discussed as examples of "ellipsis" in the language of the patient (White, 1926; Woods, 1938) or as applications of the "Von Domarus principle" (Arieti, 1955; Von Domarus, 1944). These terms refer to the fact that a number of intermediary, often tenuous associative links must be established before sense can be made of the remark, which is in effect a kind of shorthand; but they refer also to the fact that the links have a primary process quality. The associative chain has little regard for what we know as logic and proceeds on the basis of the most improbable relationships. One important effect of this process is that the relation of the response to the needs and conflicts of the patient is well hidden.

Negation is a powerful tool for hiding unacceptable needs and conflicts. If the patient is under some requirement to respond to his communicant but at the same time subject to a conflicting need whose strength is determined by how directly he says what it is that troubles him, then the addition of a *no* to the most appropriate response removes that response an infinite distance from itself. If the response that would most directly give the patient's motivation is *hate* and this is at the same time an intolerable response, he may go lower on the response hierarchy for words like *dislike, disapprove,* or *indifferent.* However, if even such responses are unacceptable, there is the expedient of negating the response by saying *not hate.* The simple but consequential fact of negation has received searching attention in psychoanalytic theory (Freud, 1925; Spitz, 1957). Freud felt that negation was a way of taking conscious cognizance of what would otherwise have been totally repressed. The idea with the negation attached is permitted into consciousness, but the repression remains effective since the negation rejects the idea.

The extremes to which the schizophrenic patient may go in his negation are extraordinary, as shown in the study of opposite speech by Laffal, Lenkoski, and Ameen (1956), which has been described in Chapter 2. In that study, the patient's reversal of *yes* and *no* served the function of dealing with unacceptable aggressive impulses. However, the opposite speech was apparent in the patient's language at large and was not limited specifically to aggressive references. Presumably the focal conflict which initiated the opposite speech was of sufficient strength to incur a generalization of the speech reversal to all situations. Since the patient had to deny his aggressive feelings, he had to deny everything in order to be safe. His ordinary conversation was therefore riddled with reversals.

It is not uncommon for schizophrenic patients to talk gibberish and to produce unfamiliar verbal forms or forms ordinarily unacceptable in the language (neologisms). The patient who speaks gibberish will also often utter sentences in which the individual words are familiar but in which the whole does not make good sense. In both cases the behavior may be understood as the appearance of disturbances designed to hide or disguise unacceptable material which is on the verge of attaining conscious expression. The kinds of conflicts which may lead to such a denudation of sense in language may be manifold, but it is a good guess that a crucial recognition is being warded off when words are stripped of their meaning. Gibberish, for example, may at one level reflect the patient's aggressive contempt for the listener, while at another it denies the murderous hostility that is close to becoming explicit in consciousness and in words; or it may reflect the patient's anxious withdrawal and effort to cloud the verbal horizon where communication threatens to bring conscious awareness to intolerable sexual wishes.

Below are reported some fragments of a therapeutic interview with a schizophrenic patient in which the patient used gibberish alternately with more recognizable but still incomprehensible language. The patient, a man of southern European descent in his late thirties, had been in treatment for over six months. His talk had been characteristically rapid, difficult to follow, repetitive, and abstract. In one session the therapist, responding to the rambling remarks of the patient, began to make such statements as, "Do you know that I have difficulty understanding what you're saying?" "How is it that I don't understand what you're saying?" "Could it be you're afraid of me?" "What are you scared about?" "Do you think I mean to hurt you?" "Do you think I don't care for you?" "Do you think I'm angry at you for something you did?" Toward the end of the session, the patient began to deny that he knew anyone of his own name, whereupon the therapist responded by saying, "Shake my hand, I want you to know I'm here." The exchange was then as follows, the dotted line indicating unclear sections in the tape recording.

Dr. Come on, shake it.

Pt. I don't shake a hand.

Dr. *(taking patient's hand)* Oh, you're leaving your hand limp in my hand.

Pt. I don't . . . . . idea . . . . .

Dr. I'm not letting your hand get away until you shake it.

Pt. Well, believe me—

Dr. What shall I call you?

Pt. I'm a very smart fellow. I don't twist in the, the same way twice, believe me. I'm a very different type of fellow.

Dr. What shall I call you?

Pt. You can call me by name. We have enough of them, and if we move that way we—

Dr. What is your name?

Pt. Well, let's say you might have thought you had something from before, but you haven't got it any more.

Dr. I'm going to call you Dean.

At this point the patient walked out of the room. In the next session, three days later, the patient came in and launched into a gibberish that sounded like a mixture of Chinese and Polish, with a distinctly conversational prosody and periodic reiteration of similar sounds. His ordinary communication was sufficiently obscure, but here it was totally incomprehensible. In addition, the patient gave other evidence of his discomfort over being in the therapeutic situation by making an effort to bolt early in the interview. He ultimately terminated the meeting by leaving suddenly. The interview went as follows:

Pt. *(speaks gibberish for three minutes)* How are you today?

Dr. Pretty good, Dean. How are you?

Pt. Not too good. How are you? You're okay? Okay, or what?

Dr. Yeah, I'm fine.

Pt. You're okay then, huh. The only other thing expected, huh?

Dr. What have you been telling me in that strange tongue?

Pt. *(speaks gibberish for 30 seconds)*

Dr. What language is that, that you're speaking?

Pt. (*speaks gibberish for 25 seconds*)

Dr. (*in French*) What are you saying?

Pt. (*speaks gibberish for 25 seconds*)

Dr. (*in Italian*) What do you say?

Pt. (*speaks gibberish for 30 seconds*)

Dr. Oh come on, cut it out, Dean.

Pt. (*speaks gibberish for 5 seconds*)
(*Doctor gets up and moves closer to patient. Patient begins to leave.*)

Dr. Wait a minute, Dean, sit down.

Pt. Whew! Boy, what a nice day, huh?

Dr. Dean, come here.

Pt. What? You said go already.

Dr. No, I didn't say go. I wanted to sit down near you, Dean!
(*Patient leaves the room, and doctor follows him into the hallway.*) Mr. Redfield, come on, I want to talk to you.

Pt. You want to talk to him? (*pointing to another patient*)

Dr. No, I want to talk to you.

Pt. Oh, we're through.

Dr. Come on, no, we're not finished yet. Come on, Dean. Dean! I want to talk to you some more.

Pt. (*returns to the room*) I personally don't believe these, these different circumstances should come to that . . . . . arousing different ideas and everything like that. I don't necessarily know that stories are—I believe, I see you had some brief ideas about different circumstances that did arise at certain times, different procedures or approaches, anything like that. Is that right? Is that right? I generally don't realize the circumstances, but—

Dr. Dean, you know you've been upset for the past few days. Can you put your finger on it, do you know what it's all about?

Pt. I did sort of mention about different circumstances, everything like that. I did bring certain things to a certain attention, but I don't arouse the idea of certain standards and everything, the . . . . . idea, approaches. But when you're feeling in love with the idea, I just don't realize that the circumstances of the

different approaches are what bring the circumstances
to the knowledge of these certain things, what knowledge of a certain thing. So you see that I don't realistically say, or that's probably I don't, well that, that's
the story of my dying. I don't realize the jurisdiction
of the, your principle . . . . . sort of . . . . . you say,
well, what's your story . . . . .

To interpret the patient's behavior strictly in terms of the events
in the therapeutic interviews, it would appear that the therapist's efforts to reassure the patient of his own and the patient's reality by
offering a physical contact (shaking hands) was received by the patient as a provocation, presumably to a sexual encounter. His gibberish would reflect the effort to keep such ideas and the consequences
they might entail from gaining verbal form.

An inspirational movement called "speaking in tongues" has been
reported among college students; it also involves the use of gibberish,
but with accompanying feelings of deep and meaningful religious communication. A newspaper account reports the phenomenon as follows:

> An extremely unusual psychic or religious phenomenon
> has been discovered among a small group of undergraduate
> Christians at Yale this year.
> A group of about 20 students have experienced what
> they describe as "the gift of speaking in tongues," or
> "glossolalia."
> They claim that the speaking in tongues—an utterance
> of apparent gibberish in what sounds like a paraphrase of
> several identifiable languages—is part of a total spiritual
> or "charismatic renewal" such as was received by the apos-
> tles of Christ at the Pentecost. . . .
> The act of speaking in tongues has been described by
> those who have heard it as "a spirit-filled gibberish." Some-
> times it resembles Swedish or German, sometimes more
> ancient languages. . . .
> Along with the gift of tongues, the Yale students claim
> to have received gifts of interpretation and prophecy.
> One of the prophecies a member of the group said he
> received was as follows: "I have spread out before you
> my gifts. . . . You have picked from among them this one
> [the gift of tongues]. . . . Now take my gift of Love, which
> is most important."

Another prophecy admonished, "You are not concerned about me, but about much show."

During the course of a conversation a student was urged by the reporter to speak in tongues, and finally did so.

The language was soft and guttural, like the chanting of a Hebrew psalm. A group of similar syllables were repeated over and over with a curious musical intonation.

Unlike most supposed mystical experiences, the student did not enter a trance-like state and was in no way changed or stimulated by the effect of his own recitation (*New Haven Register,* March 11, 1963, pp. 1–2).

The students who engaged in this activity pointed for justification to certain passages in Paul's first letter to the Corinthians where the same phenomenon is described (although with an admonition against its hazards). In the light of the foregoing discussion of disturbed language, we may hypothesize that, in part, speaking in tongues serves to provide verbal form to a conflicted wish while at the same time hiding the wish by stripping the verbalization of communal meaning. Some degree of conscious expression is allowed to the conflicted wish, but the wish itself escapes conscious recognition.

THE STRUCTURE OF FREE SPEECH

Having now examined some of the milder and some of the more extreme disturbances of speech, possibilities which must be borne in mind constantly when we attempt to understand the psychology of language, we may go on to consider the structure of free speech.

In normal free speech there is a conscious intention, and the subject has a selective interest in words relating to this intention when he undertakes to speak. But, in addition to the momentary intention, there are durable attitudes and personality configurations in each speaker which lend an underlying consistency to his vocabulary, no matter what he talks about. He has his personal style, his predilections for certain modes of expression. This is not to suggest that his language will be invariant, but that he will draw in a characteristic way from the available responses whenever he speaks.

A broad view of the subject's speech ought to show consistencies running through all his vocabulary, no matter what the topic or circumstances of conversation. On the other hand, there ought also to be major variations in his vocabulary associated with the presence of different psychological needs. If we had some good way of determining under what major need an individual were operating at any moment, we would be warranted in assuming that his choice of words reflected this need, whether the words themselves were ostensibly related to the need or not. Knowing the subject's patterns of word choice under various need conditions would permit us in turn to infer the presence of such needs whenever the subject's speech reflected one or another of such patterns. Basic information about a subject's needs is difficult to obtain, but were it possible to do so, we would be in a position to examine the flux of psychological needs within the individual by studying his language.

In the example, *He worked in a bakery but quit because he was not rising,* the word *rising* is of key interest. A study of words in close contextual association with *rising* in many samples of the subject's speech might reveal that certain words appeared with great regularity in these contexts, whereas such words did not appear so consistently in the contexts of comparable words like *going, riding, walking, sitting,* and so on. If patterns of vocabulary demonstrably related to specific need conditions were known for this subject, we might be able to compare all these associates of *rising* to the need-related patterns and conclude that the contexts of *rising* were similar to certain of these patterns, hence that the related need was operating at the time of the production of the word *rising.* This would be an indirect approach to determining whether the production of a faulty response at any moment was due to the intrusion of some particular need. At present the only procedure available for attacking this problem is one which stems from psychoanalytic treatment procedures, that is, to have the patient give his associations to the faulty response.

To make the type of contextual analyses described for a word like *rising* would require a large sampling of the subject's free speech or a structured conversation in which the subject were induced to use the word repeatedly. However, a fair estimate of the contextual associates of *rising* might be obtained if one also took as key words such other words as *ahead, succeeding, promote,* and *up, high, top,* and *climb,* which are in the same superordinate category as *rising.* The probability of several such words in a limited sample of speech is much greater, of course, than the probability of the recurrence of the word *rising,* and therefore a larger number of appropriate contexts might be analyzed in a smaller sample. The idea of superordinate categories could be applied not only to finding all the contexts relating to *rising,* but also to identifying the similarities in the contexts.

A procedure such as this was followed in the studies comparing single word and continuous word associations reported in Chapter 3.

Let us see what the same procedure reveals with respect to the structure of free speech.

The free-speech situation differs from the word-association task in a number of important respects. In free speech, the verbal stimuli impinging upon the subject occur in a relatively haphazard fashion; the intention or generating set in the situation is more likely to be determined by the speaking subject himself than by the experimenter or communicant; and there are numerous complicated instructions implicit in the verbal exchange, such as requirements to be grammatical, to be logical, to be pertinent, to be understood, and so forth. In contrast to these features of haphazard stimulation, self-determined goal, and implicit instructions in free speech, the word-association task involves controlled stimulation, a goal determined by the examiner, that is, to respond with the first word that comes to mind, and freedom from requirements to be grammatical, logical, or pertinent in the response.

Despite these differences, there is evidence that free speech and word association have much in common. Howes (1957) correlated the frequency of occurrence of words in the Lorge magazine count (Thorndike & Lorge, 1944) with the frequency of appearance of the same words in the Kent-Rosanoff (1910) tables. Although one tabulation was a count of written words, and the other of words uttered in the word-association task, he found the correlation between the frequencies to be .94. This correlation excluded certain connective words such as conjunctions, articles, pronouns, and auxiliaries which occur frequently in written language but rarely in word association. Howes concluded that the probability that a word will occur in ordinary discourse is the same as the probability of occurrence of that word in a word-association task.

In the study by Laffal and Feldman (1962) described in Chapter 3, it was shown that the word-category structure obtained by the method of single word association was substantially similar to that obtained by the method of continuous word association. The findings suggested that data developed by single word associations from a group could be taken as paradigmatic of associations developed by other methods. It was hypothesized as a result of that study that a comparable analysis of free speech would show a factorial structure similar to those in the association tasks. However, it was also hypothesized that there would be a universally high loading on a primary factor reflecting formal characteristics of the spoken language itself. A study by Laffal and Feldman (1963) explored these hypotheses by examining the response of freely speaking individuals to 8 of the stimulus words which had been used in the previous study, these words being distinctly separable into color words and animal words.

Twenty-eight university undergraduates participated in the study. The subjects were randomly paired into 14 pairs, and each pair of subjects was given 4 minutes to converse about each stimulus word. The stimulus word was visible on a blackboard throughout the time of discussion. The instructions stressed the subjects' freedom to speak about whatever came to mind but asked them to center their comments around the stimulus word and to avoid going off on tangential topics. They were also instructed to observe normal standards of politeness in giving each other the opportunity to participate in the conversation.

The stimulus words used in the study were *blue, red, yellow, green, eagle, butterfly, lion,* and *sheep.*

Following transcription of the tape recordings of the subjects' conversations, the individual words in the transcripts were sorted into categories as in the previous study. Based on a count of 1670 running words from two pairs of speakers, 55 per cent of all words received some category score. When the highly frequent unscored words, *the, a, an, and, are, was,* and *is,* were eliminated, the percentage of categorized words was 66 per cent.

In the prior study on single word and continuous word association, distributions of categories had been compared by means of overlap coefficients, and factor analyses had been done on the overlap coefficients. In the free-speech study, correlation coefficients were used in place of overlap coefficients, since the use of overlap coefficients reduces the range of possible relations to half that of the correlations coefficient, that is, 0 to 100 per cent overlap as compared to 1.00 to −1.00 correlations.

A category distribution for each of the stimulus words was derived by combining the responses of all subjects to that stimulus word. In addition, in order to compare the extent to which structuring or organization existed in the category distributions associated with each stimulus word, a random variable was generated by entering a table of random numbers for three-digit numbers corresponding to category numbers 4,000 times, the approximate average number of responses in the other distributions. The profiles were then intercorrelated, using Pearson product-moment correlations, and the correlation matrix was factor analyzed using the principal components-varimax method. Table 12 shows the correlation matrix, and Table 13 the factor analysis.

TABLE 12

CORRELATION MATRIX OF FREE-SPEECH PROFILES OF 8 STIMULUS
WORDS AND A RANDOM VARIABLE: LAFFAL AND FELDMAN
(1963, p. 500)

	blue	red	yellow	green	eagle	but-terfly	lion	sheep	random variable
blue	1.000	.847	.935	.922	.258	.277	.237	.205	.087
red		1.000	.869	.865	.299	.269	.384	.311	.103
yellow			1.000	.909	.361	.364	.386	.361	.054
green				1.000	.262	.264	.337	.301	.090
eagle					1.000	.964	.789	.775	.047
butterfly						1.000	.741	.761	.054
lion							1.000	.945	— .004
sheep								1.000	— .031
random variable									1.000

TABLE 13

ROTATED FACTOR LOADINGS OF CORRELATIONS OF 8 STIMULUS
WORDS AND A RANDOM VARIABLE IN FREE SPEECH:
LAFFAL AND FELDMAN (1963, p. 500)

	Factors				
Words	I	II	III	IV	h^2
blue	97	15	2	— 3	96
red	91	5	6	21	88
yellow	94	19	— 1	14	95
green	95	7	4	14	93
eagle	15	88	3	43	98
butterfly	15	91	3	37	99
lion	20	44	— 1	86	98
sheep	15	46	— 4	85	96
random variable	6	3	99	— 2	99
% total variance	41	23	11	21	96

The first factor had very high loadings on all of the color words. The second factor showed highest loading for the flying animals, *eagle* and *butterfly,* but with moderately high loadings as well for the other two animal words, *lion* and *sheep*. The third factor was related only to the random variable. The fourth factor showed highest loadings for *lion* and *sheep,* but was moderately highly loaded on *eagle* and *butterfly* as well.

The hypothesis that there would be a universal factor reflecting characteristics of the language at large, independent of the particular stimulus spoken about, was not borne out, as may be seen in Table 13. A related assumption was that individual speakers would show considerable self-consistency no matter what their subject of discussion. The correlations available for comparisons relevant to this assumption were: (1) speaker with himself talking about different stimulus words; (2) speaker with his partner talking about the same stimulus words; (3) speaker with his partner talking about different stimulus words. The mean correlations for all speakers were compared by *t* test. The highest mean correlation was that of the speaker with his partner talking about the same stimulus words ($r = .85$). This mean r was significantly greater at the .01 level than that of the speaker with himself talking about different stimulus words ($r = .68$) and that of the speaker with his partner talking about different stimulus words ($r = .67$). The latter two correlations were not significantly different from each other. Thus, subject of discussion appeared to be the most potent determiner of each speaker's content.

There was a remarkable similarity between the factor pattern obtained in the study of free speech and the patterns obtained previously in studies of single word and continuous word association to the same stimulus words. The common factors were a color factor, an animal factor, and a flying animal factor. The verbal response to a given stimulus thus falls into similar patterns whether it is a composite made up of single-word-association responses from many subjects, many associative responses from a small number of subjects, or free speech drawn from a small number of subjects. This finding is a significant basis for extrapolations from word-association results and theory to free speech.

It had been anticipated that the same factors would emerge in free speech as had emerged in word association, but that they would be somewhat less sharply delineated in free speech in which there is so much opportunity for the intrusion of unrelated contents. In addition, it was thought that formalistic aspects of language would tend to provide a general factor in speech which would override differences attributable to topic or stimulus. However, the distinctions between the color and animal factors were quite striking, and no general factor emerged. This would suggest that, far from being a monolithic machinery within which minor alterations may be made according to topic, language is a set of tools of different shapes and functions selectively applied by the user. This differentiation within language and selectivity in use is further illustrated by the comparisons of pairs of speakers and individual speakers. Along with the hypothesis of a general factor in free speech, it was assumed that there would be a distinct individual-difference factor which would compete very strongly with topic of discussion to pre-empt categories. The findings on the contrary indicate that an individual is significantly more highly correlated with his fellow conversationalist in talking about the same stimulus words than he is with himself in talking about different stimulus words. In addition he differs from himself when talking about different stimulus words just as much as he differs from another individual in the same conversation talking about these different stimulus words.

A most interesting point is that the color and animal factors stand out as clearly and distinctly in free speech as in single word association. Single word association is a large set of single responses drawn from many different subjects. Since each subject responds to a stimulus word with the first word that comes to his mind, there is a tendency toward heavy stress on relatively few dominant responses. Free speech must, in some way, reflect this same tendency to focus on a few dominant categories.

To shed light on this problem, one additional piece of data was sought: the relative diversity of the verbal response patterns, as shown in the category profiles. One way to examine diversity of response is by means of the entropy or information score (Shannon & Weaver, 1949).[1] High entropy would indicate greater variety of contents,

---

[1] This application of the mathematical theory of information may be illustrated by considering how an information analysis may describe a set of responses in the word-association test. In a study by Laffal (1955), 30 out of 80 subjects gave the response *bother* to the stimulus word *fuss*, 5 gave *noise*, 3 gave *fidget*, 3 gave *fight*, 2 gave *angry*, and so on. Thirty-three different words were offered by the 80 subjects to the stimulus word *fuss*, with the number of subjects offering each response varying as indicated. The best estimates of the probabilities of each of the 33 responses for a similar group of subjects responding to a presentation of *fuss* would be: 30/80 for *bother*, 5/80 for *noise*, 3/80 for *fidget*, 3/80 for *fight*, 2/80 for *angry*, and so on. From such a series of probabilities an average information or entropy value may be obtained. The entropy (H) of a set of possible signals—in our case, of possible responses—is expressed by the formula $H = - \Sigma \; p_i \log_2 p_i$ where p_i is the probability of occurrence of a given response. A stimulus word to which the group as a whole gave few different responses, with high probabilities for such responses, would have a response hierarchy of low entropy. Thus the value of $-p_i \log_2 p_i$ for *bother* ($-30/80 \log_2 30/80$) in the above example is $-.5306$, for *noise* ($-5/80 \log_2 5/80$) it is $-.2500$ and so on. The sum of these

whereas low entropy would indicate less variety of content and greater concentration of response on fewer categories. The speech patterns of single word association, continuous word association, and free speech for the same eight stimulus words were compared on this dimension. The results are shown in Table 14.

TABLE 14

ENTROPY OF SINGLE WORD ASSOCIATION, CONTINUOUS WORD ASSOCIATION, AND FREE SPEECH:* LAFFAL AND FELDMAN (1963, p. 501)

Stimulus Word	Single Word Association	Continuous Word Association	Free Speech
blue	2.8738	4.5818	5.8282
red	2.3221	4.7788	5.9232
yellow	2.7851	4.5089	5.8788
green	2.3843	4.5117	5.9877
eagle	2.7447	4.4379	5.3904
butterfly	3.1738	4.6321	5.6668
lion	3.2694	4.4935	5.7250
sheep	2.9352	4.2581	5.8321
mean entropy	2.8110	4.5253	5.7790

* The negative sign has been dropped from the entropy scores.

A progressive increase in information may be noted from single word association through continuous word association to free speech. Free speech has the greatest variety of contents and the greatest unpredictability of content at any given moment. The clarity of the factor pattern in free speech and the similarity of the factors to those found in single word and continuous word association is therefore quite remarkable. Apparently, in free speech about any particular topic,

---

separate values is the entropy of the response hierarchy for the stimulus word *fuss*.

The formula quoted above weights the responses by their probabilities in arriving at the average information value or entropy of all the possible responses to the stimulus. The entropy takes into account not only the number of different responses to a stimulus word, but also the proportions of subjects giving each response.

a wide variety of contents may be brought into play, while major emphasis continues to be placed upon relatively few categories.

There is thus substantial support for the claim that verbal processes of a discontinuous nature, such as word association, have much in common with continuous free speech. Extrapolations may be made from one type of verbal production to the other, as long as one bears in mind the differences which are likely to appear in a more detailed comparison. We have here an inkling of the fact that there is an underlying structure in language content which manifests itself in all language modalities.

5. Language and the Structure of Experience

The practical difficulties in attempting an associative analysis of the vast number of different words in free-flowing language turned us toward the possibility of categorizing words as a way, at least, of identifying and registering consistencies. *Succeeding, getting ahead,* and *rising* are not totally substitutable for each other but do contain a significant component of similarity. In greater or lesser degree, each of these words includes something of what is suggested by an idea of dominance or achievement. The ultimate judgment in such matters of verbal similarity must be an intuitive one, but it could be buttressed with objective procedures. Thus, it might be possible to ascertain the validity of one individual's intuited similarity between *succeeding, getting ahead,* and *rising,* either by having a group of individuals make the same judgments, or by having them associate freely to the words and determining to what extent the group associations for the separate words were similar.

A single judge's intuition about similarity of words depends upon accumulated experience which he applies in comparing the referents and contexts of the words being judged. The extent to which the collective phenomenon of *la langue* is represented in the judge's idiolect—which in turn is a function of how like that of others his history has been—will determine how closely his decisions of similarity match those of other judges. It is even possible that his intuitions of similarity will be more accurate with respect to *la langue* than those derived from the more objective procedure of obtaining judgments or associations from a group of individuals. In the case of associations, the overtly uttered group data would of necessity be a limited sample of *la langue* and might well be less complete and less representative than the subjectively available sample of the single individual. However, to the extent that the single individual's intuition reflected a highly idiosyncratic experience, his judgments of similarity would be invalid with respect to the group.

If one were to arrange words that appeared in a random list, such as *up, yellow, go, high, black, surprise, school, man, chair,* by what matches better with one word or group of words than with others, the grouping might look like this: *up-high; yellow-black; surprise; school; man; chair. Up* and *high* have something in common, which might be called "upness." *Yellow* and *black* have in common that they refer to color. In a pinch, one might say that *man* and *school* have something in common, or *chair* and *school,* or *man* and *chair,* but these configurations are intuitively less compelling than the *up-high* and *yellow-black* ones.

Associative responses to the stimulus word *table* seem to be of two kinds: (1) those which refer to things which have characteristics shared by the referent of the word *table* and which might fall into the category of furniture or household objects; (2) those which do not appear so classifiable in terms of a common property, but are related to *table* only in the sense that their referents occur together with the referent of *table.* This duality in the way in which words appear to be related to each other is an old one in the history of psychology, going back to Aristotle (Warren, 1921), who proposed three principles as the basis of association: similarity, contrast, and contiguity. In the subsequent development of association psychology, contrast has been considered subordinate to the other two principles and sometimes merged with similarity.

The two distinctive ways in which words may become associated with each other, by similarity and by contiguity, crop up repeatedly in studies of verbal association (Deese, 1962; Gonzales & Cofer, 1959). Whether one principle or the other is more applicable will, in some instances, be unclear. Thus, if word A is contiguous with word B, and word C is also contiguous with word B, then words A and C become associated. A and C have B in common and in this respect are similar, but what they have in common is an element that is contiguous with each of them.

The idea of contiguity, since it is essentially of a spatial or temporal nature, is not difficult to grasp, but the idea of similarity—sometimes, where words are concerned, considered more narrowly as synonymy—is by no means a simple one. Naess (1957) has given a superb discussion of synonymity which is worth quoting. He says:

> Fortunately, collective research does not seem to presuppose that all intuitions are shared by all researchers, or that they should even know of the differences, or that the intuited entities should be definite in outline and content. Thus, there may in the years to come be much fruitful research concerning synonymity by researchers with partially different *intuitive* notions of synonymity.
>
> Concerning my own intuitions not much need be said: After a rather imperfect mental introspection and *Wesensschau,* I venture to assert the following about synonymity as intuited by me:
>
> (1) Synonymity is a relation between two or more things.
>
> (2) The relation is one of identity, but only identity in one respect among others. Nothing is intuited about the degree of strictness of the identity required. Considerable laxness is permitted.
>
> (3) The identical trait or aspect is that of meaning. In the occurrences most relevant to our theme, it is that of a kind of meaning or aspect of meaning roughly suggested by the predicate "cognitive." The term "meaning" is used in this characterization partly because its indefiniteness suggests the indefinite character of the intuition.
>
> (4) The relata are words and may be also some other things. The term "word" is here chosen, not "designation" or some other more technical term, because "word" has an air of large indefiniteness.
>
> (5) One may say that two words have not always been synonymous and also that for some people this or that pair of words are synonyms whereas for others they are not. It is not a necessary condition for the synonymity of two expressions that no copies or in-

stances whatsoever are heteronymous. That is, the
expressions may be said to be synonymous without
implying an assertion covering all occurrences.

(6) The intuited relation is not one between single instances or between classes of single instances of des-
ignations. Words are conceived to have a thing
character that does not appertain to singular events
of communication, and words, rather than instances
of words, are synonymous (pp. 88–89).

Naess's analysis comes close to providing a rationale for what
we are after in a search for ways of classifying words but still excludes what we know intuitively to be similar in such words as *chair*
and *table*. Let us go back to the grouping of the response words to
table in Chapter 4. Perhaps making explicit some of the bases on which
they were grouped will reveal something of the nature of the intuited
similarity which makes it possible to bundle words even where synonymy in a stricter sense is not present.

Under the heading "furniture," the following associates to *table*
were grouped: *chair, desk, lamp, bed, tablecloth.* If we take each
one of these responses in turn and compare it to *table* with the question, "What does the referent of this word share with the referent of
table?" we may be able to make explicit some of the criteria involved
in grouping or categorizing.

The first associate to *table* is *chair*. Chairs are often found near
tables, and thus there is an experiential contiguity about the referents
of *table* and *chair*. But we are excluding contiguity as a basis of categorizing. Tables and chairs are often made of the same material,
usually wood, but although this is a basis of similarity, myriads of other
things which have no compelling affinity with *table* are made of wood
—sabots, for example. The most substantial common property of *table*
and *chair* is that they refer to implements which we call furniture. It
would probably be very difficult to define precisely the class of things,
"furniture," without listing all the things which would be included in
the classification, but no one has any problem in knowing what furniture is.

In some systems of classification of associations (Warren, 1921),
table and *chair* would be characterized as coordinate associations. The
relation of both of them to furniture would be as subordinates to the
superordinate association. Coordination, subordination, and superor-
dination refer to a feature, usually of an abstract nature, held in common. The abstract idea of furniture would be the determinant of

coordination between *table* and *chair* as references to members of the class, and the subordination of both of them as specific instances of the superordinate idea.

Desk is readily seen as a synonym of *table*, and, of course, it also has the quality of coordination with *table* with respect to the general class of furniture. *Lamp* and *bed* are likewise coordinate members of the furniture class, although one senses other dimensions of meaning in these latter words as well.

Under the general class "eating" come a variety of responses. *Food, eat, dish, fork,* and *kitchen* refer to the thing eaten, the activity of eating, the container of food, the implement of eating, and the place where food is prepared, respectively. In each case the relevance to eating is marked and sufficiently strong to warrant the assertion that eating is an integral element of reference. *Food* and *eat* clearly entail references to food; *dish* is less firmly such a reference, but in the context of these associations, it seems reasonable to maintain that *dish* refers to a container of food. In the same way *fork* refers to a utensil for eating, and *kitchen* to a place for the preparation of food. As opposed to the situation with the furniture responses, the eating responses are less distinctly classifiable as subordinates in a major class. They do, however, entail explicitly or implicitly a significant reference to the class of objects and activities involved in eating.

The basis of these classifications is, then, that the word involves some major element of reference subsumable with other references under a common rubric. Words often have more than one significant referent, and the relative importance of such components of reference in a word may be hard to come by. Nevertheless, in accordance with Naess's second assertion about synonymity, as long as there is an element of identity of reference, it is not incorrect to group words in a class, even if the identity is one among others and is not total, nor even necessarily dominant.

NAME AND ESSENCE

The discussion must take us now from the intuition of identities and categories to the magical and myth-making attitude of primitive peoples. The inherent continuity will be evident, it is hoped, in the simple fact that a basic function which language serves is either to categorize experiences or to represent a categorizing activity exercised by speakers upon their world of experience. In discussing language and the myth-making process, Cassirer (1946) noted that, if two separate perceptual experiences result in the same "essence" or inner meaning for the naïve perceiver, and he gives them a single appellation, the heterogeneity of the perceptions effectively vanishes. This is the "meta-phoric thought" which is not merely a by-product of language but one of its essential conditions. Cassirer says:

> By virtue of the "equivalence" principle, entities which appear entirely diverse in direct sense perception or from the standpoint of logical classification may be treated as similars in language, so that every statement made about one of them may be transferred and applied to the other. Preuss, in a characterization of magic-complex thinking, says: "If the Cora Indian classes butterflies, quite absurdly, as birds, this means that all the properties which he notes in the object are quite differently classified and related for him than they are for us from our analytical, scientific point of view." But the apparent absurdity of this and other such classifications disappears as soon as we realize that the formation of these primary concepts was guided by lan-guage. If we suppose that the element emphasized in the name, and therefore in the verbal concept of "bird," as an essential characteristic was the element of "flight," then by virtue of this element and by its mediation the butterfly does belong to the class of birds (p. 95).

The metaphoric, classifying activity which is a function of lan-guage is, in Cassirer's description, especially characteristic of the prim-itive mind. As it discovers and names some property in nature, it at once establishes a basis for investing this property with deific powers and for overlooking aspects of lower valence whenever the essential property is present. Cassirer finds, however, that, because language bears in itself the capability of logic, words in more advanced cultures are ultimately shorn of their myth-making and magical qualities and are reduced to the status of mere conceptual signs. However, there is an exception: in creative expression, the myth-making metaphoric function of language reasserts itself, no longer mythically fettered, but esthetically liberated and capable of remaking with language a world of illusion and fantasy.

According to Cassirer, as our attitudes toward the world around us shift from superstition to knowledge, our naming and classifying activities shift from animism to a more accurate structuring of the types of experience. Cassirer may, however, have given undue weight to the logical tendencies of modern man as opposed to the superstitions

of the aborigine. Certainly superstitious explanations are not prominent
in our understanding of the world, and the structures into which we
organize experience are, in science, submitted to rigorous definition
and test. Nevertheless, an intuitive classifying and organizing activity
is always going on in us which does not call upon science and logic
for assistance, although it may ultimately be checked against them.
This may be seen, for example, in the way we associate ourselves
spatially with sun, moon, stars, and planets. With progress in space
technology and the dissemination of notions of gravity and weight-
lessness, what we used to think of as "up" is now becoming "distant."
But we will go on for a long time talking of the sun and the moon
"up above," and, in the naïve anthropocentric view of the world which
we adopt in our daily life, they *are* up above.

There is good reason to believe that, like the primitive men described by anthropologists, we are always organizing and reorganizing
our experience in ways which highlight certain characteristics of this
experience at the expense of others and that, once such organizations
of experience have been named and categorized in language, the name
or category becomes a vital determinant of further experience. The
Cora Indians explicitly classed butterflies as birds, but the college
subjects in the study described at the end of Chapter 4 (Laffal &
Feldman, 1962) implicitly classified them in the same way, as evidenced by the fact that their associations revealed a common factor
in response to the words *eagle* and *butterfly*. Our modern subjects
would not say that an eagle and a butterfly are both birds, but they
would, in speaking about these creatures, use much the same associations! The fact that the classification is not explicit, as with the Cora
Indians, does not reduce the experiential similarity of the two objects.
Modern man perhaps has an advantage in his unwillingness to group
butterfly and *eagle* explicitly: he is therefore able to discriminate their
differences more readily and, if need be, shift them to different categories where the context demands it. His behavior is more flexible, but
his experience, like that of the Cora Indians, still invests the names
butterfly and *eagle* with much the same associative meaning.

Cassirer's account of the power of names in metaphoric thought
is sometimes reflected in the behavior of disturbed patients. Laffal,
Lenkoski, and Ameen (1956; also see Chapter 2) described a patient
who reversed *yes* and *no* in his language. This same patient, in one
of his agitated periods, literally illustrated the awful significance which
names may assume under some circumstances. Part of a recorded
interview with the patient is quoted below.[1]

---

[1] Five dots indicate small portions of the tape recording which were

Pt. All they were saying is my name and my initial, and just riding right by my house. That's all they were doing.

Dr. Well, why would they do that?

Pt. . . . . .

Dr. Why would they do a thing like that?

Pt. Why? I know why myself. I can, I went downtown and started hollering like hell and start calling the cops and say I want them to do something. They thought I was the chief of police.

Dr. You, you thought you were?

Pt. Sure I was. Sure I was chief of police. Even in every store I went into, I . . . . . Even your initial. Right out.

Dr. Why were they doing that? To make you angry?

Pt. You can tell me? I know. I know why. Just for the hell of it. Just to get on your nerves. That's why. One person does it, all right. But you get a number, doing it all the time, that's all changed to a difference. That's all they do. . . . . .

Dr. When did they stop?

Pt. When they stopped? They stopped okay. Even during the ball game on the radio at night. I can listen to the ball game and be, get so mad I almost broke that thing. I just grind my teeth and start pounding things. I almost jumped off the floor an inch.

Dr. Are they men? Women? Who's calling you?

Pt. Even on the radio, broadcasting over on the radio. They had to say me in the outfield. I was in the out-field.

Dr. How did they say it? Roberts is in the outfield?

Pt. Yeah, they didn't, didn't say me out there. Yeah, by, by your last name. But by your full name? Let you know right to people? People you know? Probably you would. But if they keep the name, you know, like in a, in a, in a vault like my army papers there— something like that—and say your name over and over again. It could drive you nuts if you want to pay attention to it. It could drive you to do something.

unclear. The interview was conducted while the patient was under the influence of amytal.

Dr. To do what?

Pt. To go over and punch him.

Dr. Who?

Pt. Some people's, from in the names of, in the door right here is my mother's name.

Dr. Your mother's name?

Pt. Yeah. Gloria Roberts. Why, she used to get so much in the habit of saying her name right in here, in the dayroom. I had to holler at her. My father used to say his own name right here in the living room, in the waiting room there, or in the visiting room . . . . . And people used to repeat right after her. I told them: repeat you all the time! Only one person. Always a bunch of people repeat me all the time.

Dr. What does that mean when they repeat your name? What does that mean?

Pt. I think they're making, it means they're making a fool of me. Always sit there, repeat your name. How are you supposed to feel if somebody is always repeating your name? How the hell would you feel?

Dr. You seem to be angry.

Pt. Certainly—

Dr. They seem to be taking—

Pt. Certainly not—

Dr. —taking something away from you when they repeat your name.

Pt. Yeah.

Dr. What do they take away from you?

Pt. Well, when they repeat my name they take it away from me. The thing is, all right, say Joseph A. Roberts. Okay. But say, say your name, your, your initial and where you live! I got, I got my army papers sent here on television.

Dr. I don't understand that, Joseph. What do you mean?

Pt. Last night in the fights. I, of course, you guys, you fellows are here at night. I know if you listen to fights at home. I got my, my army read right from T.V.: Forty-third infantry. You're in heavy mortar. You need the—

Dr. Joseph, what, what is it when they, when they say your full name? That seems to be special.

Pt. When they say my full name, Doc, I can tear the country apart. I liked it.

Dr. What do—

Pt. Even your first and last name. It's the same thing, isn't it? Suppose they keep saying you over television. You start to hear it over and over again. This—

Dr. Well—

Pt. You mean to tell me people could help? How in the damn couldn't they? Unless they do it the right way. Is supposed to be said. No, they got to say your name along with it again and again. You're supposed to be said.

Dr. Why, Joseph, why do they say your name?

Pt. Mainly people know themselves. I think they know themselves. They could be half off their rocker I think. Saying so many names all the time. All right in line like picket lines when you're going on strike.

Dr. When did it first start? When did people start saying your name?

Pt. When they started was last summer.

Dr. Last summer?

Pt. Yeah.

Dr. That was when you were where?

Pt. Believe I left Sandusky. I went on about a six month leave before I came back here. That's what Father Wilton prescribed. He said, you're better off to go back in the V.A., so I came here.

Dr. What's going to happen?

Pt. What's going to happen?

Dr. Think they'll stop saying your name?

Pt. I hope not. I hope they don't, do say my name over. All right you say good morning, Joseph, how the hell do you do? Are you going home tomorrow? Are you going out for some air? Let's hear the broadcast or something. But just sit down like a dumb bastard in a chair and say Joseph Roberts all day long, is that any sense? It could get on my brain. Of course, it gets on the other guy's bed, brain that's saying it. Come to the door: I'm B. G. Roberts!

Dr. Who says that?

Pt. Many a visitor up here said that in the dayroom when

they came up. What the hell am I supposed to be, the trash? I gave initials to people, other people? To strangers? I can see they asked for it. I had to give them the . . . . . papers . . . . . I brought the damned army papers and just handed it to them, that, that would be it. As soon as I said Roberts, probably they'd know my initial. But there's other Roberts too. I'm Joseph A. Roberts. Now my head feels a little bit, starting to clear up.

Dr. Starting to clear up? Feeling better now? Do they say anything else besides just your name? It is always just your name?

Pt. Just my name and then nineteen, you were in the forty-third, you need the bronze star, coming right from television.

Dr. Why the bronze star? Did you do something that should get you the bronze star?

Pt. I know, myself. Probably, probably right on T.V. They said your father is, is going in the . . . . . And they say his name, initial, and rank and serial number right on T.V. For what? Maybe they say yours, right there in the picture . . . . .

Dr. Somebody said it right in the picture.

Pt. Right in the damn picture.

Dr. Is something wrong with the name, Joseph?

Pt. There's something wrong with my name.

Dr. What's wrong with it?

Pt. Just that, that I like to be said outside. I like to kid around, I like to fool. I like to get in with, with guys and talk about things that make sense, talk over: when you guys going home; or, let's, let's go in the rec hall and why don't we go down and get some coffee and; what are you going to buy; or something: when's Christmas coming? Sit down on a chair like a goddamn egg and start saying someone's name all the time!

Dr. Who does that?

Pt. Hell, man! I was said up here! Guys right there in the dayroom, every goddamn . . . . . and his wife said me.

Dr. Said you?

Pt. Yeah, so what! I think they know themselves!

Dr. Joseph, the way you say it, it sounds as if when somebody says your name he's doing something to you.

Pt. Sure he isn't.

Dr. What is he doing?

Pt. If I want to mind it, Doc, if I just sit down and mind it, really make it, make it make me, get on my brain. If I just sit down there then it wouldn't, it would bother me. But if it does, if I don't make it bother me, I'll do anything. I'll start coming around here and pounding on the office window . . . . . I'm going to punch this and that, just for the hell of it, because I'm feeling too much at the time which I don't. I'm nuts, I'm all in my, I'm not in my senses. What the hell is it?

Dr. Do you wish you were somebody else?

Pt. Yes! I wish I was somebody else. When I go down town, I heard me said right on Church and Chapel. In the bank, as soon as I walk in the door they used to say my name. Right to people! Strangers! I know?

Dr. Your whole name they'd say?

Pt. Yeah. My full name, my mother's full name, every damn thing. Might as well give them the bank book.

Dr. Why would they say your mother's name?

Pt. I know why. And they come around, "Well, you got the bronze star." Christ, this went on for about six months. In the summer my mother was said. Yes, I'll say it now, I'll admit that.

In the patient's fantasy, others have gotten hold of him, and of his mother as well, by means of his and his mother's names. If others have his name, they might as well have his bank book, they are making a fool and trash of him, they put him in places where he does not want to be, they reveal him to strangers. The patient experiences a profound frustration in everything he does; wherever he turns, he appears to be blocked and impotent. He projects the source of his frustration and sense of impotence into the world around him, on to people who use his name for purposes which are not his own, and he suffers a sense of motor and psychical inhibition due to outside control. This is a familiar clinical picture in a paranoid psychosis, where the patient is unable to accept his own impulses, and deals with them by attributing them to the world around him, responding then to the projected impulses with rage and denial. The modality of the projection in this case is the significant point that bears on language. People make him suffer *by doing things with his name.*

THE MYTHIC MODE, PRIMARY PROCESS, AND EGOCENTRIC AND INNER SPEECH

Susanne Langer, in a commentary on Cassirer's theory of language and myth (1949), pointed out that, although Cassirer found himself in disagreement with Freud on the nature of basic motivations of man, there was a close and vital agreement between some of their ideas. She saw Freud's description of the dream work as almost exactly identical to the mythic mode which Cassirer attributed to primitive ideation, in which intense feelings are expressed in symbols formed by the excited imagination. In these symbols the meanings remain implicit and hidden, and the emotions appear instead to belong to the image which may be a vision, a gesture, a sound, a word, or an external object.

Jean Piaget has described certain aspects of language and thought in the child (1926; 1928) which also echo Cassirer's "metaphoric attitude" and Freud's "primary process." In one series of observations of a boy and a girl of six, the remarks made during play appeared to fall into two fundamental groups: egocentric speech and socialized speech. In egocentric speech the child speaks only for or about himself and does not attempt to influence or to communicate with his audience. Socialized speech is a communicative nonegocentric speech, in which the child tries to influence his neighbor or to communicate some information.

Up until the age of about five, in Piaget's study, the child works almost always alone. From five to seven, little groups are formed, but these groups are transitory and irregular. Between the ages of seven and eight, there is an impetus for work with other children, and it is in this period that the proportion of egocentric speech declines.

Egocentric thought (to which egocentric speech is inseparably tied) is basically intuitive and syncretistic. It leaps directly from premise to conclusion without intermediary steps and without attention to paradoxes. Personal schema of analogy and memories are applied. Proof is not required; belief is engendered by a kind of vision or intuition of the whole. Visual schema and judgments of value play an important part in the thought. This is contrasted with communicable or socialized thought, in which deduction is prominent, in which explicit rendering of relationships and steps is required, in which there is an emphasis on proof, and in which personal judgments of value are subordinated to collective judgments of value.

After the age of seven, according to Piaget, children do not show much syncretism in perception, but they do show it in verbal intelligence. Although they tend to see objects in more correct and logical relationships, their verbal reasoning still takes syncretic forms. In one experiment, about 40 pupils between the ages of eight and eleven were given proverbs and asked to match the proverbs with sentences having corresponding meanings. They were then questioned as to the basis of their matching. There were a large number of incorrect choices, but the children always justified their choices with an explanation. Piaget's analysis of the mental processes of the children is as follows. As the child reads the proverb, he makes a schema in which such things as the symbolic meaning of the proverb, the mental imagery, the rhythm of the words, the position of the words, and punctuation all enter as elements. The child then undertakes to explain his matching, and, having the general schema available for projection into words, he searches for and finds the appropriate words and phrases that will "explain" his comparison. The existence of the schema will even distort the child's understanding of the corresponding sentence, and in turn, in whatever way the schema changes as a result of the corresponding sentence or of the need to explain the matching, all of the parts—the proverb, the sentence, and the explanation—will alter in order to fit in the schema. Piaget's account of the desire for justification as a universal law of verbal intelligence in children is very close to Cassirer's description of the mental processes of aborigines. In the child's syncretistic reasoning everything is related, everything is connected to everything else, and everything is perceived through a pre-established network of general schemas built up of imagery, analogous details, contingent circumstances, and whatever other mental manipulations are necessary to bring discordant facts into harmony. There is no room for the accidental or the unaccountable in the child's view, and he will find or make a reason for everything, although his reason will reflect his still egocentric organizing schemas rather than the objective reality. Piaget points out that such justifications by children, rooted as they are in childish syncretism, sometimes have the quality of pathological interpretations by patients who have regressed to more primitive modes of thinking.

In a critique of Piaget's view, Vygotsky (1934) maintained that the progression of the child's language was not from egocentric to socialized speech, but on the contrary, from socialized to egocentric speech, with egocentric speech ultimately becoming inner speech which is part of the process of thinking. In Vygotsky's conception egocentric speech is a phenomenon which represents a transition from the inter-psychic, social to an intrapsychic, individualized functioning of language. According to Vygotsky, speech for oneself is derived from speech for others, and egocentric speech is a stage on the way to inner speech. Egocentric speech does not merely accompany the child's activity as a kind of nonfunctional by-product, but serves mental orientation and understanding, helps overcome difficulties, and furthers the solution of problems. The fate of egocentric speech is thus quite different from that described by Piaget, who maintains that it gives way to socialized speech. Vygotsky holds that egocentric speech develops rather than declines but becomes increasingly internalized and changed into silent inner speech which in turn is a significant component of thought.

Ultimately, in Vygotsky's view, when vocalization drops away from egocentric speech, this heralds the development of a new ability to think words instead of speaking them. Vygotsky's further discussion of the idea of inner speech is reminiscent of Freud's primary process, Cassirer's mythic mode, and Piaget's syncretistic thought. Inner speech, he says, shows a preponderance of the sense of a word (the sum of all the psychological events aroused in our consciousness by the word) over the meaning of the word, the prevalence of agglutinations as ways of forming word-combinations, and the fluid interpenetration of the senses of different words. In inner speech, "a single word is so saturated with sense that many words would be required to explain it in external speech. No wonder that egocentric speech is incomprehensible to others" (p. 148). Thus, Vygotsky describes a language that is personalized, unstable, and quite different from the language which we know in *la langue.*

The utterance of communicative language is not a simple vocalizing of inner speech. It is a complex process involving the transformation of the fluid internal, unvocalized process into a structure which is acceptable in *la langue* and will be understood by others. Vygotsky believes that in the final analysis verbal thought is engendered by motivation and so has its roots in the personality. In order to understand thinking one must understand the needs, interests, and emotions of the individual.

Finally, the very personal nature of verbal thought is indicated as follows: "We come now to the last step in our analysis of verbal thought. Thought itself is engendered by motivation, *i.e.,* by our desires and needs, our interests and emotions. Behind every thought there is an affective-volitional tendency, which holds the answer to the last 'why' in the analysis of thinking" (p. 150).

LANGUAGE AND THE STRUCTURE OF EXPERIENCE

How language structures and organizes experience, and in itself becomes a determinant of the nature of experience, has occupied linguists and philosophers for some time. Johann Gottfried von Herder (1744–1803) and Wilhelm von Humboldt (1767–1835) are credited with having originated the view that the conceptual development made possible by and embodied in language in turn influences the nature of experience. B. L. Whorf introduced the idea to American psychologists in the form of a theory of cultural relativism as a function of language differences (Brown & Lenneberg, 1954; Carroll & Casagrande, 1958; Fishman, 1960; Whorf, 1956). Of special interest in the present discussion is the work of a number of German and Swiss linguists, among them Hallig and Wartburg (1956; 1963), Trier (1934), Wartburg (1946), and Weisgerber (1938). Under the influence of developments in Gestalt psychology and of the work of Kurt Goldstein (1948) with aphasic patients, they evolved what has been called the "field theory" of language (Basilius, 1952; Ullmann, 1959). Goldstein (1948) had pointed out that the problem in brain-damaged aphasic patients was broader than that of evoking or dealing with word images. The difficulty in finding and using words was part of a total personality change which involved an impairment of the abstract attitude, a loss of ability to categorize events and objects. Since the meaning of a particular event or object is derived from the class of things of which it is a part, the problem of meaning assumed central importance in Goldstein's interpretation of aphasic symptoms.

Field theorists maintain that languages incorporate unique ways of cognitively organizing the world, and they stress vocabulary as the bearer of the cultural burden. A basic proposition of the field theorists is that there is a conceptual intermediary world, a *Zwischenwelt* (Weisgerber, 1938; 1953) in each language, which is not simply a reflection of the external world but an ideational organization of this world, and which involves the speaker intimately and irrevocably in the culture of his group. This *Zwischenwelt* is the product of long years of cultural development.

The concept of semantic fields was formalized by Gunther Ipsen in 1924 (Reuning, 1941) as *Bedeutungsfeld* (field of meaning). However, as Ullmann has pointed out (1962, p. 244), the idea had its antecedents in phenomenology and in Cassirer's teachings about the influence of language on thought, as well as in Saussure's (1915) picture of language as a structured whole whose elements define each other and derive their value from the whole which they form. In 1931, Jost Trier produced a study on the history of German vocabulary in the area of intelligence, entitling it the study of a "linguistic field" (*sprachliches Feld*). The essence of the meaning of a word, according to Trier, is in its place in the field. The vocabulary of a language is a structure, an organized network, wherein the meanings of the units, the words, are determined by their integral relationship with other units of the network. The word gains its meaning from the whole of the structure, and, vice versa, the structure gains its meaning from the individual words. A given word is conceptually related at one level to other words, and this group of conceptually related words (for example, *shrewd, wise, clever, crafty, cunning, witty, learned, educated, accomplished*) is in turn integrally related to other con ceptual groups, which together form still higher organizations.

The vocabulary of a language, according to field theorists, is a finely articulated grand structure built up out of these conceptual fields of various orders. This is the cognitive structure which languages impose on the world. It should be noted that field theory has been criticized (Betz, 1954; Ullmann, 1962, p. 249) for suggesting that words, in a close-fitting mosaic, neatly cover the field of meaning without gaps and overlap. Languages are not so tidy, according to these criticisms, and there are, rather, focal clusters consisting of words of close meaning, along with gaps where, hypothetically, there could be experiential discriminations statable in words. This is clear, for example, with respect to the idea of anxiety. Words like *fear, anguish, panic, apprehension, dread, fright, alarm, terror, horror, upset, distress, uneasiness, worry, concern, disquiet, trouble, disturb, misgiving, shame, guilt, remorse,* and *foreboding* are not easily fitted together into a continuous map. One might employ dimensions of intensity and of outerness and innerness with respect to the self as bases for ordering such words over a range of possible experiences, but actual usage would repeatedly controvert the pattern. Anxiety is a highly subjective experience, most difficult to define with consensual precision despite the fact that the language community would acknowledge the general area intimated by such words. Speakers might not readily discriminate between *fear* and *anxiety* and the precise references of these words, but they would concur about differences between *fear* or *anxiety* and *happiness* or *gaiety.* In this sense one could speak of a distinct field of reference containing such words as *anxiety, fear,* and the like, even though the field itself had little articulation.

THE POSSIBILITY OF A CONCEPTUAL DICTIONARY

The arrangement of word lists by subjects is an old story, as Buck points out (1949, p. xiii). However, the development of field theory has been of considerable importance for modern semantics. It has given rise to studies of both a descriptive and a historical nature (Reuning, 1941; Tinsley, 1953) and has also—a natural outcome of its stress upon words and meanings of words—led to significant new approaches to dictionary- and thesaurus-making. Hallig and Wartburg (1956; 1963) have given substance to the possibility of developing a universally applicable conceptual scheme under whose rubric uniform comparative studies could be made either of separate languages or of one language at different times. The possibility of revealing differences in conceptual field distributions of languages either longitudinally or in cross section brings linguistics into close union with social history and anthropology. One lexicologist (Matoré, 1953) has gone so far as to maintain that lexicology is a sociological discipline using certain linguistic materials, namely, words, and that lexicology is related naturally not to such linguistic matters as syntactics or phonetics, but to sociological interests.

Mezger (1956) pointed out some of the advantages which might accrue from a conceptual dictionary. One language might be compared with another in terms not of the meaning of individual words, but of the range of meanings in coherent groupings of words referring to the same area. Languages might be compared with respect to their distributions of and predilections for various subject matters defined by the dictionary, and it might also be possible to compare the state of a given language at one epoch with its state at some other time. Mezger suggested the following structure of classifications for a conceptual dictionary:

A. *World, Nature, and Life*
  I. World, inorganic matter, chemical and physical properties of matter, aggregate conditions
  II. Organic world, plants, animals, man as part of nature—the body, senses and their activities, activity, conditions and needs of the body (sleep, food, motion), bodily defects, diseases, life, reproduction, death, destruction
B. *Man*
  I. As a thinking, feeling, and willing being
    a. Thought and expression

        b. Individual emotions and relations between men
        c. Activity and will, character, honor, and morals
     II. Creative and organizing man
        a. State and people, family and descent
        b. Customs, law, justice
        c. Property, housing, dwelling and settlement, work, household, family, technique, professions, crafts and service, tools, weapons, military, transport
        d. Religion
    III. Man and world
        a. Existence and relation, time, space, area, position, shape and form, quantity, size, degree, number, motion

An analysis of several languages, applying such broad classifications, might reveal that in one language words for world, nature, and life predominate, whereas, for another, words for property, housing, professions, and the like predominate. This would reflect a fundamental fact about the conceptual orientation of the speakers of these languages and could well provide a key to understanding their history and their social structure. Such a basic fact would also undoubtedly reach down into the life of the individual member of the community.

Linguists usually orient themselves toward language phenomena of groups and in this sense toward an average or normative language. Therefore they have not clearly raised the possibility that linguistic relativity or differences in the *Zwischenwelt* of a language might extend as far as individual speakers of the same language. Studies of individual authors (Fermin, 1954; Keller, 1953; Wartburg, 1946, p. 161) have usually been taken as illustrative of a period or of a class of speakers. Nevertheless, if, as linguistic field theorists suggest, the vocabulary of a language is informed and organized with a conceptual model, then surely it should be possible to examine differences between individual speakers of the language in their predilections for certain aspects of the model or for fields of the total vocabulary. With this extension of the *Zwischenwelt* view to individual differences, we come back to the province of psychology.

The basic problem in creating a conceptual dictionary—whether such a dictionary aims at revealing the *Zwischenwelt* of a total language or of an individual speaker—is to find concepts which adequately represent man's experience. This is fundamentally a psychological issue, although it may also be dealt with as a logical one.

Roget's famous thesaurus (1852) is an example of a logical conceptual ordering of language. Roget, of course, had a practical aim in mind: to help the writer (or speaker) find the word that would best suit his purpose. Given the idea, the writer could look up a list of words related to this idea and choose from among them. In describing his basis of grouping words, Roget said:

> Eschewing all needless refinements and subtleties, I have taken as my guide the more obvious characters of the ideas for which expressions were to be tabulated, arranging them under such classes and categories as reflection and experience had taught me would conduct the inquirer most readily and quickly to the object of his search. Commencing with the ideas expressing abstract relations, I proceed to those which relate to space and to the phenomena of the material world, and lastly to those in which the mind is concerned, and which comprehend intellect, volition, and feeling: thus establishing six primary Classes of Categories (p. v).

The six classes which Roget established were: (1) abstract relations, including existence, resemblance, quantity, order, number, time, power; (2) space, including motion or change of place; (3) material world, including properties of matter such as solidity, fluidity, heat, sound, light; (4) intellect, including acquisition, retention, and communication of ideas; (5) volition, including voluntary and active powers such as choice, intention, utility, action, antagonism, authority, compact, property, and so on; (6) sentiment and moral powers, including feelings, emotions, passions, and moral and religious sentiments.

In practice, Roget's thesaurus fulfills its aim not because the writer, in his pursuit of the elusive word, follows a route from the most general idea to some logical subdivision in which his word may be found, but because he has a good idea of the specific area within which to search and simply looks up a word which he knows to be in that area, so finding other related words and the particular one best suited. If I want a word that expresses a certain subtle dexterity, I simply pick a common word like *skill,* which comes close but does not satisfy, and look for the grouping of words around *skill.* There I find *finesse* which fits my intention. In Roget's system, the subgroup of *skill* is in the following logical hierarchy:

Class 5. Volition
  Division 1. Individual volition

Section III. Voluntary action
Part 2. Complex voluntary action
"Skill"

The scheme itself contributes very little to locating the desired word. In all probability the more inclusive classes were arrived at by construction from the primary subdivisions, but the ordering of classes reflects not the compelling qualities of experiences or processes of thought but an *ad hoc* logical arrangement. Nevertheless, the fact that within the logical structure the classes do have an experiential unity makes it clear that logical considerations are not irrelevant in the task of ordering language.

By contrast, let us look at the scheme which evolved from Caroline Spurgeon's study of Shakespeare's imagery (1935). Spurgeon believed that memory is not merely a storehouse but a device for selecting aspects of experience which have special meaning and attraction for us and that an individual's temperament may be revealed by a sampling of his memory. One could therefore gain information about the personality of the poet by studying his images, since he would tend to draw such images from the objects he knew best, thought about most, or to which he was in some way most sensitive. Some reservations have been expressed regarding this thesis. Ullmann (1962, p. 202) points out that arguments *ex silentio* cannot be taken to reflect an absence of interest in particular areas on the part of the writer, and he illustrates this in the fact that Izaak Walton, author of the *Compleat Angler,* did not use a single image derived from fishing in his *Life of Donne.* However, it is worth noting that a more sophisticated approach to the contents of a writer's language would not necessarily see these contents as mirroring directly the central preoccupations of the writer, but as presenting cues to underlying psychological configurations. Thus, Ullmann maintains that it would be naïve to attribute the numerous insect images found in the works of modern novelists to an absorbing interest in entomology or to trauma associated with insects but concedes that Sartre's obsessive concern with insects may have a psychological motivation.

Spurgeon took all the images from Shakespeare's plays and from the writings of some of his contemporaries and classified them according to theme or subject matter. The definition of image was left somewhat vague: "I use the term 'image' here as the only available word to cover every kind of simile, as well as every kind of what is really compressed simile—metaphor" (p. 5); this is a weakness of her study

(Foakes, 1952). However, her findings are striking enough to warrant the belief that she did indeed secure a representative sampling of the language of Shakespeare and his contemporaries. For example, in classifying the images of Marlowe and Shakespeare, she ascertained that there were distinct differences in the subject matters characteristic of each writer. Thus, Shakespeare stressed nature, animals, everyday and domestic things, the body in health and sickness, indoor life, fire, light, food, and cooking. Marlowe, on the other hand, drew heavily on images derived from the classics and from the sun, moon, planets, and heavens. A preoccupation with dazzling heights and vast spaces was the dominant note of Marlowe's imagery, where Shakespeare found his inspiration among the green fields of earth and the ordinary lives of men.

The classification scheme which evolved from Spurgeon's analysis of Shakespeare, Marlowe, and Bacon is as follows:

A. *Nature*

    I. Growing things: flowers, trees, plants, fruit, weeds

    II. Weather: cold, storm, wind, rain, cloud, mist, changes

    III. Sea and ships: ships and sea-faring, sea

    IV. Celestial bodies: sun, stars, shadow, moon

    V. Elements: water and river, earth

    VI. Gardening: various, canker, grafting, ripeness, growth

    VII. Seasons: spring, night and day, winter, summer

    VIII. Farming

    IX. Natural features

B. *Animals*

    I. Four-footed animals: domestic various, dogs, wild various, lions, various

    II. Birds: single, kinds, general (wings and flight), falconry, snaring, fowling

    III. Insects, etc.: various, bees, flies, spiders, general, mollusc

    IV. Reptiles

    V. Fabulous

    VI. Fish

C. *Domestic*

    I. House: indoor, out

    II. Textiles: clothes, material, needlework

    III. Jewels
    IV. Light and fire: fire, light and darkness
    V. Human relations: children, women, various, babes, boys, men
    VI. Life and death: death, life, birth
    VII. Indoor games
    VIII. Miscellaneous

D. *Body*
    I. Body and bodily action: action, body, senses, sleep, torture
    II. Food and drink: food, cooking, drink
    III. Sickness and medicine: sickness, medicine, and treatment

E. *Daily Life*
    I. Classes and types
    II. Sport and games: sport, outdoor games
    III. War: various, weapons and armor, explosives
    IV. Trades and building: trades, building
    V. Substances and metals: substances and liquids, metals
    VI. Money
    VII. Town life
    VIII. Roads and travel
    IX. Topical
    X. Buildings
    XI. State and government
    XII. Village life
    XIII. Commerce classes
    XIV. Miscellaneous

F. *Learning*
    I. Classical: mythological, historical
    II. Religion: various, simple beliefs, Biblical, superstitious
    III. Law
    IV. Proverbial and popular
    V. Reading, writing, and books
    VI. Science
    VII. Facts from books

G. *Arts*
    I. Visual and decorative
    II. Music
    III. Drama

H. *Imagination*
> I. Personification: qualities, states and emotions, nature, various
> II. Imaginative
> III. Abstraction and concretion
> IV. Fantastic
> V. Miscellaneous

If Spurgeon had studied more writers, other categories might have found their way into the system. Still, as it stands, this is a significant achievement which clearly establishes the individual differences of several great writers.

It is readily shown that idiosyncratic preferences exist in writers or speakers not only for classes of images but also for classes of words. Such a fact strikes us immediately, for example, in the writing of Jonathan Swift. The following is the opening passage of Chapter 1 of "A Voyage to Lilliput":

> My father had a small estate in Nottinghamshire; I was the third of five sons. He sent me to Emmanuel College in Cambridge at fourteen years old, where I resided three years, and applied myself close to my studies; but the charge of maintaining me (although I had a very scanty allowance) being too great for a narrow fortune, I was bound to apprentice to Mr. James Bates, an eminent surgeon in London, with whom I continued four years, and my father now and then sending me small sums of money, I laid them out in learning navigation and other parts of the mathematics useful to those who intend to travel, as I always believed it would be some time or other my fortune to do. When I left Mr. Bates, I went down to my father, where, by the assistance of him and my uncle John and some other relation, I got forty pounds, and a promise of thirty pounds a year to maintain me at Leyden; there I studied physic two years and seven months, knowing it would be useful in long voyages.

There are at least 15 references to number and quantity in this paragraph. A perusal of *Gulliver's Travels* will reveal that this is neither an accident of opening passages nor of the particular episode described. It pervades the whole work, and in varying degrees is characteristic of all of Swift's writing including his poetry. Such a fact is surely related in fundamental ways to Swift's world view. In *Gulliver's Travels* these quantitative references lend an air of scientific objectivity and exactitude to the fantastic log of an imaginary traveler, so helping create the illusion of reality. This does not alone reflect a brilliant irony on the part of the writer, but an inevitable and happy application of his native bent.[2]

Spurgeon's approach stands in contrast to that of Roget. Where Roget began with a set of logical preconceptions and an a priori scheme, Spurgeon permitted the writer's words to group themselves into categories which became the conceptual scheme for describing his psychological concerns.

Modern linguists steer a course between these two approaches. An outstanding example of the construction of a conceptual dictionary is in the work of Hallig and Wartburg (1952). In their monograph, they point out first of all that their concern is with the classification of concepts rather than with words as such and that a conceptual dictionary must establish the underlying concepts which may be represented in words. However, they make it clear that these concepts must stem from prescientific aspects and possibilities in language rather than those which have developed from scientific knowledge and sophistication. They also require that the concepts be arranged and organized according to a unitary viewpoint and that everything be integrated into a unified whole.

Hallig and Wartburg go on, in their study, to distinguish between "meaning" and "concept," following some work of H. Güntert. The total meaning of a word is composed of a "logical universal" (general meaning), connotations which give a subjective coloring to the word for each individual, the feeling tone of the word which derives from its use, and the occasional meaning which in a given situation becomes delimited from the general meaning. It is the logical universal which Hallig and Wartburg seek as that isolate from the total meaning which may form the basis of a structural description of language.

Having established that it is the logical universals, the concepts, which the dictionary-maker is after, Hallig and Wartburg then go on to discuss the position from which their system of concepts is derived. The issue, as they see it, is to find an all-inclusive approach to dividing up man's experience and the objects in his universe into conceptual units and subdivisions. To some extent the structure is already determined by a given vocabulary, since implicit in the vocabulary are the

---

[2] See Appendix I for a more detailed analysis of some passages from *Gulliver's Travels*.

concepts which give meaning to words. They stress that the structure of concepts which will, hopefully, define the essential qualities of man's experience must reflect the natural prescientific viewpoint of the gifted average individual who observes the world with naïve realism, rather than the sophisticated view of the modern scientist or philosopher. Their psychological approach is thus a kind of phenomenological survey of man and his experience. A good example of a discrimination that the ordinary individual might not make, that the scientist would, is in the classification of *whale*. In the first edition of their system (1952) Hallig and Wartburg place *whale* in the general class "fish of the sea." In their second edition of the same work (1963) they place *whale* in the class "marine animals," since the whale is a warm-blooded mammal. Nevertheless they argue (1963, p. 35) that, despite our scientific knowledge of this animal, it is in the common conception still a fish because it lives like a fish.

Hallig and Wartburg find that the first product of this simple, natural, prescientific approach to man's experience is the discovery of a dichotomy: the self and the objective world.

The objective world provides the first main division of their system, and is labeled, *The Universe*. This division is readily subdivided into the states, appearances, and processes of nature, and to it are assigned concepts which refer to objects and circumstances of inorganic and organic nature, exclusive of man.

The second major division is *Man,* and this includes man as a biological creature separate and distinct from other living things, his experiences of self, his work, and his capacity for thought. In this division are also placed the objects of material culture which have been created by man.

A third large division is designated *Man and Universe,* and to it are assigned two major subdivisions, one called "The a priori," and the second, "Science and technology." "The a priori" refers to man as a thinking and observing being in opposition to himself and the world. Hallig and Wartburg intend to subsume under this category the ultimates or givens of consciousness, the kinds of knowledge that the individual simply has and uses with instinctive certainty, such as discrimination of dimension, shape, weight, and physical form; sensory experiences; and perception of contrast and similarity, number and quantity, space and distance, time, movement and change. The subdivision "Science and technology" includes all that thought and research have introduced in all areas of being; here are subsumed the subject matters of the individual sciences and all aspects of technological development.

In this framework, Hallig and Wartburg hope to encompass everything that a simple, phenomenological world view might contain, and they believe that they have achieved a structure of concepts in which the major divisions and subdivisions are bound together by a natural relationship without being forced. In this system they begin with nature and naturally given objects, place man in a central position, and finally include man's interaction with nature. The major divisions and subdivisions of the scheme proposed by Hallig and Wartburg are as follows:

A. *The Universe*
    I. Heavens and atmosphere
    II. Earth
    III. Vegetation
    IV. Animals
B. *Man*
    I. Man as physical being
    II. The soul and the intellect
    III. Man as social being
    IV. The social organization
C. *Man and Universe*
    I. The a priori
    II. Science and technology

Some applications of the Hallig and Wartburg scheme appear designed primarily to reveal the variety of terms available for any particular area of reference. Thus Keller (1953), in a study of the twelfth-century author Wace, and Fermin (1954), in a study of Bifrun's sixteenth-century translations of the Gospels, merely group the usages of these authors under the various headings provided by the Hallig and Wartburg system (or a modification of it) without any indications of frequency of occurrence. It is of interest that they apply the system to the work of individual authors, although the intent is ultimately to provide a picture in the one case of the French language of the early twelfth century and in the other of sixteenth-century Romansh.

The category system of Spurgeon was derived empirically from the examination of a limited selection of vocabulary from several authors, whereas that of Hallig and Wartburg is an all-inclusive scheme capable of subsuming any selection of vocabulary, large or small. Spurgeon's classifications emerged from a grouping process in which, with each image considered, the question asked was: "With what other

images does it have a referential similarity?" The system of Hallig
and Wartburg, on the other hand, reflects a certain theory of the
psychology of man. Although there is a logical flavor to their scheme,
they develop it from a phenomenological position which seizes immediately upon the self-and-world distinction (man and the universe)
as the crucial fact of experience.

However, the question may be raised whether there are not more
pertinent or more fundamental psychological grounds on which to base
a method for the analysis of language, particularly where there is interest in discriminating between different speakers or between the utterances of a single speaker under various conditions.

It is a long way from the experiments of Bousfield, Cofer, and
Deese to the analysis of the writings of Shakespeare and to the possibility of intercultural comparisons of language. Nevertheless, there is
an unmistakable unifying principle. The existence of categories, which
revealed itself in clustering of associates and in factor analysis of associations, is a fact operative on a vast scale in individuals, determining, as Spurgeon has said, what the individual attends to, registers, and
draws from his memory. The linguistic *Zwischenwelt* is characteristic
of the culture at large, but even within a broad cultural orientation,
individuals are uniquely stamped by their vocabularies. Whether it is
more correct to say that the language of an individual takes on a cast
which reflects his attitudes and experiences or that his attitudes and
his experiences are determined by the cast of his language, the readiness for selective experiencing is mirrored in the fields of language.

How this idea of categories may be applied in elucidating the
underlying themes of an individual's language will be illustrated in the
next chapter. Again, the source materials will be the language productions of schizophrenic patients.

6. Analyses of Psychotic Language

A familiar assumption in clinical work is that, even in periods of severest incomprehensibility, when his listener may be at a loss to understand him, the psychotic patient is talking pertinently about matters of vital concern to himself. This is opposed to the view sometimes taken that, although the verbalizations of the patient reveal the presence of serious conflicts, they are not necessarily related to these conflicts.

Efforts at understanding what the disturbed patient says often follow the example of psychoanalytic interpretations of dreams; the disturbed speech is regarded as a kind of manifest content, and, as in dream analysis, the latent content related more directly to the patient's conflicts is sought in associations to the elements of the manifest content. In dream interpretation use may be made of symbols occurring in the manifest content; these may reveal something of the latent content directly without the mediation of associations. The interpretation of dreams and the parallel interpretation of the disturbed language of the psychotic patient require intuition and skill on the part of the clinician in perceiving connections and understanding symbols.

Psychotic patients are usually not in a position to comply with a request for associations to the elements of their disturbed language, and securing such asso-

ciations for an adequate clinical interpretation of latent content poses
a serious problem. Therefore interpretations of what the patient says
in his periods of disturbance are usually without the benefit of associations and instead utilize extensive information about him and
familiarity with him gained from therapeutic contact and observation.
This knowledge of the patient's typical behavior patterns and attitudes
is brought to bear in giving meaning to his disturbed remarks. However, obtaining associations remains a desideratum of utmost value in
understanding disturbed language. The present chapter illustrates a
contextual approach to the problem of obtaining verbal associations.

Words appearing in proximity with each other in an individual's
language are, by this fact, psychologically associated with each other.
Words are related also by synonymy or similarity of reference. These
two aspects of association, contiguity and similarity, have already received attention in the previous chapter. They have a direct application in the exploration of meaning in the disturbed language of the
schizophrenic patient. Let us assume that an obscure statement of a
patient were the object of study. If a large sampling of the patient's
speech were available, say from tape recordings of previous conversations, in which the words in the obscure statement recurred, it would
be possible to determine the typical kinds of words which appeared in
close contiguity with the key words of the obscure statement. Further,
if the availability of the large sampling of the patient's language made
it possible to determine the typical contextual word associates of other
key words, it might be possible ultimately, by comparing the associates
to the words in the obscure statement with the associates to other key
words, to draw inferences about the similarity of the associative meaning of the obscure statement to the associative meaning of other words
or statements. The facts of synonymy and of similarity of reference enter in making such analyses feasible. Synonymous words or words with
similar reference could be grouped as instances of the same class or
category, and the comparison of contextual associates could utilize
category commonality rather than word commonality as the criterion of
closeness of meaning.

Obviously nothing near a complete sampling of a patient's language is ever available. But it is possible, using recordings, to take
what the patient says on many different occasions and to use this as
the sampling of his language in which to search out the uniformities in
context characteristic of any given words. If the various contexts in
which particular words of interest occur are noted, it might be possible to arrive at something like a group of associatively related statements, phrases, categories, or words which, in the conglomerate, would

point to the latent content associated with the key words as reliably as might a single chain of associations produced in response to the key words. Some of these associates taken from context would undoubtedly reflect uniform idiosyncratic features of the patient's language as a whole, as well as broader cultural uniformities, but others would be uniquely related to the key words. Where several key words were searched in this manner, the over-all uniformities characteristic of the patient's language at large and of his culture would appear consistently in the contexts of all key words. But beyond this, the differences pertinent to the key words would also materialize.

This may become clear with an illustration from the language of a schizophrenic patient, a twenty-eight-year-old man. The patient was born of parents of Irish descent. The father had graduated from an Ivy League college and had a supervisory, but not highly paid, position in a large firm. The mother was about twelve years younger than the father, but psychiatric personnel who had numerous contacts with the parents in connection with the patient's hospitalization felt that she was both the dominant member of the family and a source of major difficulty for the patient.

The mother was a somewhat large woman, bigger physically than her husband. Being the only woman among four men, she found them demanding and self-centered, felt overwhelmed by the household chores, and often wished that she had a daughter to help her. She had the distinction of being one of the first dental hygienists in the United States, and for a while during the patient's adolescence she returned to this profession to better the economic standing of the family. In this connection, it is reported that the patient, as an adolescent, had the fantasy that children are spit out of their mothers' mouths, and on one occasion he wrote something to his mother in which the only comprehensible part was the sentence, "I shall amount to something in spite of my dental mother."

The father was a mild, soft-spoken man who found his son's illness completely baffling but staunchly tried to be of help and always remained sincerely interested in his welfare. In a somewhat unrealistic way, he held out for the patient the possibility of high achievements and seemed to feel that the patient was truly a man of great potential. But on a simpler level, he often took the patient to sports events, was proud of his achievements, and corresponded regularly with him during his hospitalization.

The patient was the youngest of three sons, the first being three years old when he was born, and the second, one year old. The patient liked to assert that he had been born by Caesarean section. However, according to the mother he had a normal delivery. At his birth the mother had a breast abscess so that she and the patient were kept in the hospital for five weeks, the baby remaining in the nursery and being brought to her only once a day for a brief period each time. The mother felt that the patient may have remembered this failure on her part to care for him and that his psychiatric condition was in some way related to these early events.

At the time of his birth the mother had very much wanted a girl, and she had been disappointed at having a third boy. The patient himself maintained that she at first treated him like a girl, but finally gave up and let him be a boy. The mother found him not nearly as affectionate as the other children, and she always regarded him as distinctly different from them. She felt it was difficult to get near him, that he was cold, withdrawn, and self-willed. She was frank in admitting that she had never been able to love him. He was mischievous and odd as a young boy, preferring to stay by himself and to read and rarely playing with other children. In his childhood he was closer to his next older brother than to anyone else, but he resented the fact that his brothers were held up to him as models. The parents were strict and formalistic in their rearing of the children, insisting on perfect grades at school and perfect manners. It is reported that the children were expected each morning to greet their parents with "Good morning," and, if they did not do so, they were reprimanded.

The patient began school at the age of five. He made good grades but missed nearly a year of high school at the age of fourteen because of a bicycle accident in which he sustained a skull fracture. He also suffered from hay fever which caused him to lose considerable time from school.

In high school the patient belonged to the dramatics club and was on the school newspaper staff. When he was fifteen his mother sent him to dancing school in order to have him make more friends, particularly among girls whom he tended to avoid. When the patient was eighteen he was seen by a physician. At this time he was isolating himself in his room, refusing to go to school, and behaving in a negativistic manner. The physician felt the boy was schizoid, but the parents always denied that the visit to the physician had anything to do with a nervous breakdown. They stated that the patient had been slow in growing, that he had remained immature and underweight longer than they considered normal, and that he had been taken to the physician for endocrine therapy to further his physical development.

The patient graduated from high school at the age of twenty, and for a short time worked as a copy boy on a newspaper in a distant city, refusing, despite his family's urging, to consider college. The father especially was greatly upset about this, since the patient had always said he intended to take up writing as a career. The father felt him to be the most brilliant of the three sons, since he wrote so much better than they, who also aspired to be writers.

The patient left his newspaper work to enlist in the Army, and after basic training he was sent to Korea. He was in front-line combat for several months before being wounded in the chest. He was hospitalized for a short time in Japan, then returned to Korea. After this he was extremely fearful and one evening discharged his revolver in such a manner as to have the bullet pierce his leg, fracturing a bone. He was returned to the United States for hospitalization. Shortly after discharge from the hospital he was referred for psychiatric examination because of continual complaints of physical ills, and at that time the examining physican expressed disbelief that it had been possible for this man to get through eight months of combat. Around this time the patient developed the habit of inhaling fumes from a pot of glue "because it helped him to lose himself." One day, while sniffing glue, he got up suddenly and began to shout. A week later he began to be disturbed by auditory and visual hallucinations, and he was committed to a psychiatric ward.

Those who had anything to do with the patient found his talk bizarre, tangential, and disconnected. Many of his answers were seemingly irrelevant, with big words and complicated phrases. His manner was stiff, pompous, and overpolite, and there was a good deal of stereotypy in his behavior and his speech. He appeared evasive when questioned, but at times would freely express his delusional ideas. He was easily distracted, and constantly interrupted himself to comment on objects in the office or sounds in the hall. He was inclined to pun a great deal and to speak aphoristically. Thus, when asked, "How are your spirits?" by an examining doctor, he responded, "I don't know, I don't drink." When asked what his occupation was, he replied, "Soldier by instinct, and a man of peace by design." Early in his illness his plans included going to college since that would be necessary to manipulate the public in his future career. The future career which he contemplated at the time was high political office, since that would give the greatest scope to a genius such as his.

In the Army hospital the patient declared that he was in possession of an unusual sense of power and that he was being controlled by a source of energy which was located at Army headquarters. He stated that the birds had voices and talked to him. He felt that he had been selected for a position of importance such as brigadier general or a seat in the Senate. This knowledge was communicated to him through telepathy. He was hyperactive, disturbed, and noisy. At this time he was treated by insulin coma, receiving 30 comas.

After the treatment he was still stiff, withdrawn, and overpolite, and his planning was egocentric and unrealistic. He desired to go home and write a book. It was judged that, although he had a social and work incapacity, he could be allowed home, and he was discharged to his family. He was twenty-three years old at this time.

His adjustment at home was poor from the start. He tried to get work and did in fact obtain two successive jobs but was dropped after a few weeks in each case because he was sarcastic and insulting to his fellow workers and to the customers and could not tolerate authority. After these experiences he did not seek further employment but stayed home, where he was seclusive and withdrawn, but not a serious problem until the return of his next older brother, who had been in Europe studying for about a year. The third and oldest brother had, since entering the service, married and settled in a foreign country.

The patient was intensely jealous of his next older brother and resented his return; thereafter, he rendered life practically impossible for the family. He was unruly and insulting and would brook no criticism or discipline. He persecuted his mother at every turn. When she tried to take a nap in the afternoon, he would go about the house stamping, slamming doors, and singing or whistling loudly. When guests came to the house he was insulting to them and used vile language. He accused his father of being a drunken old bum and his mother of carrying on with other men during his father's absence from home. When the mother's mother and stepfather came to visit and the mother kissed her stepfather the patient shouted at her that she had better go to confession and tell the priest the kind of relation she had with her stepfather. This type of behavior went on for two months. One day they had a woman guest to dinner, and the patient began making obscene remarks to her. The mother insisted that he leave the table and go to his room. He complied, but when she went to see him later he threw a glass of water in her face. On another occasion he tried to push her down the stairs when she remonstrated with him. Once, when he was persistently disturbing her rest, she got so angry with him that she went out into the hall with a strap in hand and told him that she would hit him with it if he did not keep quiet. The patient seized her arm and twisted her wrist to make her drop the strap. At this point the family decided they could not tolerate the patient's behavior any longer, and he was brought to a Veterans

Administration Hospital. He consented willingly to go, but commented to his mother and brother, "Now I suppose you two can make love to each other as much as you like." Throughout this period the patient had been increasingly and obsessively religious, insisting that the family attend services daily and that they participate in all religious observances.

Three years after coming into the hospital, the patient entered a prolonged psychotherapeutic treatment with a therapist, which lasted for seven years. Throughout this period the patient remained in the hospital, although occasionally returning to his parents' home for a visit. Fantasies regarding other men on the ward and homosexual concerns were prominent in his discussions. There were times when the patient angrily refused to see his therapist, and periods when he was very disturbed and had either to spend time in a locked ward or on heavy doses of tranquilizing drugs.

Despite persistence of some typical character patterns which had been noted throughout his life, such as the abstruseness in language and the formality and overpoliteness of his manner, the patient ultimately came to an open psychiatric ward where he lived without medication and which he made his home while he began a college career. He at first aspired to be a teacher, hoping, as he said, to start by teaching kindergarten and working his way up to the higher grades. However, he did not do well in teacher's college, and dropped out. He then went to a college within walking distance of the hospital and successfully completed a two-year program in journalism. After that, he continued to pursue his interest in writing by taking evening writing courses at another college in a nearby town. On his ward the patient came to be regarded by everyone as a salutary influence, even if he was somewhat distant and hard to understand, and he was often gracious and amusing. It had been made clear to him that he need not fear displacement from the hospital. In this setting of security the patient, while not able to leave the hospital for an independent life, was able to achieve substantial gains.

Psychotherapeutic interviews with the patient had been recorded, and thirty of these in the first year of the patient's treatment (his twenty-seventh year) were transcribed. Thus, a sizable body of the patient's language was available for reference. In the first recorded interview, the patient made the following remark in response to an invitation from the therapist to comment about the fact that tape recordings were being made of the therapy sessions.

In the, the halls of the Justice Department there is an

understanding of a bona fide agreement between any
people scheduled to meet within government circles, within
government triangles, within government rectangles or any
place else. It is hard to speak with a language which has
an idiom of opposition. I mean insofar as there are so
many bulwarks in historical content representative of a,
the revolutionary victory won over an English prosidium.[1]
It's made this country great in its self-containment. It might
be of interest but it's hard to understand what I mean
through a nonutilization of English grammar books. A small
faction usually arises to call themselves leaders, forever after
apologizes for it, who oppose learning. I don't know whether
that's wholly correct or not, but Jimmy Cagney in one of
his movies specified the fact that people who come up from
the depths usually have a right to authority. The depths of
the Anglo-Saxon language has no use for anything that is
nonutilized, that is nonutility. What I mean is that progress
is foolish when you consider the fact that through language
and leadership you can augment the process of future
generations being of foreign parentage.

This selection contains three references to *government* and three
to *language*. The task was set of locating, among the available
interviews of the patient, all contexts in which he used these words.
A context was defined as that segment of the patient's language
which included one sentence immediately preceding the sentence in
which the key word was used, and one sentence immediately following the sentence with the key word. In some instances—for example, where the patient made a remark consisting of only a single
sentence—the context included only the single sentence. It will be seen
in the segments quoted below that defining a sentence itself is an
arbitrary matter when it comes to the spoken language of a schizophrenic patient, as often is the case in the spoken language of normal
individuals.

Since the number of contexts for *language* was somewhat smaller
than that for *government* in the patient's language, contexts for *English* (used twice in the quoted segment) and *England* were also sought
out as related to *language* and as a way of providing a roughly equivalent amount of associated material for the comparison with *govern-*

---

[1] The neologism *prosidium* may be a combination of the words *prose
idiom* and *presidium,* which would combine the patient's preoccupations with
language and with government.

ment. All the contexts of the various key words occurring in the thirty interviews are quoted below. The numbers preceding each of the contexts indicate from which of the interviews the selections were taken. A succession of five dots indicates that the tape recording was obscure at that point.

Contexts of GOVERNMENT

1. In temperance due I don't see any reason why two men can't proceed as popular as ever both in themselves as a duocratic and as a democratic premise. I mean the God-given greatness of this country, and I hope that there are no more triangular conflicts in a two-party GOVERNMENT. It can only lead with little self-control to disaster and, with a great deal of self-control, upset. That's why we have our monitor in the brain and controlling element, the pituitary, in GOVERNMENT the judiciary, as black-masked as need be to suit the situation. I wish the president all the success in the world, and I'd like to tell him he no longer has to fear the start of any war or fatigue caused by the regulation of myself.

2. Hardly just died. You know, I wish this GOVERNMENT the best I can.

5. None of it is essential to coop, communicate . . . . . The GOVERNMENT always has some propaganda on the postage. Maybe that's what he [father] was sending me, this message.

5. Every time you go to help you get shot. For the president, in a GOVERNMENT position, you'd better forget that. That's off the record.

5. Yes, today is a good day. I wish. . . . .all hope the GOVERNMENT all the luck they want. If they need to use me, why they can just explain themselves to me.

6. I express myself simply in terms of death being. . . . . necessary to my papers. . . . .But I don't like the GOVERNMENT to dig up the scales when I think that they have done something. Instead of questioning me as to the results, take on the, what they assume to be a dangerous thing to say.

7. Well, that's probably the way I'd come out at this time, irrational. I suppose it had something to do with the

diet, the fact that the, the GOVERNMENT doesn't want to feed you no matter who you are. You can be St. George, and they won't feed you.

9. The very fact that he [brother] always had a habit of falling apart, it seems, and then coming up with some very tangible statements. Which is good GOVERN-MENT. But the fact that he [brother] was rather un-diplomatic was strange to me.

9. That great headache. But no GOVERNMENT ever tied two brothers together. I don't think any GOV-ERNMENT ever tried to do anything but break up the family for the good of its separate members. To coop-, copy the, and analogous system of the fam-ily. . . . .

10. I tried going out without the help of the spirit. That old reliance on Christianity and this great GOVERN-MENT of ours. Reciprocate.

10. I'd say the best thing to do is remember the spirit, the happy inspiration, elevation and thought which is probably responsible for Christian organization. It's funny, I, I, I blame, I blame the GOVERNMENT for almost everything.

10. Of course you understand that a person would have to be in the GOVERNMENT frame of mind. Pardon me.

13. All the only people that can see it are my family and the cat. The seeds of GOVERNMENT were in good hands. The self-restraint of involving myself. . . . .over the week end I wish I had them home, my boat, my, vivacious friends and family, friend and family.

13. Call, call it what you will, it's an, it's an awful prob-lem. I appreciate the man's genius in understanding the problem of the GOVERNMENT, not only the theoretical. . . . .philosophical standards, but the prob-lems at hand, last week's, and today's and tomorrow's . . . . .And my idea of psychology and my problem psychologically is to put them down in some sort of a form which may be helpful and generically to put some sort of an obstacle in my path which I can meet and use, utilize.

15. The world is full of an awful fight. It needs a good GOVERNMENT. The world, not the country.

15. Well, GOVERNMENT is held to remind future generations there is an association between struggle and attainment as there was in the Pilgrims. They were the fathers of the country.

17. I hope the GOVERNMENT will take notice of that. We might as well find how to avoid this trip to the Casbah.

18. Very becoming. The history of the people is diverse and is a good form of GOVERNMENT. Push that out and you have a general idea of no war at all.

18. When they see a cop their mouth drops open. GOVERNMENTS testify themselves according to law. As for getting the point, they sue the doctors.

18. Now there's another factor I'm fighting. I mean to get on top of the building, you are getting on top of GOVERNMENT property, you are getting on top of the president's cosigned area. You are getting on top, therefore, in my own words, of the patient.

18. There's no gainsaying of any emolument, aggrandizement when you've lost a patient. The GOVERNMENT can't pay. . . . .Unless we tar, tarheaded thing to face, tar and garter.

18. That don't worry any boats who didn't understand. If we could overlook a number of hypnotic GOVERNMENTS, they could stop them dead or turn them about, unless they. . . . .with no disturbance except that which may come to them. Now in the Army there's battering Caesars.

19. Let the GOVERNMENT, let the GOVERNMENT retire. The GOVERNMENT hours are all through. You can always laugh at a man whose candidate is Truman.

20. But I'm not in Congress any more. Fine nurse for children, grow up with the congressman's. . . . .through their own GOVERNMENT. It certainly won't stay there forever.

22. The medicines are his [doctor's]. But, unless he is a GOVERNMENT doctor I think that, therefore, it is a fight instilled to see which has a more right to the medicine. And a doctor's fight would be toward private entry, of course.

23. So melancholy, so melancholy, so melancholy. The

GOVERNMENT, the GOVERNMENT has their eye
very carefully on my money. They, they've done very
practical with it, the last two years or more so they're
trying to get rid of me to Perry Point.

23. Friendship is, is evidently more of a parody necessary
to them [the Russians] at this time than anything else.
They're just creeping into a new thought of GOV-
ERNMENT which was depraved by the revolution
but brayed forth from it and started with revolution
as a truce. Among them were. . . . .and World War
II destroyed something.

25. My idea was to take an oil well and try to make some
money. But I got the advice if you buy oil wells, if you
buy oil fields, through the GOVERNMENT. Money.

26. Say, I'm, I'm the chairman of patient GOVERN-
MENT meeting downstairs.

26. He'd [the president] be the chairman probably. I think
a real good GOVERNMENT needs a president who
is able to be recipient of the fact that there is a chairman outside of himself. By inviting the Congressional
chairman, Mr. Rayburn.

26. I mean, I think top man is considered to be president,
rather than chairman, so that gives them [the Russians]
a lot of insecurity that they [the Russians] don't have.
They [the Russians] should be taught the GOVERN-
MENT. I mean taught for good, for keeps, not, not
the art of GOVERNMENT but the fact that medita-
tions, distress, as in this country, has been put on the
presidency which is not the continuous name, that is,
that his name is really the secretary general. He is the
leader and the, the broadcaster of each meeting.

26. Men who are trying to make their name in letters, like
Tolstoy. They're trying to do with the GOVERN-
MENT. They're well satisfied, and try to make a name
for themselves.

30. I'd like to do good. I'd like to do anything I could to
cut down that GOVERNMENT expense in the first
place and to give it to another federal organ, an organ
which in some way is. . . . .depends upon the GOV-
ERNMENT thus alleviating the GOVERNMENT
expense.

30. Well, through my organization I'd give them some

money. The other GOVERNMENT organ is the State of Delaware which gives my father compensation.

30. I expected to go out on one meeting with a GOVERN-MENT agency that would clear everything up. That's never. . . . .I've had about a hundred of them.

30. I've had lots of contacts. It's that something seemed to blah with me in the GOVERNMENT. Mistrust, and lackadaisical attitude.

Contexts of LANGUAGE

4. I can't say that because of self-analysis as a basis of recording. You speak of LANGUAGE of reflection. If you're going to have a suitable expedition or expression you have to have the reverberation of what you say.

4. Some day my forebears, my ancestors, will come, my, some day, my offspring will have great precocious hygienic precept, even more so than I. When my grandfather came over here in the middle, no he came over here about the end of the nineteenth century which means that I like to talk a lot because of the fact that he was learning the LANGUAGE then as his favorite passtime. My great great great great great great, my great grandfather on my father's side, great grandfather. . . . .

4. Say your father came over at the beginning of the nineteen, twentieth century, and he'd be learning the LANGUAGE. That would put in your ears a great deal of the semantics of the situation.

4. That's true. My great, great grandfather was, of course, accustomed to the LANGUAGE and by the time I came along, on that side, that is, why we were accustomed to LANGUAGE, that's my mother's side. The maternal projection is toward adjudication.

4. I laugh. . . . .I laugh is what I say. I suppose that has to do with the fact that we used the LANGUAGE on my mother's side, and I can't help laughing hysterically. . . . .if I could master self-analysis.

7. I have the idea it would be a good idea if there was something unusual to give, to stir the mind of the sick, ...fine, finer points of music being shared between

the audience and the group, so that they, they'd both
be virtuosi instead of just one of the group. In the
LANGUAGE of the spheres, the music is sometimes
put on the New Year's side. You're not only memo-
rizing a routine for making an organization. . . . .
what they call a response.

7. It was a religious hymn. It opened a vista for the group
who were singing it into a foreign LANGUAGE, and
also into a foreign approach.

7. I'm not eluding the sense of the whole thing. Well, anything that comes out in this dispersed LANGUAGE
and speed confuses. Those two go together so there
wouldn't be any stratification.

10. I am becoming prejudiced against the ENGLISH
LANGUAGE. Very common, common term, like the
cominform.

12. We're both suffering from tuberculosis. Peace, as the
Bible says, I love you. . . . .universal LANGUAGE.

13. So I know my goal when I'm thinking politically and
yet I have no difficulty in expressing it. And I sometimes use obscene LANGUAGE as a sort of relief, an
outlet as you in psychology say.

14. From nonsense comes nothing. From nonsense comes
the ENGLISH LANGUAGE.

16. It follows that advice upon LANGUAGE and its origins.

17. The essentials of being quite severe in your own restrictions as a lay person, as a person of priestliness
and so, no great problem. Papal warrant occasionally
is mysterious LANGUAGE open much, but they don't
prompt the papal crown in this country. They don't
prompt the papal state.

18. Well, it's just LANGUAGE.

18. Mostly for the LANGUAGE. I went, I went through
so much in Greek class.

18. The LANGUAGE itself is ENGLISH. Now, I hate
ENGLISH so much that I'd rather give it to another
person's ears for good or evil, which means nothing to
me.

20. Going beyond my needs. Why I think it's apparent that
both floors in seeing their reflection, recognize the fu-

ture some one and most of all the LANGUAGE. Well what was the word, was it, *horrors?*

27. I hate to distort the word *adjective*. It just gives off so much of an aura of classic meaning without which its sense is nil and yet it has a basis in LANGUAGE of vocation. Similar to the vocation of making ships.

Contexts of ENGLISH and ENGLAND

2. The fact that he was down to the bare simile of co-operation, to communication method he had to hit me, probably because it was the last, Jesus, I don't know what to say, the last straw. You see, you get the ENGLISH all. . . . .wings that the angels are supposed to have, and I know the one to keep away from. And the, another man, German, Dutchman, kicked me to break me down to trash.

8. Oh, I'm not a competent judge. But he's [brother] found his stratum which is at least half satisfactory, that he's working for a Gaelic which means that he's half, half set, I mean, he has a. . . . .that he gets his working in, and then he can rest reassured, being half ENGLISH and half Irish. If you work for an Irishman you go home and have your ENGLISH tea, and then—

10. French and ENGLISH. Friendship and ENGLISH. I'd say friendship in French because they sound alike and they're a mystic and obstreperous thing.

12. I think that if I worry about you, I have a commission that might have something to do, an activity to undertake, an appointment, which jolly well gives me a good feeling of security, fulfillment, and if no irrationality comes. . . . .individual. It sounds extremely fatal, but the ENGLISH never could reason anyway. Their reasoning is terrible.

14. Well, they're descendants of the ENGLISH people. If I talk directly, they may hear me.

18. Well, in ENGLAND, that would be called an offensive speech. It would probably be more action to the deaf.

18. Psychiatry is a substance in ENGLAND of a last virtue. It's a, one that's aspired to. In ENGLAND they don't have in these funeral parlors where people are locked

in. But they, if they are mentally sick, have these reasons continuously, and if they do not make what is
commonly known as an agreeable salutation, they are
thus bereft of life.

18. This ENGLAND fascinates me. . . . .It's a small—

23. What a dream I had last night. I was falling through
space and I ended up in a court in ENGLAND before
the prince, and the prince looked just like this little doll
I have here. He was about the. . . . .he was, in other
words, he was a child, but he was dressed very effem-
inately just as a prince should be.

27. That's why the, the factors of pugilism are so finesse.
Why so complex is that school based upon the great
intellectualism of ENGLAND. Unlike baseball which is
the subconscious is. . . . .not sublimation.

27. They're funny people. They learn how to speak ENG-
LISH and then they express themselves in thanks.

27. Beneficial, beneficient. . . . .beneficious, beneficient,
with most benefit, beneficient. Speaking in modern
ENGLISH I come against the cognomer of violence,
the cognomen of violence is what I come up against
speaking in modern ENGLISH. You come up against
people who are, that, they're tough.

In order to discover whether there were any differences in the
associates which appeared in these various contexts, words and phrases
which could be classified under certain general headings suggested in
the contexts themselves were listed for *GOVERNMENT* and for
LANGUAGE. Pronouns were identified by the nouns to which they
referred. The listings are presented below, with all the relevant words
as drawn from the 30 interviews. With the words arranged in this
manner, some striking differences are apparent between the *GOV-
ERNMENT* and *LANGUAGE* contexts.

1. There were more words and phrases relating to leadership,
dominance, greatness, power, achievement, and control in the contexts
of *GOVERNMENT* than in those of *LANGUAGE* and related words.

   a. *GOVERNMENT: popular, God-given greatness, lead,
   self-control, self-control, monitor, brain, controlling
   element, pituitary, judiciary, president, success, he
   (president), regulation, president, St. George, great,
   self-restraint, genius, attainment, fathers of the country,*

>   cop, doctors, get on top of, getting on top of, president,
>   getting on top of, aggrandizement, Caesars, candidate,
>   Truman, Congress, congressman, his (doctor), he (doc-
>   tor), doctor, doctor, he (president), chairman, chair-
>   man, president, chairman, Congressional chairman, Mr.
>   Rayburn, top man, president, chairman, presidency, sec-
>   retary general, leader, make their name, Tolstoy, make
>   a name for themselves.

b. *LANGUAGE:* great, precocious, adjudication, master, virtuosi, restrictions, great, papal, papal crown, papal state.

c. *ENGLISH, ENGLAND:* competent judge, have a commission, prince, prince, he (prince), prince, great.

2. There were more words related to aggression, destruction, and violence in the contexts of *GOVERNMENT* than in the *LANGUAGE* contexts.

a. *GOVERNMENT:* triangular conflicts, disaster, war, died, you get shot, death, don't like, dangerous, falling apart, undiplomatic, break up, blame, awful fight, struggle, push that out, war, sue, fighting, gainsaying, lost a patient, stop them dead, disturbance, Army, battering Caesars, laugh at, fight, doctor's fight, get rid of me, parody, depraved, revolution, revolution, World War II, destroyed, mistrust.

b. *LANGUAGE:* prejudiced, obscene, hate, evil, horrors, hate, distort.

c. *ENGLISH, ENGLAND:* hit me, last straw, kicked me, break me down, obstreperous, fatal, offensive, funeral, bereft of life, pugilism, come against, violence, come up against, come up against, tough, opposed.

3. Words having to do with psychological upset and with illness were more prevalent in the *GOVERNMENT* contexts.

a. *GOVERNMENT:* upset, fear, fatigue, headache, awful problems, problem, problems, my problem psychologically, their mouths drop open, worry, melancholy, melancholy, melancholy, insecurity, distress, seemed to blah with me, lackadaisical.

    b. *LANGUAGE: hysterically, the sick, confuses, suffering, tuberculosis, difficulty, problem, went through so much.*

    c. *ENGLISH, ENGLAND: worry, mentally sick.*

4. References to money and property predominated in the contexts of *GOVERNMENT*.

    a. *GOVERNMENT: property, emolument, pay, money, it (money), oil well, make some money, buy oil wells, buy oil fields, money, expense, expense, give some money, give compensation.*

    b. *LANGUAGE:* none.

    c. *ENGLISH, ENGLAND:* none.

5. Equally distributed among the two contexts were words with a cognitive, ideational aspect (other than references to education).

    a. *GOVERNMENT: reason, premise, brain, forget, think, assume, irrational, suppose, think, remember, inspiration, thought, understand, mind, appreciate, genius, understanding, theoretical, philosophical, psychology, psychologically, remind, take notice of, idea, getting the point, understand, thought, mean, meditations, clear everything up.*

    b. *LANGUAGE: self-analysis, reflection, precocious, precept, means, adjudication, suppose, self-analysis, idea, idea, mind, memorizing, sense, confuses, know, thinking, nonsense, nonsense, advice, means nothing, think, recognize, meaning, sense.*

    c. *ENGLISH, ENGLAND: know, know, judge, means, mean, suppose, think, irrationality, reasoning, mentally, reasons, intellectualism, subconscious, reason, find out, noted.*

6. References to friendship, satisfaction, and good were about balanced between the two sets of words, although the contexts of *LANGUAGE* itself had few such references.

    a. *GOVERNMENT: popular, success, like, wish the best, help, good, hope all the luck, good, good, help, reliance, happy, elevation, good, friends, friend, helpful, good, becoming, good, fine, friendship, truce, good, inviting, well satisfied, do good, alleviating.*

b. *LANGUAGE: suitable, hygienic, good, finer points, love, relief, good.*

c. *ENGLISH, ENGLAND: cooperation, half satisfactory, rest reassured, friendship, friendship, good feeling, security, fulfillment, virtue, agreeable salutation, thanks, beneficial, benefit.*

7. Words referring to communication showed some interesting features. Those words which referred in a general way to speaking, writing, records, and communicating were equally distributed among the contexts of *GOVERNMENT* and *LANGUAGE*. However, in the *LANGUAGE* contexts there were many more words dealing with music, sounds, and hearing. These latter are listed at the end of each series.

a. *GOVERNMENT: tell, communicate, propaganda, message, off the record, explain themselves, express, in terms of, papers, questioning, say, tangible statements, say, call it what you will, testify, in my own words, name, make their name, in letters, Tolstoy, make a name.* Sounds: *brayed forth, broadcaster.*

b. *LANGUAGE: say, recording, speak, expression, say, talk a lot, say, semantics, call, responses, says, Bible, expressing, say, word, word, adjective.* Sounds: *reverberation, ears, music, audience, music, religious hymn, singing, ears.*

c. *ENGLISH, ENGLAND: communication, simile, say, talk, called, speech, salutation, in other words, speak, express, speaking, cognomen, speaking, wrote, names, speeches.* Sounds: *sound alike, sounds extremely fatal, hear me, obstreperous, deaf.*

8. Differences in favor of the *LANGUAGE* contexts were found in words dealing with learning and education.

a. *GOVERNMENT: taught, taught.*

b. *LANGUAGE: learning, learning, Greek class, classic meaning.*

c. *ENGLISH, ENGLAND: school, learn.*

9. In the contexts of *GOVERNMENT* there were several men-

tions of the Russians, whereas in the contexts of *LANGUAGE* the stress was on Europeans and unspecified foreigners.

> a. *GOVERNMENT: Casbah, them* (the Russians), *they* (the Russians), *them* (the Russians), *they* (the Russians), *they* (the Russians).
> b. *LANGUAGE: foreign, foreign, papal state, Greek class.*
> c. *ENGLISH, ENGLAND: German, Dutchman, Gaelic, half Irish, Irishman, French, French.*

10. Religion and mysticism were referred to slightly more frequently in the *LANGUAGE* contexts.

> a. *GOVERNMENT: spirit, God-given, St. George, spirit, Christianity, Christian, Pilgrims.*
> b. *LANGUAGE: religious, hymn, Bible, lay person, person of priestliness, papal warrant, mysterious, papal crown, papal state.*
> c. *ENGLISH, ENGLAND: Jesus* (expletive), *angels, mystic.*

11. References to origins, beginning, and ancestry predominated in the *LANGUAGE* contexts.

> a. *GOVERNMENT: start of war, seeds of government, future generations, new thought, first place.*
> b. *LANGUAGE: ancestors, forebears, offspring, beginning, came along, from nonsense comes nothing, from nonsense comes language, origins, opened a vista.*
> c. *ENGLISH, ENGLAND: descendants.*

12. References to children, family, and home were interesting. There were more such references in the *LANGUAGE* contexts, and in addition, there seemed to be an emphasis on ancestors, offspring, and mother in the *LANGUAGE* contexts.

> a. *GOVERNMENT: he* (father), *he* (brother), *he* (brother), *two brothers, family, its* (family), *separate members, family, my family, home, family, family, future generations, fathers of the country, children, father.*
> b. *LANGUAGE: forebears, ancestors, offspring, grand-*

father, he (grandfather), *he* (grandfather), *his* (grandfather), *great grandfather on father's side, great grandfather, father, he* (father), *great, great grandfather,
mother's side, maternal projection, mother's side.*

c. *ENGLISH, ENGLAND: he* (brother), *he* (brother),
he (brother), *he* (brother), *he* (brother), *he* (brother),
home, he (brother), *he* (brother), *home, descendants,
little doll, a child.*

It is possible to discover other dimensions in these contexts which
might prove discriminating or interesting. However, what has been
presented is only intended to make the point that such an analysis is
feasible. The associations to *GOVERNMENT* reflect leadership,
strength, control and power, money, conflict, and the Russians, whereas
the associations to *LANGUAGE* are characterized by reference to
music, learning, Europeans, religion, origins, maternity, and family. It
might be said that for this patient *GOVERNMENT* is weighted on
the paternal side and *LANGUAGE* on the maternal side. Within the
narrow limits of the quoted contexts, it is not possible to say whether
the associations that the patient produced would be similar to those
produced by anyone else using the same key words in free speech.
References to leadership and conflict seem to fit well in a cultural
sense with *GOVERNMENT* and references to learning, music, and
to Europeans would seem to follow from the fact that *LANGUAGE*
refers to spoken words and from the fact that *ENGLISH* was also
taken as a key word. However, some of the additional associates in
the areas of religion, origins, maternity, and buying and selling would
not be readily predictable on a priori grounds.

The suggested paternal and maternal characterizations, when
applied to the original remarks of the patient, appear to make a good
deal of sense. Bearing in mind that the contextual analysis has by no
means given us the clear right to call *LANGUAGE* a substitute for
MOTHER and *GOVERNMENT* a substitute for *FATHER*, let us
see nevertheless how such suggestions help translate the patient's remarks. The interpretation, based on our analysis, is given at the right.

1. In the, the halls of the
Justice Department there
is an understanding of a
bona fide agreement be-
tween any people sched-

uled to meet within government circles, within government triangles, within government rectangles or any place else.

It is all right to meet in a paternal setting.

2. It is hard to speak with a language which has an idiom of opposition.

I find it difficult to speak with the oppositional language of Mother.

3. I mean insofar as there are so many bulwarks in historical, in historical content representative of a, the revolutionary victory won over an English prosidium.

Mother has been overthrown in the past by force.

4. It's made this country great in its self-containment.

The victory has led to great independence.

5. It might be of interest but it's hard to understand what I mean through a nonutilization of English grammar books.

It is hard to understand me because I do not use Mother's language.

6. A small faction usually arises to call themselves leaders, forever after apologizes for it, who oppose learning.

Newcomers (children) calling themselves fathers—to their eternal regret—oppose Mother.

7. I don't know whether that's wholly correct or not, but Jimmy Cagney in one of his movies specified the fact that people who come up from the depths usually have a right to authority.

People who come up from the depths (children) claim the right of fathers.

8. The depths of the Anglo-Saxon language has no

Mother has no use for any-use for anything that is nonutilized, that is non-utility.

9. What I mean is that progress is foolish when you consider the fact that through language and leadership you can augment the process of future generations being of foreign parentage.

one who does not use her language.

There is no point in trying to accomplish anything since mother and father alone determine whether the child will be alien.

With the help of an analysis of contextual associates, the patient's remarks gain a meaning which was not apparent at the outset. This example is not presented as conclusive, nor will it be utterly convincing. But it is suggestive of an approach. In actuality the situation is far too complex to permit the simple equation of *LANGUAGE* with *MOTHER* and *GOVERNMENT* with *FATHER*. Nevertheless, that there is some significance in the relationships is supported by what emerges when the scheme is applied to the patient's remarks.

The interpretations which are made possible by such a contextual analysis may go to the very center of a patient's conflicts and shed light on many of the obscurities of his language. The present patient's history indicates that he felt either cut out or spit out of his mother rather than born like a normal child. His mother's disappointment at not having given birth to a girl and her early separation from him in the hospital provide a substantial psychological basis for his feeling of alienation. In the patient's associations he not only despairs of overcoming this alienation, but he finds the relationship with his mother an engulfing and inhibiting one, against which he must rebel constantly.

The picture of his father as the one in whom the potential for successful rebellion is vested is, by the patient's history, only a wishful one, for the father was in fact a submissive and unassertive individual. His father should have been the one to challenge the selfishness and the coldness of mother, but he failed in this and instead left the task to the weak and helpless child.

The close connection between language and mother, toward whom there are at the same time such angry and such fearful feelings, suggests some interpretations of the patient's language distortions. It is mother who has given the gift of speech to the patient. The association of the mother's profession as a dental hygienist with oral speech may be important here, as well as the more general association implied in the phrase *mother tongue*. This tie between mother and language is certainly supported in the contextual analysis of the patient's references to *language*. If the patient speaks, it is with mother's language, and indeed speech has become the field of conflict. His language is a constant rebellion in which, if he must use language, he will at least subvert communication and so frustrate mother. But behind this rebellion there appears to be a depressive note; it is a struggle he cannot win, and the blame is as much on the passive father who will not fight the battle as it is on the mother who rejects the child.

The patient's defiance of his father's wish that he become learned like himself could be part of his negativistic attack on language and learning. It was only after long years of treatment that the patient undertook an educational venture. The attempt may be understood in terms of his discovering in the therapist a person who did provide an image of strength and who offered a secure place, the hospital, for the patient. In this setting of a strong father (therapist) and a tolerant home (hospital), the patient could approach learning with less ambivalence and less need to destroy the very thing he wished to achieve.

The foregoing illustrates the possibility of constructing a matrix of associations out of contexts in which key words appear and of interpreting the key words in terms of the associations. Such an approach brings one quickly to the subject's core conflicts and significant psychological configurations. In all probability, it would make little difference what words one took as the key items for analysis; the analysis would, if pursued far enough, lead to the central issues of the speaker's psychology.

In the example given, the categories were derived *ad hoc* from the available words in the patient's language. As a further illustration of the use of contexts to provide associations and also as an illustration of the power of this type of analysis, let us turn to a study using pre-established categories (Laffal, 1960).

In this study, the possibility of getting at associative meaning of certain critical words by collating the contexts in which the words were used was applied to a theoretical issue in psychoanalytic literature.

Daniel Paul Schreber (1903) was a doctor of jurisprudence and a prominent judge at the end of the last century, who, after becoming psychotic, published an account of his delusions in the belief that he was making a contribution of value to science and the knowledge of religious truths. Without having known Schreber personally, Freud

(1911b) undertook, on the basis of the published autobiography, to trace the etiology of Schreber's delusions and in his study formulated the now famous paradigm of homosexuality and projection in paranoia. Macalpine and Hunter who published an English translation of Schreber's autobiography (1955) disagreed with Freud's interpretation and maintained that a wish for ambisexuality and self-contained procreative powers was at the root of Schreber's illness. They pinpointed the difference between their view and Freud's by contesting Freud's account of the symbolism of the sun in Schreber's delusions (Macalpine & Hunter, 1955):

> If the sun was not a father symbol for Schreber, Freud's theoretical deductions only partially cover the facts. The passive homosexual wish-fantasy, ultimately derived from his infantile relation to his father and evidenced in his relation to the sun, could not afford the whole explanation, but would throw light only on one aspect, however important, of his psychosis and the content of his delusions.
>
> All the evidence goes to show that the sun, far from representing only the father, mirrored Schreber's own ambisexuality, being both male and female (p. 378).

If Schreber used the same terms in writing of the sun as he did in writing of father figures, this could be taken as evidence that his associations to the two were alike and that, in effect, they meant the same thing to him, as Freud maintained. If, on the other hand, Schreber wrote about the sun the way he wrote about women, this could be taken as evidence for the Macalpine and Hunter view that the sun had important feminine aspects for Schreber. The problem, as posed in the study, was to compare the contexts of various key words in order to determine their relative similarity to each other. To make such an analysis of contexts feasible, it was necessary to categorize the words in the contexts of the key words, somewhat in the manner already illustrated in the speech of the patient just discussed.

A set of categories, which had been derived from the sorting of words in various samples of patient language, was available for this purpose. The heading words of these categories are shown in Table 15. A more elaborate category system which has subsequently evolved is defined and illustrated in Appendix I. Many of the heading words remain the same, and the reader may refer to them in Appendix I for details.

Unfortunately, the third chapter of Schreber's autobiography,

TABLE 15

WORD CATEGORIES USED IN THE CONTEXTUAL ANALYSIS OF SCHREBER'S LANGUAGE:* LAFFAL (1960, p. 475)

agree	durable	illness	separate
back	earth	individual	sharp
begin	end	join	slow
big	essential	living	some
body feature	forward	near	strong
body function	group	play	structure
change	hear	possess	up
come	help	real	upset
dirty	hollow	ruin	want
disagree	hurt	see	work
down			write

* Definitions of most of these categories may be found in Appendix I.

which dealt intimately with members of his family, was deleted from the work by official censorship, so that there are practically no references to Schreber's father in the autobiography. This makes a direct comparison of language related to *father* with language related to *sun* impossible. However, there are some indirect ways of approaching the problem. It is clear in Freud's discussion that God is the father figure par excellence. Macalpine and Hunter do not accept this view and, consistently with their position about the sun, speak of "his [Freud's] conviction that God and the sun were 'nothing but' father symbols for Schreber; he ignores their obvious female significance. . . ." (p. 378). Some fairly definite predictions arise from these differences of view.

If Freud's contention that *sun* and *God* were both father symbols for Schreber is correct, there ought to be a strong similarity in the way Schreber wrote about both of these, and both ought to be more similar to the way Schreber wrote about male figures than to the way he wrote about female figures.

If the Macalpine and Hunter view is correct, then there ought also to be a strong similarity between the way Schreber wrote about *sun* and *God,* but how he wrote of both of these ought to be very similar to the way he wrote of females. Their view would seem to entail the prediction that the *sun-female* and *God-female* relationship would be at least as strong as, and possibly stronger than, the corresponding *male* relationships.

Two papers by Niederland (1951; 1959) adduce considerable evidence, based on a study of Schreber's father's life and works, that the accusations which Schreber directed against God, especially relating to body torture, were also appropriate to Schreber *père*. The older Schreber wrote extensively on the theme that, in the earliest years of the child's life, a maximum of pressure and coercion should be used in the inculcation of physical and emotional restraint. He devised mechanical instruments for enforcing correct body posture, not only in waking, but during sleep, and he believed in strict disciplinary training measures, including corporal punishment. Niederland maintains that not only God, but Schreber's physician, Dr. Flechsig, who is mentioned often in the autobiography, was a father symbol for Schreber: "First Flechsig, and then God, is reinstated in the place of father" (1951, p. 591). Freud does not make this direct relationship between Flechsig and God and Flechsig and father. Freud believes that Flechsig and God belong to the same class in Schreber's mind, but that Schreber's homosexual feelings toward Flechsig are derived from those toward an older brother, whereas the homosexual feelings toward God reflect such feelings toward his father.

These remarks about Dr. Flechsig suggest that the contexts surrounding the physician's name might also provide some data about the male-father symbolization of *God* and *sun*. Freud maintains at least that Dr. Flechsig and God were both the subject of homosexual longings of the patient. In this sense both stood in the relation to him of a dominant male figure. Niederland goes further than Freud in equating Flechsig with father. If the analyses of Freud and Niederland are correct, there ought to be a strong relationship in the way Schreber wrote about *Flechsig* and *God,* and both of these ought to be more strongly related to the way Schreber wrote about *male* references than the way he wrote about *female* references. Macalpine and Hunter are not specific in interpreting the symbolism of Dr. Flechsig in Schreber's psychology, but they appear to suggest also some element of identity with God: "Endowed with this divine power as head of the 'Nerve-Institute,' Flechsig was supernatural and partly a soul . . . in direct contact with God. . . . Herein lies the easy passage from Flechsig to God . . . and 'God Flechsig' " (p. 396).

Passages in the text of Schreber's autobiography, as translated by Macalpine and Hunter (1955), which contained only one of the words *sun, God,* or *Flechsig,* or one *male* or *female* reference, were marked for transcription. A passage was defined as a sequence beginning three lines before a line containing a key word and ending three lines after a line containing the key word. A roughly equivalent number of such passages was taken out for each key word. It happens that the word *sun* occurs alone least often in the autobiography, and the total number of passages available for *sun* was used to determine the number of passages selected for each of the other key words, since it was desired to have approximately equal numbers of categorized responses in the ultimate comparisons of contexts. For all key words other than *sun* (for which no additional passages were available), an additional equivalent number of passages were taken out for reliability determinations.

The words in the selected passages were categorized in accordance with the categories in Table 15, plus certain other categories which were subsequently eliminated for reasons given below. In order to study reliability of associated categories for those words in which enough passages were available, the lines were randomly divided into two sets, each containing an equivalent number of lines in which the key word appeared and an equivalent number of lines one, two, and three lines above or below the key-word line. There were thus two profiles each of distributions of responses associated with *male, female, God,* and *Flechsig,* and one profile of responses associated with *sun.*

Inspection of the distributions of categories revealed that there were some categories which rarely occurred in Schreber's writing and some categories which occurred consistently and with great frequency. These categories were taken to reflect Schreber's over-all idiosyncratic language style applicable to *all* of his writing no matter what the specific subject and were eliminated from the analysis, since they would have contributed only to a general increase in apparent similarity of all contexts and not to the discrimination between the contexts associated with the various key words. Further, the specific categories under which *man, woman, sun, God,* and *Flechsig* were scored were also eliminated from the comparisons, since selection of the critical passages had been made on the presence of one and the absence of the other categories. The total number of categories was in this way reduced to the 42 in Table 15. The number of associated words remaining in the category profile for each key word ranged from 192 to 258.

In Table 16 are shown the reliabilities of the category profiles of the associated contexts for all the key words except *sun,* for which no reliability was available, and the intercorrelations of all of the category profiles. The correlations are Pearson product-moment correlations obtained by comparing frequencies of occurrence of the 42 categories in the contexts of the key words.

The contexts for *female* were the least reliable ($r = .566$). The

TABLE 16

PEARSON PRODUCT-MOMENT CORRELATIONS BETWEEN
CONTEXT PROFILES OF KEY WORDS: LAFFAL (1960, p. 476)
$N = 42$ categories

		male profile		*female* profile		*God* profile		*Flechsig* profile	
		1	2	1	2	1	2	1	2
male	profile 1								
	profile 2	.706*							
female	profile 1	.667	.561						
	profile 2	.457	.437	.566*					
God	profile 1	.226	.475	.166	.420				
	profile 2	.451	.534	.413	.352	.679*			
Flechsig	profile 1	.679	.645	.576	.504	.446	.598		
	profile 2	.556	.662	.516	.319	.552	.636	.737*	
sun		.523	.330	.678	.356	.136	.444	.511	.397

* reliabilities

reliability of the *male* contexts was .706; for the *God* contexts it was .679; and for the *Flechsig* contexts it was .737.

It will be noted that, for the contexts of *male, female, God,* and *Flechsig,* 4 intercorrelations were available for each pair. The test of significance took advantage of this fact. Thus, to test the hypothesis that the way Schreber talked about *God* was more like the way he talked about *male* than the way he talked about *female,* the 8 correlations involved (4 for *God-male* and 4 for *God-female*) were compared with each other, making 16 comparisons. The *God-male* correlations were greater in 13 of the comparisons, the *God-female* correlations were greater in 3 of the comparisons.[2]

[2] In this study, a sign-test analysis (Johnson, 1949) of the sets of correlations showed that the *God-male* correlations were significantly greater than the *God-female* correlations. However, the sign test calls for matching of independent pairs, whereas, in the study, each correlation was compared once with the 4 correlations in the opposing set. The pairs were thus not entirely independent. To determine the applicability of the sign test in this situation, an

With respect to the relationships between *sun* and *male* and *sun* and *female,* a problem arose. Since only one *sun* context was available, only 2 *sun-male* and 2 *sun-female* correlations were possible. However, as a test of the different viewpoints of Freud, and of Macalpine and Hunter, comparisons were made: for the Freud prediction, between the *sun-male* and *sun-God* correlations and the *sun-female* and *God-female* correlations; and for the Macalpine and Hunter prediction, between the *sun-female* and *sun-God* correlations and the *sun-male* and *God-male* correlations.

In neither instance was the difference significant. Inspection of the table of correlations for the contexts of the key words will show that the contexts of *sun* are not related in any consistent way either to the contexts of *God* and *male* or *God* and *female.*

Certain other comparisons of the correlations in Table 16 were made, bearing on the way Schreber wrote of *Flechsig* and the way he wrote about *God, male,* and *female.* The correlations between *Flechsig* and *male* were greater than the correlations between *Flechsig* and *female* in 15 out of 16 comparisons, greater than *Flechsig* and *God* in 14 out of 16 comparisons, and greater than *God* and *male* in 16 out of 16 comparisons. In addition, the correlations between *God* and *Flechsig* were greater in 13 out of 16 comparisons than the correlations between *God* and *male.*

Several aspects of Freud's position were supported in the study. Thus, the contexts of *God* in Schreber's autobiography were more like the contexts of *male* than of *female;* the contexts of *Flechsig* and *male* were more alike than those of *Flechsig* and *female.* The relationships between the contexts of *God, male,* and *Flechsig* also suggested that, in the slight difference of opinion between Niederland and Freud, the Freudian position was stronger. Niederland saw both *Flechsig* and *God* as father symbols in Schreber's writing. Freud maintained that, although both *Flechsig* and *God* were in the same class, *God* was the father substitute and *Flechsig* stood in the relationship of a brother. Since not enough contexts of *father* were available to make direct comparisons possible, it was necessary to use contexts of *male* to test the various hypotheses. Schreber wrote about *Flechsig* more in the way he wrote about *male* than about *God.* He wrote about *God* more in the

---

empirical test was made on 2500 sets of 8 random numbers to determine how often by chance one group of 4 numbers would be larger in various proportions than another group of 4 numbers. The probability of obtaining a ratio of 13:3 was .15; the probability of a ratio of 14:2 was .11; the probability of a ratio of 15:1 was .04; the probability of a 16:0 ratio was .02. These probabilities are all somewhat higher than those given in tables for the sign-test comparison of independent pairs.

way he wrote about *Flechsig* than about *male*. If the matrix of associations around *Flechsig* were seen as composed of *male* and *father* words, with *male* words predominating, and the matrix of associations around *God* as composed of *father* and *male* words, with *father* words predominating, this could account for the strong relationship between *Flechsig* and *male,* the moderately strong relationship between *Flechsig* and *God,* and the comparatively weak relationship between *God* and *male*.

With respect to the relationship between *sun* and *God* as symbols, the findings supported neither Freud's nor Macalpine and Hunter's views. Freud saw *sun* and *God* in the autobiography as father symbols, and Macalpine and Hunter ascribed feminine qualities to both of them. Unfortunately *sun* was not written about enough in the autobiography for tests of the reliability of the distribution of its contextual associates and for enough comparisons with other contexts to provide meaningful statistical tests. The comparisons which were made combined two predictions from Freud and two predictions from Macalpine and Hunter: that *sun* was like *God* for Schreber and that both were either like *male* or like *female*. The differences between correlations of *sun-God* and *sun-male* versus *sun-God* and *sun-female* were insignificant, in part because *sun* and *God* were not very highly correlated.

Table 17 shows the average correlations between the category

TABLE 17

AVERAGE CORRELATIONS RANKED FROM HIGHEST TO LOWEST:
LAFFAL (1960, p. 477)

Context Profiles Correlated	Average Correlation
male - Flechsig	.636
God - Flechsig	.558
male - female	.531
female - sun	.517
female - Flechsig	.479
sun - Flechsig	.454
male - sun	.427
male - God	.422
female - God	.338
sun - God	.290

profiles of contexts for all key words. These averages were arrived at by taking all the intercorrelations in Table 16, 2 for *sun* with the other words, and 4 for all the other words with each other, and dividing by the number of correlations. The table shows *female* and *sun* to be more highly related on the average than *male* and *sun*. Of the 4 direct comparisons between these correlations available in Table 16, 3 show the *female-sun* correlation higher, and 1 shows the *male-sun* correlation higher. The tendency of the data is thus slightly in the direction of the prediction derived from the Macalpine and Hunter view that *sun* is a feminine symbol in the autobiography.

Since the word *sun* was used in isolated contexts relatively infrequently in the autobiography, as compared to words like *God, Flechsig,* and words categorized under *male* or *female,* it is likely that both Freud and Macalpine and Hunter were forced to speculate more freely on its symbolism and relationship to other aspects of Schreber's thinking. In each case some striking context of the word seems to have been taken as the key to its interpretation. Thus, Macalpine and Hunter referred to the fact that Schreber called the sun a whore. In addition, they pointed out that the sun is of feminine gender in German[3] and that there is folk-mythological support for the idea of the sun as a feminine thing. Freud laid emphasis on the fact that Schreber himself identified the sun sometimes with the "upper" and sometimes with the "lower" God. Freud also drew on evidence from other cases, from literature, and from mythology to support his assertion that the sun was a father symbol for Schreber. It is possible that Freud and Macalpine and Hunter, in relying heavily on universal interpretations of the sun as a symbol and having relatively little textual material relating to the sun available in the actual autobiography, failed to evaluate correctly its significance in Schreber's system. The complexity of sun symbolism is well illustrated in a paper by Abraham (1913) who, while adhering to the position that the sun is a father symbol, pointed out the many ways in which it is also a female symbol.

This study of symbolism in Schreber's autobiography further illustrates the application of a category analysis of contextual associates in free-flowing language. The study itself highlighted many of the problems involved in developing and applying a system of categories. Considerable work was done, subsequent to this study, on refining a category system and standardizing the procedure for applying it. The principles guiding the development of a set of categories, the definitions of the categories, and examples of their use may be found in Appendix I.

---

[3] Sun and moon tend to have opposite genders in various languages, but the distribution is arbitrary: German *die Sonne-der Mond,* but French *le soleil-la lune.* I am indebted to Professor Stephen Ullmann for pointing this out.

7. Language in Psychoanalytic Theory

The preceding chapters have developed the idea of a structure of language and have demonstrated the possibilities of its application. The material brought forward was drawn in part from linguistic, philosophical, developmental, and experimental psychological sources, and in part from clinical case material. Throughout, the emphasis has been upon the role of a sociocultural norm as embodied in *la langue* and upon the role of individual motivation in language behavior. In the present chapter we turn to a theoretical analysis of language from a psychoanalytic point of view.

From the earliest days of his concern with aphasia (1891) and with the cathartic treatment of hysterical illness (Breuer & Freud, 1893), Freud gave thought to the psychological nature of language. His most systematic discussion of the subject is to be found in his "Project for a Scientific Psychology" (1895), and he recurred to themes set forth there throughout his subsequent writing.

Freud developed a conceptual model of language which dealt with the role of language in consciousness, the relation between language and thought, the development of language in the child, the origins of language as an instrument of social communication, the function of language in the restitutive efforts of schizophrenic patients, and the moti-

vated nature of language parapraxes and distortions (Laffal, 1964a).
We shall consider some of the criticisms which have been directed
against this psychoanalytic model of language and show how the
model relates to the theory of language as a structure of fields of
reference. Illustrations are drawn from the psychotherapeutic study
of an aphasic patient and from an examination of language changes
in a schizophrenic patient. The presentation is divided into four sections: language and consciousness, psychoanalytic theory of language
and aphasia, psychoanalytic theory of language development, and
schizophrenic language.

LANGUAGE AND CONSCIOUSNESS

The most striking, and at the same time the most puzzling, thing
that Freud had to say about language was that it provided the distinction between a conscious and an unconscious idea. In its simplest
and most often quoted form, the proposition may be found in "The
Unconscious" (1915): "The conscious presentation comprises the presentation of the thing plus the presentation of the word belonging to
it, while the unconscious presentation is the presentation of the thing
alone" (p. 201).

The role of language in consciousness was adumbrated very early
in Freud's writing when he applied a distinction between the "idea of
the word" (word concept) and the "idea of the thing" (object concept) to the study of aphasia (Freud, 1891). These ideas have already
been alluded to in Chapter 1. He hypothesized that brain damage
which affected only the areas contributing to the "idea of the word"
led to verbal aphasia, a disorder in which associations between verbal
elements were primarily disturbed; whereas damage which interfered
with the associations between the word concept and the object concept
led to asymbolic aphasia, a disorder in which the naming of objects
was affected. The distinction between the "idea of the word" and the
"idea of the thing" subsequently entered into his hypothesis that the
development of speech was the important *modus* through which "ideas
of things" became conscious. However, in one of his last writings, *An
Outline of Psychoanalysis* (1940, p. 42 ff.), Freud no longer maintained that connection with the memory traces of speech was a pre-
requisite for preconscious or conscious processes as contrasted with
unconscious processes, and emphasized, instead, certain differences in
the psychic energy associated with ideas as the basis of their being conscious or unconscious.

The apparent shift on Freud's part with respect to the role of language in the distinction between unconscious and preconscious encouraged the view among some psychoanalysts that his earlier ideas were mistaken (Holt, 1962, p. 201; Kris, 1950, p. 543; Rapaport, 1951, pp. 698 f.). Schilder (1936) offered an explicit criticism of Freud's idea:

> Freud has developed the rather complicated idea that the difference between the conscious and the unconscious idea is not that they are different records of the same content situated in different parts of the mind but that the conscious idea comprises the concrete idea plus the verbal idea corresponding to it while the unconscious idea is that for the thing alone. The relation between sign and reference is so fundamental that it is hard to believe that it should not be present in what Freud calls "unconscious thinking" (p. 206).

Bearing in mind these reservations regarding Freud's use of language as a criterion to distinguish between conscious and unconscious, we may go on to examine in detail his thinking in this area. In *The Interpretation of Dreams* (1900, p. 574 f.), Freud offered a description of consciousness as a sense organ for the apprehension of psychical qualities arising from excitations from various sources. Originally consciousness was capable of receiving perceptual excitations from the periphery of the organism, and excitations of pleasure and displeasure from inside the organism. However, the presence or absence of pleasure offers only a crude basis for bringing ideas into consciousness, and in the course of human development a more subtle mechanism for the production of psychical quality, namely speech, came into play as a source of internal excitation. By virtue of the psychical qualities which accompany the auditory-verbal discharge in speech, whether spoken or internal, consciousness has become capable of following more intricate thought processes not dependent either upon perception of external objects or sensations of pleasure and displeasure.

Freud thus postulated that the auditory-verbal discharge in mnemic residues of speech provided the qualities necessary to attract consciousness and to permit consciousness to follow an intricate train of ideation. However, it is important to note that he had already indicated, in "The Project for a Scientific Psychology" (1895, p. 445), that other modalities such as the visual and the kinesthetic could also provide the necessary qualities for consciousness. In "The Ego and the Id" (1923, p. 21) he again made this explicit in accounting for certain preconscious fantasies involving visual thinking. He cautioned against the oversimplification of regarding verbal residues as the only source of conscious or preconscious stimulation and pointed out that thought processes could become conscious by a reversion to optical mnemic residues. Nevertheless, he felt that what becomes conscious in such visual recall is as a rule only the concrete subject matter of the thought, whereas the relations between the various elements of the subject matter, which especially characterizes thought, cannot be given visual expression. Visual thought is therefore only fragmentary and is nearer to unconscious processes, whereas thinking in words is a more fully conscious process.

The path open to consciousness is thus broader than that provided by language alone. It includes the mnemic residues of sensory modalities other than the auditory, residues which are capable of making conscious the "concrete subject-matter" of past perceptions but not, as may the verbal residues, relations between such subject matters. Although it is clear that access to consciousness was not limited, in Freud's conception, to the verbal modality, he often spoke of word presentations as the *only* vehicles of consciousness, to the exclusion of such modalities as the kinesthetic and visual. Perhaps this was because he believed that the qualities associated with verbalizations permitted, as did no others, the highest development of objective thought: *"Thus, thought which is accompanied by the cathexis of indications of thought-reality or of indications of speech is the highest and most secure form of cognitive thought-process"* (1895, p. 431).

We have seen that Freud drew on the qualitative nature of language in describing the relation between language and thought. What is the nature of the quality provided by language which makes thought processes available to consciousness? In the work which he did with Breuer on the hypnotic treatment of hysterical neuroses, Freud characterized language as a discharge mechanism. He found that symptoms would disappear if under hypnosis the patient recovered the traumatic memory and described the disturbing event in detail, giving utterance to the affect. The curative result was in part accounted for by the fact that the strangulated affect was able to find an exit through speech. "The injured person's reaction to the trauma only exercises a completely 'cathartic' effect if it is an *adequate* reaction—as, for instance, revenge. But language serves as a substitute for action; by its help, an affect can be 'abreacted' almost as effectively" (Breuer & Freud, 1893, p. 8).

This energic discharge aspect of language may be understood more clearly from the discussion of language and quality in the "Project for a Scientific Psychology" (1895, especially pp. 417–422). Here Freud attempted to show how speech, since it also possesses the kind of quality which is characteristic of perceptions, makes possible conscious thought. The discussion may be summarized as follows.

Perceptions give rise to indications of quality which excite consciousness and attention. The outcome of the energy flow related to external and psychical quantity in perception is that memories are laid down. In order for attention to range systematically over these memories laid down as a result of perceptions, some indications of quality, such as those which arise in perception, must be available to guide the attention. If there were a *discharge* associated with the passage of psychic quantity, this would give rise to indications of quality which could guide attention. Speech associations provide such discharge opportunities. The manner in which they do so is as follows. Excitation, presumably associated with initial attention, passes via a branch stream from the memory image to the associated auditory image, to the verbal *motor* image, and thence to discharge. Reports of discharge give rise to, or are themselves, indications of quality, which in turn lend consciousness to the memories. There is thus a mechanism—tied to verbal images—which permits attention to bring systematically into consciousness a connected series of memories. This is conscious, observant thought.

Speech associations, because of their indications of quality, also put thoughts with which they may be linked on a level with perceptual processes and make it possible to remember thoughts. Thus, not only perceptions, but also thoughts, may be remembered.

Freud repeatedly stressed the verbal *motor* aspect of language. This was because the ideas of energy discharge and the attendant consciously perceivable quality were crucial in his discussion. The clinical application of this energy-discharge concept has already been alluded to in reference to Freud's use of the "talking cure" (1893, p. 38) in the treatment of hysteria. In the "Project," Freud was explicit about the role of language as an energy-discharge mechanism associated with thought:

> Thus we have found that the charactertistic thing about the process of cognitive thought is that the attention is from the start directed to indications of the discharge of thought —that is, to indications of speech. It is well known that what is known as "conscious" thought is accompanied by a slight motor expenditure (1895, p. 424).

It is in order here to point out some striking parallels between the language theory of the behaviorist John B. Watson and some of the psychoanalytic ideas which have been outlined. The similarities exist in several respects.

First, Watson, like Freud, stressed that experience was multifaceted, with sensory, motor, visceral, and verbal components merged in the reaction of the individual.

Second, both stressed the intimate relation between language and thought. Watson felt that *"the term 'thinking' should cover all word behavior of whatever kind that goes on subvocally"* (1930, p. 243). Freud gave a central role to speech in cognitive thought, and the motor-energic aspects of thought were referred to by both men as minimal motor expenditures associated with speech, as may be seen in the remarks from Freud's "Project" just quoted and in the following remark of Watson:

> My theory does hold that the muscular habits learned in overt speech are responsible for implicit or internal speech (thought). It holds, too, that there are hundreds of muscular combinations with which one can say either aloud or to himself almost any word, so rich and so flexible is language organization and so varied are our overt speech habits. . . . Soon *any, and every* bodily response *may become a word substitute* (Watson, 1930, p. 239).

Third, if we bear in mind that Freud (1895, p. 422) used the term "memory" to include unconscious ideational processes and that Watson used it to refer only to conscious memories, then the similarity of their views of the nature of conscious recall is apparent in Watson's remark that *"memory is really the functioning of the verbal part of a total habit"* (1930, p. 256). In terms of Freud's discussion of language, this would be "the conscious presentation [which] comprises the presentation of the thing plus the presentation of the word belonging to it" (Freud, 1915, p. 201).

Fourth, the difference in the two authors' conceptions of "memory" is also echoed in Watson's critique of the psychoanalytic idea of the unconscious. Watson was unwilling to accept the idea of repression, a crucial notion in psychoanalytic thought, but his description of what Freud called "unconscious" does not appear to be inconsistent with Freud's view. Watson says:

1. An enormous number of manual habits are formed, es-

pecially during infancy, without corresponding verbal habits. 2. A still larger amount of visceral organization (organization in unstriped muscles and glandular components) is constantly forming without verbal organization, not only during infancy but also throughout life. 3. The assumption seems to be reasonably grounded that this unverbalized organization makes up the Freudian's "unconscious" (p. 264).

He goes on to say:

> I believe that when subjective psychologists have given verbalization its due place in the whole process of bodily organization they will be ready to admit that being "conscious" is merely a popular or literary phrase descriptive of the act of *naming our universe of objects both inside and outside* (p. 264).

Fifth, finally, Watson and Freud both emphasize the importance of verbal features in the structure and organization of thinking. Watson says:

> I should like to say here emphatically that *whenever the individual is thinking, the whole of his bodily organization is at work (implicitly)*—even though the final solution shall be a spoken, written or subvocally expressed verbal formulation. In other words, from the moment the thinking problem is set for the individual (by the situation he is in) activity is aroused that may lead finally to adjustment. Sometimes the activity goes on in terms of (1) implicit manual organization; more frequently in terms of (2) implicit verbal organization; sometimes in terms of (3) implicit (or even overt) visceral organization. If (1) or (3) dominates, thinking takes place *without words* (p. 213).

The similarities between the Freudian and Watsonian theories of language do not, of course, obliterate the differences. The basic disagreement lies in the fact that Watson strictly excluded mentalistic notions and sought to account for higher-order phenomena in terms of muscular and visceral innervations and conditioning, whereas Freud's concepts ultimately split away from physicalism and dealt with psychic acts and energy.

The contribution of language in making conscious thought possible raises the question of the relationship between language and primary and secondary process. The role of language in secondary process was succinctly stated by Freud in "The Unconscious" (1915) :

> The system *Ucs.* [unconscious] contains the thing-cathexis of the objects, the first and true object-cathexes; the system *Pcs.* [preconscious] comes about by this thing-presentation being hypercathected through being linked with the word-presentations corresponding to it. It is these hypercathexes, we may suppose, that bring about a higher psychical organization and make it possible for the primary process to be succeeded by the secondary process which is dominant in the *Pcs.* (p. 201).

But what of words which appear in dreams, whose forms are determined by primary process? Does the presence of words in dreams contradict the statement that word presentations make it possible for primary process to be succeeded by secondary process? In *The Interpretation of Dreams* (1900), Freud indicated that the dream work could not actually create speeches as we do in our normal waking discourse. Speeches which figure in dreams are shown, on analysis, to be fragments of speeches which have been made or heard while awake, rather than originating in the dream. The dream work deals with such fragments in an arbitrary fashion, dragging them out of context and putting them together in a new order.

This was clearly an effort to distinguish between language as utilized by primary process and language as a secondary-process phenomenon. Freud reiterated these ideas about dream speech in his "A Metapsychological Supplement to the Theory of Dreams" (1917, p. 228), where he pointed out that words carried over to the dream from the day's residues are not expressions of thoughts in the dream, but appear as if they were objects perceived like any other objects in the dream.

This differentiation between language in primary process and language as a secondary-process phenomenon may, I believe, be given further definition by drawing on Saussure's (1915) distinction between *la langue* and *la parole*. It would appear that Freud was groping for a distinction, such as that made in Chapter 1, between idiosyncratic and consensually valid use of language. In primary-process usages, either the word is not communally accepted or there is a disjunction between communal word (word presentation) and communal experience (thing presentation). Thus, if the patient refers to the object "horse" with the word *gryx,* this would be a primary-process usage of language. By the same token, *Emperor of Tartary,* in the language of the old man in *Nicholas Nickleby* (see Preface), to the extent that it does not have reference to a communally shared (or possible) experience, reflects a primary-process usage.

In the light of the foregoing discussion, a careful reading of the relevant part of *An Outline of Psychoanalysis* (1940, pp. 42 ff.) will reveal that Freud was not abandoning his idea of the role of language in the distinction between unconscious and preconscious, but that he was essaying a more general characterization of the difference which would not be so intimately tied to the specific manifestations in language. We have already seen that Freud attributed access to consciousness to all indications of quality, including visual and kinesthetic as well as verbal. In the *Outline,* Freud went on to attempt a distinction between preconscious and unconscious in energic terms:

> We seem to recognize that nervous or psychical energy exists in two forms, one freely mobile and the other, by contrast, bound; we speak of cathexes and hypercathexes of the material of the mind and even venture to suppose that a hypercathexis brings about a sort of synthesis of different processes—a synthesis in the course of which free energy is transformed into bound energy. Further than this we have been unable to go. Nevertheless, we hold firmly to the view that the distinction between the unconscious and the preconscious condition also lies in dynamic relations of this same kind, which would explain how it is that, whether spontaneously or with our assistance, the one can be changed into the other (p. 44).

In his discussion of Freud's concept of bound and free cathexis, Holt (1962) pointed out that one important meaning of binding is that "the cathectic charge becomes increasingly more difficult to separate from its idea, a state that is aptly called bound. A bound cathexis stays with a content, at least for the most part, contributing to the sustained identity of thoughts" (pp. 517–518). Further, Holt offered the following definition:

> *Binding is a synthetic process, carried out by hypercathexes, wherein drive cathexes are stably linked to mental representations.* It is a quantitative, not an all-or-none, con-

cept, so that free energy can be thought of as becoming increasingly bound, as we go from the primary-process pole along the continuum of thought toward the secondary-process pole (p. 521).

In the learning of a language, particular words are learned and experienced by members of the community as referring to (bound to) a particular set of events. Thus the idea of binding appears to fit language as a consensually learned and consensually valid event. It is important to note that we have here introduced via language a communal criterion of binding, or of secondary process, which is ultimately the criterion of the reality of a thought process. The language of an individual, then, to the extent that it reflected a shared reference— that is, was consistent with *la langue*—would be a manifestation of the binding of drive cathexes. That is, it would indicate that the individual accepted and used the name given by his community to a particular experience. The consequence of this contract is nothing less than the acculturation of the individual. To the extent that the individual's language was inconsistent with *la langue,* his language would reflect primary process and absence of the communally valid reality. The schizophrenic patient who calls people by a number code rather than by name would be using language in a primary-process manner since the code would not be shared by others, even if it were thoroughly learned and consistently used by the patient.

This discussion of Freud's views of language emphasizes the dimension of communal reality in language as a secondary-process phenomenon. Gill (1963) has stressed that there are exceptions to the parallelism of the conscious and unconscious and secondary-process and primary-process dimensions in psychoanalytic theory. Freud regarded language (that is, consensually valid language) as a nodal phenomenon through which unconscious could become conscious and which at the same time was a sure criterion of the presence of secondary process. Since word presentations carry indications of quality, language of either a consensually valid or idiosyncratic type could never be an unconscious event. Therefore, language in dreams and schizophrenic language, that is, idiosyncratic language as distinct from *la langue,* is not "unconscious language" but necessarily conscious although under primary-process control.

PSYCHOANALYTIC THEORY OF LANGUAGE AND APHASIA

How can Freud's distinction between idea of the word and idea of the thing (which originated in his study of aphasia) and his extension of this distinction to the differentiation of conscious and unconscious be applied in the psychotherapeutic treatment of aphasia? Freud never carried his theory that unconscious representations were those which lacked the idea of the word back to its logical conclusion that the aphasic patient suffered at least in part from excessive repression in that much was being denied to consciousness which *could* become conscious. Language incapacity in aphasia is not usually regarded as a motivated difficulty, even by those who describe it as an organismic or total-organism disorder (Goldstein, 1948). Instead, it is seen as the loss of a capacity, essentially biologic in nature, for higher-level functioning, the therapeutics of which involve relearning and retraining. But Freud's discussion of aphasia lends itself to the view that at least what we call expressive aphasia (Wepman, 1951) may be a motivated exploitation of an organic difficulty. This would say that, like the hysterical individual with conversion symptoms who has denied consciousness to unacceptable material, the aphasic patient is warding off awareness by turning a language disability into a generalized failure of language. It is a fair hypothesis that what the patient is warding off is recognition of the serious assault upon his body and his loss of ability to function in his customary manner. When recognition is forced upon the patient by a demand he cannot meet or a task he cannot perform, we see in what Goldstein has called the "catastrophic reaction" the extreme anxiety which may be mobilized by such an acknowledgment.

If one takes the view that the language failure is equivalent to a pervasive repression in connection with the need to deny consciousness to whatever might stimulate the recognition of the extent of body damage, the problem of rehabilitation of the patient's language becomes more than a retraining problem. It is a problem having to do with language as the key to his psychological defense against awareness of loss. Such a problem lends itself to a psychotherapeutic as opposed to a retraining approach, for the patient has more to permit himself to use language again than he has to relearn it. The dilemma of the psychotherapeutic treatment lies in the fact that the very modality of treatment, language, must be avoided by the patient in order to keep out of consciousness his recognition of the body damage.

The fact that a certain amount of language retraining is possible does not necessarily controvert this view of the dynamic significance of the aphasia. The learning of specific words in retraining usually takes place in such a manner as to encapsulate the words as discrete phenomena acquired *de novo*, without the extensive associations developed by a lifetime of familiarity with the words. Relearned words

come into use for the patient shorn of their associative meaning and
so constricted as referential tokens that they do not pose a serious
threat of evoking what is defended against. The fact that language has
been hit broadside by the aphasia is not far removed from the massive
change which is introduced in all of a patient's language when he
speaks gibberish or when he reverses *yes* and *no*.

A serious psychotherapeutic effort with an aphasic patient must
have as its goal the reduction of the defense against conscious recognition of his body damage. Some therapies stress the supportive aspect
of treatment and urge repeated and hearty praise for successes. Thus,
Longerich and Bordeaux (1954) say:

> As the days go by, call to the aphasic's attention every
> tiniest success or advance and heartily praise each one. The
> most despondent patient, given sincere and enthusiastic ap-
> proval, eventually thaws out and begins himself to call at-
> tention to his victories. Never stop a patient from doing
> this. Instead, take time to analyze orally the various means
> by which he achieved the victory. Call these to his attention
> and emphatically state that he is doing much better (p.
> 165).

Such "supportive" treatments appear to deny the very possibility that
the patient must face—namely, that he has only a limited apparatus
and will probably encounter many failures. In this sense, they play
into the psychopathology which supports the aphasia. Of course, this
is not to say that the patient must be faced inexorably and unremit-
tingly with the fact that he has lost precious functions. As with any
other psychotherapeutically treated patient, he must be helped to face
consciously what is unpleasant and frightening when denied awareness
but what may be divested of some of its intolerability when brought
into clear light.

Some recorded segments from two psychotherapeutic interviews
with an aphasic patient are presented below. The first segment is from
an interview at the very beginning of treatment, the second from an
interview a little more than three months later. Psychotherapeutic
treatment began six months after the stroke which had left the patient
aphasic and hemiplegic on his right side. The patient was seen three
times a week for half-hour sessions. In this treatment the patient was
encouraged simply to utter words without any regard for what he was
saying. It was noticeable that, when specific questions were asked or

demands were made, the patient encountered great difficulty in producing speech. However, he appeared to be able to keep up a flow of speech as long as there were no specific demands.

The selections merely illustrate the approach, whose object is to encourage the patient to expand his spontaneous language and to keep to the fore the idea that at some point the patient must deal with the crucial problem of his impairment. Dotted lines indicate incomprehensible segments in the recordings.

Early Interview

PT. Good. All right. And. . . . .the boys went. . . . . out there Saturday morning and over there, and over there in the corner there. Saturday morning I gave someone cigarettes, I suppose, over there, corner.

DR. Could you speak a little louder, Mr. Wilson?

PT. All right.

DR. So I can hear you?

PT. And I gave him something over there.

DR. Who, who are you talking about?

PT. Over there, there, over there. . . . .too, I guess, I gave him something too. God Almighty, and then I gave him something over there. I gave him cheese and everything else, I guess. I gave him something over there. I gave him something over there.

DR. What did you give him?

PT. Yes, I know. And I gave him something.

DR. What did you give him?

PT. Cookies, chocolate, something else, over there. God Almighty, I gave him something over there in the corner, over there, I gave him something, I. . . . .over there in the corner over there, once. Once I gave him something that, I gave him something, God damn it, I gave him something, something. I gave him something. And I gave him something, God Almighty. I gave him something too. I gave him something, also. Also I gave him something.

DR. To whom did you give something? To whom, to whom did you give something?

PT. There in the corner over there.

DR. Who was it?

Pt. I. . . . .

Dr. Who was it?

Pt. God Almighty, I gave him something. God damn it,
I gave him something. (*patient cries*)

Dr. Take it easy, Mr. Wilson. Relax. You don't have to
cry if you can't think of the word.

Pt. All right?

Dr. Take it easy.

Pt. I gave him something, God damn it, I gave him something too. I gave him something. . . . .I gave him
something and ah, and ah, and ah, and I gave him
something. I gave him something, gave him something, over there, corner. God Almighty, I gave him
something over there.

Interview Three Months Later

Dr. You're exercising your arms?

Pt. Yes, I know.

Dr. Uh huh.

Pt. And well better and better I guess, huh? And later on
I'll find that things are good again, huh? Well. . . . .
to, because of weather and happening things out there
longer, short things, why? Because I don't know. Because the weather perhaps. Saying things too. I don't
know. But because the weather out there, saying things
and hoping things, good and strong, I, I don't know.
Perhaps the weather out there is miserable weather
and things are great thinkers too. I don't know, because God Almighty, sometimes aggravating, huh?
Well, by and by I'll speak these things are great
thinkers too, huh? A, and a long time I talk, talk
decently and things are great thinkers too and, by and
by I'll find things of importance, and things are great
and. . . . .I suppose. It's all right too, huh? And, and,
things are great and thinkers are good thinkers too
perhaps. I know it, God Almighty. Because over there
and over there, why? Because the weather, well, over
there, and over there. . . . .Okay, kid almighty, God
Almighty too, huh? Oh God, it's miserable, huh?

Dr. What's miserable? What's miserable?

Pᴛ. Over there, over there.

Dʀ. Your leg and your arm?

Pᴛ. Yeah, yeah. Things are great, I suppose, huh? And well. . . . .well understood, understood perhaps. I know, God Almighty! Thinkers. But when I go there, now on, I find that thinkers good thinkers too, huh? Over there is, oh God, why? Perhaps later on I'll find that, and that, I don't know. I don't know because over there, over there okay, over here is all right. And later on I hope that, I hope that thinkers are good perhaps, huh? God Almighty. When I go home the other day I'll find that, find that girls and boys are good thinkers again. But later on I'll find that, over there and over there is all right again. And, and we, God Almighty, wonderful. . . . .wonderful, gorgeous . . . . .something, God Almighty. Something wrong, but hell with it, huh? Oh God, murder! (*laughing*) Okay Joe, it's all right. It's all right because later on I'll, it's all right, too. Hmph. Okay, Joe, perhaps, over there, hand and face and hands and everything, good enough, I suppose. And, and later on I'll find that words and sentences, sentences are good. And money perhaps and figures, and sentences good.

The treatment attempts to bring the patient to consider and talk about his loss. It does not shy clear of the material most designed to produce the catastrophic response, but relies upon the therapeutic relationship to help the patient through such crises. It is to be anticipated that full awareness of the loss, which would entail ability to verbalize the loss and its implications, will be most difficult and most disturbing to the patient. Theoretically, however, if the patient can reach this point, he will no longer need to employ language failure as a defense and will be able to use his language to the maximum capacity remaining.

PSYCHOANALYTIC THEORY OF LANGUAGE DEVELOPMENT

The "Project for a Scientific Psychology" (1895) provided an account of the earliest phases of language development which stem, on the one hand, from experiences of pain and, on the other, from imitative tendencies in the infant. Certain objects perceived by the infant cause him to scream in pain. The association between the sound of the scream and the painful perception emphasizes the hostile character of the object and attaches a verbal quality to the object which would otherwise not be clearly characterized because of the pain. This association of a verbal report with an object that causes pain is the means by which memories which caused pain may be made conscious and subjected to attention, when otherwise they might be avoided because of the painful association. According to Freud, the first class of conscious memories are thus painful ones, and what makes it possible for them to become conscious is their association with a verbal report (the screaming). A second basis for language development is the tendency to imitation. The infant imitates noises which he hears from objects and from people around him. The auditory-verbal qualities associated with these sounds thus also permit the related memories to become conscious. The final step in the development of speech occurs when deliberately produced sounds are associated with perceptions.

These ideas relating to the experience of pain were in part forerunners of what, in later psychoanalytic theory, became the "reality principle" (1911a), for the screaming of the child is the early paradigm of verbalization associated with painful reality which leads ultimately to the capacity to permit ideas associated with displeasure into consciousness (as opposed to repressing them) so that impartial judgment may be passed upon them. Freud devoted a long section in the "Project" (pp. 437–440) to a discussion of how memory images of a painful sort became "tamed" and of how the release of displeasure associated with such images either could be taken as a signal by the ego in the case of practical thought to abandon that particular path, or could be disregarded by the ego in the case of theoretical thought.

It is of interest to note that the social function of speech as communication was seen by Freud as a secondary acquisition:

> The innervation of speech is originally a discharge in the nature of a safety-valve . . . a part of the path to *internal change*, which is the sole means of discharge until the "specific action" has been discovered. This path acquires a secondary function by attracting the attention of some helpful personage (who is usually the wished-for object itself) to the child's longing and distress, and thenceforward it serves the purpose of bringing about an understanding with other people and is thus absorbed into the specific action (1895, pp. 422–423).

The primary role of speech, in its earliest stages, is as a mechanism for the moderation of psychic energy prior to the discovery of the specific action. This earliest function of speech, as described in the "Project," is like the discharge function given such an important measure of responsibility for the curative effects in treatment of hysteria (1893). A secondary, acquired function of speech is that of communication with others, which follows from the fact that the child's screaming attracts the reinforcing person.

Other psychoanalytic writers have focused on the role and relation of language to infantile body needs, bodily actions, and body development. "In order to understand the growth of language one must observe closely what the child wants, what parts of the body become involved in the process of wanting, and ultimately how he learns to speak and think of different parts of the body and of the desires and feelings associated with them" (Kubie, 1934, p. 430). Spitz (1957) has given a detailed account of the development of the headshaking *no* from the rooting behavior of the infant and believes that this gesture is the visible indicator that the abstraction of refusal or denial has been achieved by the child. This abstraction is the first step in the development of a vaster verbal symbolic function in the second half of the second year.

Two papers by Ferenczi (1911; 1913) trace in great detail the genesis of language in the child in terms of the child's bodily needs and psychic state.[1] The earliest period of psychic life is that of the infant prior to birth. This, according to Ferenczi, is the period of unconditioned omnipotence in which needs are continuously, automatically, and immediately met. After birth, when the mother, in effect, recreates the comfort of the prenatal period, there is a period of magical-hallucinatory omnipotence. In this period, the child's needs lead to the hallucinatory representation of the need-gratified condition, but at the same time the mother anticipates and fills the needs. The need, the hallucinatory wish fulfillment, and the actual gratification come very close together, although not perfectly so, and the child is in a state in which, as far as he is concerned, the need brings along with it the gratification.

However, since timing of the gratification brought by mother is not always exact and since the appropriate gratifier is not always presented, certain actions, such as crying and body gestures, are evoked. These actions are responded to by the mother as signals, and the child is thus in a phase of omnipotence by help of magic gestures in

[1] Compare Latif (1934) for a behavioristically oriented account of the development of language in the child.

which his vocal and other gestures bring the gratification.

The child gradually discovers that some things in the world do not gratify and do not obey his will. He is faced with the necessity of distinguishing between his own feelings and wishes and the sensations which arise from stimulation by the world around him. There is an animistic period in this development in which the child still ascribes to the outer world the qualities he is aware of in himself. He seeks to find in every object his own organs and their activities. The child is exclusively concerned with his own body and with the satisfaction of his needs for sucking, eating, contact with his genitals, excretion, and so on. His attention is arrested by those processes in the outer world which remind him of these experiences:

> Thus arise those intimate connections, which remain throughout life, between the human body and the objective world that we call *symbolic*. On the one hand the child in this stage sees in the world nothing but images of his corporeality, on the other he learns to represent by means of his body the whole multifariousness of the outer world. This capacity for symbolic representation is an important completion of the gesture-language; it enables the child not only to signalize such wishes as immediately concern his body, but also to express wishes that relate to the changing of the outer world, now recognized as such (Ferenczi, 1913, p. 228).

The development of speech permits the representation of a much greater multiplicity of objects and processes of the outer world than was possible with gesture language, and speech rapidly gets substituted for gesture. Certain sounds are brought into close associative connection with definite objects and processes and are gradually identified with them. From this accrues the great progress—there is no longer a necessity for the cumbersome figurative imagination and dramatic representation. Words allow a far more precise and economic conceptualization and expression of wishes and relationships. However, even with the development of speech, the child still preserves his feelings of omnipotence, because his entourage responds quickly to his words and his efforts to indicate his needs. For the child the illusion is further propagated that he is in possession of magical capacities. This period is called by Ferenczi the period of magic thoughts and magic words.

This period seems to fit the language phenomena described by Piaget (1926) among young children and Cassirer (1946) among primitive people. The child uses his words in a magical fashion; he acts upon the world with them in the innocent hope that, now that he has a handle for things, he can move them around with it. Although language marks the advent of a new state of mental development, a means of ordering and dealing with psychic events and of broadening the range of action of the individual, the child initially uses language in a manner reminiscent of primary process, the only model that he knows, for the purposes of gratification, security, self-protection, and maintaining his central role in the world around him. In the same way that the infant's earliest response to a wish is the conviction that it has been or is about to be fulfilled, the child at first uses words as if they themselves will bring about the wish fulfillment.

Once language is within the child's grasp, it becomes an integral and crucial part of his total experience. Naming something gives it a distinctiveness and an identity, but body skills and sensitivities must have matured to the point where the discriminations entailed in the naming have become possible. Freud (1925) suggested that the earliest discrimination was between what is desirable to take into the body and what must be spit out. This is the ontogenesis of the idea of "no." When "in" and "out" have become distinctly different experiences, dimensions have been established which may be named and which are firmly grounded in a body event. As the child develops, the naming process assists in identifying and stabilizing new experiential dimensions. In turn, once experiences have been named, other experiences which evoke the paradigmatic body responses are classed as familiar events. Naming thus assists discrimination and organization of experience, but may also, as Cassirer demonstrated, limit experiences to the discriminations which have been labeled. The functioning of such experiential dimensions or "spheres of meaning" even in normal adults has been aptly demonstrated by Werner (1956). He provides several examples of how normal individuals grope to identify tachistoscopically presented words and shows how impressions of broad spheres in which the words belong may be present prior to the clear perception of the words themselves. Organismic bodily experiences of an emotional or kinesthetic nature may be important in this early form of cognition. Werner found that aphasic cognitions had an organismic bodily character similar to that of the normal subjects in the tachistoscopic experiments. This type of response is on a continuum with the childish use of language which strives to impress the most familiar bodily experiences on the world and to subsume all that is new under what is already familiar and defined.

The experiences of the child are inevitably influenced by his social milieu, and in this sense cultures impress patterns of discrimination on the individuals in the group. Nevertheless, individuals reorganize and stress for themselves certain aspects of these culturally determined dimensions. Idiosyncratic differences stem from the unique constitutional and experiential combinations which befall individuals. Out of the possible dimensions of human experience and out of the culturally preferred dimensions, the individual evolves a structure of experiences, tied to language, which is his special approach to life problems. Some day, when studies of the epigenesis of experience (Erikson, 1959) have produced the necessary detailed information, it may be possible to trace the growth of experiential dimensions and discriminations and at the same time to show the parallel development of related vocabulary.

SCHIZOPHRENIC LANGUAGE

The human needs which seek gratification and discharge are channeled by this experiential structure, which is designed to mesh the individual with the world around him in a way which ensures him maximum fulfillment without damage. Where the opportunities for discharge provided by the structure keep the needs of the individual within bounds and where gratifications come in sufficient amounts and opportunely, the structure may be said to function effectively. However, where there is increased pressure of drive without appropriate gratification, the structure may become oriented toward the dominant unsatisfied needs, losing its value as a mediator between the individual and reality. The modes of functioning may then shift radically, and, instead of operations on reality, autoplastic operations such as characterized earlier developmental stages may become the method of reducing the drive level and achieving gratification.

We know that earlier modes of functioning persist in higher-order developments and that language is never completely emancipated from its infantile origins. In schizophrenia, language may become more openly contaminated or recontaminated with infantile aims and methods. The structure of language then may serve—in strong competition with, but not to the total exclusion of, its organizing functions—as a means for the achievement of regressive aims.

Freud's discussion of schizophrenic language (1915) takes up a suggestion by Tausk (1919, p. 75) that schizophrenic symptoms are an "organ language" in which concepts which might be conveyed in words, such as "This part of my body does not belong to me" or "I renounce the outer world," are expressed by the patient in such bodily forms as *flexibilitas cerea* or catatonic stupor. In commenting on a case described by Tausk of a schizophrenic woman who complained that her "eyes were not right, they were twisted" and who attributed this to her lover, who was an "eye twister" or "deceiver," Freud points out that in schizophrenia, language may take on the character of "organ-speech," literally translating words into bodily experiences.

The magical use of language is echoed in such examples of schizophrenic speech. The word has now assumed for the patient a compelling quality which determines the nature of his experience with only limited regard for reality. The instrument for coping with the world through communally adopted and shared techniques, which originated in the bodily experiences of the individual, has now, in a sense, arrogated to itself the selection of what bodily events shall be experienced. The patient's special needs and conflicts are, of course, the basis of this selectivity, and his language has become a narrowly channelized but highly important means of finding again and again among all the varieties of experience those features which reflect his unmet needs.

This reorientation of language reduces its value as a means of coordinating the individual with communal reality. The pre-eminent instrument of the secondary process has begun to show evidences of primary process, with the most irrational equivalences and substitutions taking place:

> In schizophrenia *words* are subjected to the same process as that which makes the dream-images out of latent dream-thoughts—to what we have called the primary psychical process. They undergo condensation, and by means of displacement transfer their cathexes to one another in their entirety. The process may go so far that a single word, if it is specially suitable on account of its numerous connections, takes over the representation of a whole train of thought (Freud, 1915, p. 199).

Remote associative links and farfetched parallels become as potent a basis of substitution and equivalence as synonymy itself; and the word, no longer serving as a communal token of *la langue,* takes on now all of the many meanings which are in any way connected with it, now a single idiosyncratic meaning.

Freud saw the increased importance of words in schizophrenia as evidence of an effort on the part of the patient to recapture the world of reality which had been lost to him:

> It turns out that the cathexis of the word-presentation
> . . . represents the first of the attempts at recovery or cure
> which so conspicuously dominate the clinical picture of
> schizophrenia. These endeavours are directed towards re-
> gaining the lost object, and it may well be that to achieve
> this purpose they set off on a path that leads to the object
> *via* the verbal part of it, but then find themselves obliged
> to be content with words instead of things (1915, pp. 203–
> 204).

The language structure thus becomes to some extent independent of
reality and itself the thing operated upon in order to establish the
patient's position in the world of men and to secure some moderation
of his pressing conflicts.

One study (Laffal, 1961) may be adduced to show how schizophrenic disorganization and reintegration influence the structure of the
patient's language. The patient studied was the same one from whose
interviews the associates of *government* and *language* were drawn in
Chapter 6. The material in that chapter suggested that for this patient
speaking of government and of language was at the same time speaking of father and of mother. The equivalences were subtle and by no
means absolute; nevertheless, they were clearly present. Such con-
taminations of adult language reflect the breakdown of communal
language distinctions and language structure.

The problem posed in the study was to examine changes in the
free-flowing vocabulary of this patient in the course of a year
of psychotherapy in which certain gross, readily identified and characterized behavioral changes took place. At the beginning of the
treatment, the patient was on a locked ward, but had occasional
privileges to leave the ward in his own custody. He was unpredictable
in his behavior, showed inappropriate affect by laughing and smiling
apparently in response to his own thoughts, and tended to become in-
comprehensibly abstruse in his conversation. Around six months after
the beginning of treatment, the notes in the patient's chart indicated
that in the therapy the patient was verging closer to significant material about the relationship with the therapist, but along with this
were reports of increasingly psychotic ways of speaking and of hal-
lucinating during the treatment hours. There were also reports of the
patient's shouting at and purposely bumping into sicker patients. There
followed a period in which the patient was restricted to the ward and
in which he was extremely difficult to communicate with, refusing to
come to the doctor's office or walking out after a few minutes if he did

come. At the end of the year, the patient was communicating better in therapy, talked about passes at home, and had assumed a privilege card in order to work in the library. That this progress was not transitory was evidenced by the fact that shortly afterward the patient went to an open ward, where he was elected president of the patient government. In the first year of treatment, the patient made a clearcut social improvement, and subsequently, as may be seen in the more detailed description of him in Chapter 6, he was able to go to college while living in the hospital. It seemed reasonable to suppose that, with the patient's change toward social adaptation, his language might also show some changes with respect to choice and distribution of word categories.

Before looking in detail at the way the patient's language changed, verbal material from two additional sources was analyzed in order to establish that the technique of category analysis was capable of discriminating between the styles of speech or writing of different individuals. In a prior study of the Schreber case (Laffal, 1960; see also Chapter 6), a large amount of written material had already been categorized. A number of psychotherapeutic interviews with another psychotic patient, Mr. B, provided additional material. Thus there were available separate profiles of categories from three sources: the written autobiography of the patient Schreber, the interview material of patient B, and the interview material of patient A discussed above.

The speech samples were categorized as outlined in Appendix I, and profiles of the category distributions were constructed.[2] Reliabilities of category profiles were determined by randomly splitting the speech sample from each patient into two subsamples, taking alternate lines of text or transcription. All comparisons were made by means of Pearson product-moment correlations. In these comparisons only 34 categories, rather than the full 94 available, were used, in order to accentuate differences which might exist. The remaining categories were eliminated by the application of certain systematic procedures designed to identify those categories which appeared consistently throughout the profiles and which would hence not discriminate between the profiles (see Laffal, 1961, p. 424).

Table 18 shows the reliabilities and intercorrelations of speech samples from the therapeutic interviews with patients A and B and from Schreber's autobiography. There were marked differences between the various profiles; hence it was clear that the technique of category analysis could discriminate among individuals.

The technique was then applied to the analysis of the therapeutic

[2] At the time of this study, only 94 categories were in use.

TABLE 18

RELIABILITIES AND INTERCORRELATIONS OF CATEGORY PROFILES
FROM PATIENTS A AND B AND SCHREBER'S AUTOBIOGRAPHY
$(N = 34$ CATEGORIES $)$: LAFFAL (1961, p. 424)

		Patient A		Patient B		Schreber
		A_1	A_2	B_1	B_2	S_1
Patient A	A_2	.801				
Patient B	B_1	.099	.027			
	B_2	.159	.127	.833		
Schreber	S_1	—.008	—.031	—.472	—.398	
	S_2	—.057	—.136	—.537	—.510	.935

interviews of patient A. Four interviews in August and September of one year, four interviews in February and March of the second year, and five interviews in October of the second year were taken for the analysis. The selection of these particular interviews was determined by their relatively close groupings in a series of thirty interviews which had been recorded during the year of treatment. The first four interviews were at the beginning of treatment of the patient; the second four occurred about six months after treatment began; and the third group of interviews was about a year after treatment began. The third group was made up of five interviews, since two were relatively brief.

The initial hypothesis tested was that the three groups of interviews would show a shift in the profiles of vocabulary, reflecting improvement in the patient's psychiatric condition. It was predicted that the profiles of the last interviews would differ sharply from those of the early and the middle interviews, since the last interviews were obtained under conditions of relative psychological integration.

Table 19 shows the reliabilities and intercorrelations of the profiles of categories taken from the early, middle, and late interviews. The reliabilities for the early, middle, and late interviews ranged from .704 to .752. The early and middle interviews correlated moderately with each other, but differed markedly from the late interviews.

Changes in the structure and diversity of the category profiles of the various interviews were examined by computing entropy or average information (Shannon & Weaver, 1949) of the profiles.[3] The information scores are shown in Table 20.

[3] In this analysis, all 94 categories were used. See footnote, Chapter 4, for a description of the use of information scores in this type of analysis.

TABLE 19

CORRELATIONS OF PROFILES OF CATEGORIES DERIVED FROM
EARLY, MIDDLE, AND LATE INTERVIEWS OF PATIENT A
($N = 34$ CATEGORIES): LAFFAL (1961, p. 425)

		Early		Middle		Late
		E_1	E_2	M_1	M_2	L_1
Early	E_2	.752				
Middle	M_1	.323	.400			
	M_2	.300	.380	.707		
Late	L_1	—.033	—.078	—.044	—.189	
	L_2	.156	—.012	.110	—.175	.704

TABLE 20

INFORMATION SCORES OF EARLY, MIDDLE, AND LATE INTERVIEWS
OF PATIENT A: LAFFAL (1961, p. 426)

Interviews	Information Scores of Category Profiles*
early 1	5.7758
early 2	5.6257
early 3	5.5800
early 4	5.6188
middle 1	5.6874
middle 2	5.7546
middle 3	5.6767
middle 4	5.6642
late 1	5.5762
late 2	5.5742
late 3	5.3250
late 4	5.7087
late 5	5.3778

* The negative sign has been dropped from these scores.

These entropy scores may shed some light on the nature of the patient's language changes during psychotherapy. High entropy scores indicate greater unpredictability of response, and lower scores accordingly indicate increased organization and predictability. The Mann-Whitney test applied to the ranked information scores showed those of the late interviews to be significantly smaller, at the 5 per cent level of statistical significance, than those of the early and middle interviews. In view of the available evidence that the last interviews occurred during a period of relative integration, as compared to the early and middle interviews, it would appear that for this patient psychological integration was accompanied by greater structuring of the category profile or by reduction of the diversity and dispersion of category choices in his speech.

This conclusion suggests, if the present patient is typical, that movement in the direction of recovery from schizophrenia may be attended by an increased structuring of the vocabulary. The fluidity of associations in the psychotic state, which reflects primary process, has given way to more consistent and regular application of the dimensions of language. The structuring reveals itself in increased predictability of the improved patient's language.

This study of the language changes of a schizophrenic patient demonstrates how the idea of language structure may provide a measurable approach to the psychological analysis of free-flowing language, capable of taking into account the broad pattern of the subject's vocabulary. The theoretical considerations which have been presented in this chapter suggest many possibilities for study. Genetic studies of vocabulary development from childhood to adulthood may provide valuable information about the growth of experiential discriminations. Studies of shifts in vocabulary structure under strong need conditions or under stress may reveal that underlying drives and conflicts are associated with particular categories. The detailed study of vocabulary structure in schizophrenia and organic brain damage may tell us a great deal about symbolism and about which dimensions are more prone to intrusions by pathology and which are more stable and durable even under such conditions. We know very little about ways of influencing the total language pattern of an individual. To what extent does experiential reorientation change the vocabulary structure, and to what extent may manipulations of the vocabulary structure produce experiential reorientation?

Questions such as these can, at present, only be asked, not answered.

Appendix I
A System of Categories

In this appendix a system of categories is outlined, with definitions and examples, which has grown out of studies, such as those reported throughout the book, on word association and free speech. The outline forms the basis of a more extensive dictionary of definitions and examples which requires a volume in itself.

Most content analyses classify language productions in terms of a particular psychological hypothesis to be tested, comparing, for example, the number of aggressive items or the number of dependency items in the samples under study. They select and characterize only those items which are relevant to the hypothesis. In this sense, the language is merely the vehicle for a limited number of tokens and is not itself under consideration as a psychological phenomenon. Here, however, we are interested in a total vocabulary analysis, and for any language sample we wish to know what references of all types are present. Every word must come under consideration.

In what follows, the general principles which have governed the development of a set of categories are described, and the categories themselves are defined with examples.

PRINCIPLES OF CATEGORIZATION

1. Categories are the results

of grouping words from many different language samples. In this sense, categories emerge from the language itself rather than from preconceptions of what ought to be categorized.

2. Categorization is on the basis of relatedness of reference, including, but not limited to, synonymity. Thus, *book, newspaper, read, write, pencil, alphabet, language, ink,* and *print* may all be grouped in a single category on the ground that all are or may be related to writing and written language. A category is thus a unity of area or field of reference rather than of specificity and synonymity of reference. For a word to be made part of a group it is only required that some component of the total word meaning lie within the common area of reference.

3. Grammatical form as such is not a category determinant. Nouns, adjectives, verbs, and adverbs which are referentially related are placed in the same category. Thus *bird* (noun), *high* (adjective), *fly* (verb), and *up* (adverb) would be placed in the same category as having a common element of reference.

4. In determining reference of a word or a phrase, a hypothetical "average speaker" is kept in mind. This is a principle put forward by Hallig and Wartburg (1952). Subtle connotations contribute to categorization only in an ancillary way. Categorization is on the basis of generally accepted meaning and references which the ordinary intelligent speaker would readily identify. In some instances—schizophrenic language, for example—it is possible that the speaker has a unique, idiosyncratic sense in mind for a particular word. However, categorization must be related to *la langue* as a social, consensually interpreted behavior.

5. Categories will not always be distinguishable from each other. Each category will have a unique, distinct core of reference different from the core of all other categories, but there may be border and overlapping areas in which it will not be easy to distinguish which of two or more categories is being referred to. There may therefore be some degree of unreliability in placing words in categories. Clarification in particular instances might be achieved by querying the speaker as to his intention, but where this is not possible, a judgment must be made as to the most likely category to apply.

6. An important criterion of a good category is that it occur neither too frequently nor too rarely. Categories which occur very frequently in all language samples lack power of discrimination between the samples. By the same token, categories which occur only rarely lack sufficient weight to provide meaningful distinctions. Thus,

to be useful, a category must not be so limited as to subsume only a few words nor so broad as to subsume an inordinately large number of words. The "right-left" distinction provides an example of an infrequent category. There are few words in our language that make these particular references, and the category "handedness" or the categories "right" and "left" would therefore have limited usefulness. At the opposite extreme would be a category such as "nature" or "man-made" which would include many words and would occur with such consistently high frequency as to be undiscriminating between most samples of speech.

7. The dictionary-maker cannot know beforehand what dimensions will emerge from his studies of language, but he must have some conception of what might be psychologically important. He need not have a theory which clearly defines important categories, but he must at least operate within a psychological framework which would help him identify and discriminate categories that might be of importance in man's experience.

This may be illustrated by a specific comparison of the present approach with that represented in the system of Hallig and Wartburg (1952). Most developmental theories (for example, psychoanalytic theory and Piaget's theory) hold that the child's corporeality is the basis of his experiences of the world around him. Whether something is *in* or *out* of the body, for example, would be a basic bodily experience and an important discrimination. These qualities of "inness" and "outness" are indeed enthroned in our verbalizations, and a search of words will produce many that fall into these categories.

In the system of Hallig and Wartburg, words referring to "in" and "out" are lumped under the general heading of "space" within their third large subdivision (*Man and Universe*). Words like *up* and *down* and *forward* and *back* are likewise lumped under the general heading of "space." Their system appears to overlook important dimensions when it groups all of these under a single general heading.

8. The classification of individual words has to be a reliable process; and the system of classification must have demonstrable validity by discriminating between separate speakers and otherwise producing meaningful results in studies of language samples.

9. Once the category system has evolved, there will be words that do not readily fall into any of the categories. To accommodate such words, new categories may be added or the existing categories may be broadened. However, assuming a wide sampling of vocabulary has already been taken, new words are placed in the existing system by

finding the category which seems to best include the major denotation of the word. In case no category seems appropriate, the word is simply not categorized.

10. Categories may range from simple to extremely complex areas of reference. Thus, spatial "upness" is a relatively uncomplicated phenomenon of experience. But "friendliness" and "violence" are complex human experiences. It is not possible to tell beforehand whether one or another of these dimensions is of greater utility or importance for a psychological analysis. Two speakers may differ from each other, for example, in the fact that one makes many references to "up" while the other has many references to "violence." In free-flowing language, such different complexities of reference occur in close succession. There is no a priori reason for assigning relative weights to the categories in terms of their presumed psychological significance, although further study may show that there is some basis for doing so.

11. The system does not begin with a logical framework, but seeks to evolve categories from actual content presented in language, while applying a psychological orientation as to possible significant discriminations. There is therefore no superordinate scheme such as appears in the logical system of Roget. It is possible that analysis of the associations of the categories with each other may reveal that there are higher-level bonds between the categories themselves, and this might ultimately provide the basis for superordinate arrangements of the categories. At present each category is given independent and equal status within the system.

12. In the case of homonyms (different words identical in sound), the precise word is identified as far as possible by the context. Where single words are being categorized and there is no context available, whatever circumstantial evidence may present itself is utilized to determine which of the homonyms is being used and, accordingly, which categories would be appropriate. Since association may occur along a dimension of similar-sounding words, there is reason to bear in mind the possibility that homonyms with apparently different meanings may also entail implicitly the dimensions of their similar-sounding cognates. The strength of this involvement would undoubtedly differ for different homonyms. One way of determining the extent of the relatedness of homonyms would be to estimate the degree of similarity in their contexts, somewhat on the order of the study of associative similarity of words in Schreber's autobiography (see Chapter 6).

However, expediency requires us to limit the number of categories which may be applied to any word, and, for all intents and purposes, homonyms with different meanings must be regarded as different words. The same reasoning would apply to polysemes (words with a number of different meanings, depending on context). The context determines the major categories of reference entailed in the word. In many, but not all, instances of polysemy, there will be a consistent core of similar meaning and an additional unique meaning depending on the particular usage. Thus: *After the flood the river had a sanguine color; He is a man of sanguine temperament; Cannibals are a sanguine people.* The reference to blood is present in all of these usages of *sanguine,* but in one instance for its color value, in another for its implications of good health and cheer, and in the third for its aggressive overtones.

13. A special problem arises in dealing with opposites. Some areas of reference are clearly divisible into opposing extremes (Ogden, 1932), although this is not a universal characteristic of language reference. Ullmann (1962, p. 143 f.) makes the point that synonyms may often be distinguished by examining the appropriate antonyms. Thus *decline* is like *reject* when it means the opposite of *accept,* but not when it is the opposite of *rise.* Examination of appropriate antonyms may thus serve to clarify meaning similarity. We have already seen there are good grounds for the view that opposites may be closely related and that logical extremes may be psychological neighbors, especially since the addition of a negation readily creates an opposite. This is an area that will require considerable investigation. In the present system, opposites are not joined under the same heading, but left distinct. It may thus be possible to examine more clearly the extent to which they imply each other in terms, for example, of contextual similarity.

14. The category system is directed at the common vocabulary, in a broad sense. It may not be readily applicable to special discussions in which the content involves refinements of reference within a limited area of experience. Thus, a treatise on color in which individual color names were mentioned frequently and characterized differently might require a variation of the category system to permit the broad category "color" to be replaced by specific color names or by subgroupings of colors. In such cases, either a new, specially applicable category system would have to be devised for the unique problem at hand, or certain of the categories described in the existing system might be subdivided as required.

The product of the application of these principles is a set of 114 categories capable of tapping some aspect of almost all the words in the English vocabulary. Words which do not appear to fit into the category system are generally those which serve a strictly grammatical rather than a referential function in the language, and words which are so finely compounded of separate meanings that attempts to categorize them are futile.

Table 21 lists heading words for the set of categories arranged alphabetically. The heading words merely suggest the areas of reference and are not themselves to be regarded as the key or defining words. Definitions of the categories are products of the words which constitute them.

TABLE 21

ALPHABETIC LISTING OF CATEGORIES BY HEADING WORD

1. ABSURD	35. DOWN
2. AGREE 1 (SYMPATHY)	36. DRINK
3. AGREE 2 (AGREEMENT)	37. DURABLE
4. AGREE 3 (SIMILARITY)	38. EARTH
5. ALL 1 (WHOLE)	39. EASY
6. ALL 2 (MUCH)	40. EAT
7. ALL 3 (FREQUENT)	41. END
8. ANIMAL	42. ESSENTIAL
9. ART	43. FALSE
10. ASTRONOMY 1 (SPACE)	44. FAR
11. ASTRONOMY 2 (WEATHER)	45. FAST
	46. FEATURE (BODY)
12. BACK	47. FEMALE
13. BAD	48. FORWARD
14. BEGIN	49. FUNCTION (BODY)
15. BIG	50. GO
16. BLURRED	51. GOOD
17. CALM	52. GROUP
18. CHANGE	53. HAPPENING
19. CLEAN	54. HEAR
20. CLOTHING	55. HELP
21. COLD	56. HILL
22. COLOR	57. HOLLOW 1 (DWELLINGS)
23. COMMERCE	58. HOLLOW 2 (OBJECTS)
24. CONFINE	59. HOT
25. CONFLICT 1 (HARM)	60. HOUSEHOLD
26. CONFLICT 2 (HATE)	61. ILLNESS
27. CONFLICT 3 (DISAGREE)	62. IN
28. CRIME	63. INDIVIDUAL
29. CURE	64. JOIN
30. DEAD	65. LANGUAGE 1 (SPEAK)
31. DIFFICULT	66. LANGUAGE 2 (WRITE)
32. DIRTY	67. LAW
33. DOMINANCE 1 (STRONG)	68. LITTLE
34. DOMINANCE 2 (LEAD)	69. LIVING

70. MALE
71. MATERIAL
72. MEASUREMENT
73. MECHANISM
74. MONEY
75. NEAR
76. NEGATION
77. NUMBER
78. OPEN
79. OUT
80. PLACE
81. PLAY
82. POSSESS
83. REASON 1 (COGNITION)
84. REASON 2 (EDUCATION)
85. REASON 3 (SCIENCE)
86. SACRED
87. SEA
88. SEE
89. SELF-REFERENCE
90. SEPARATE
91. SEX
92. SHARP 1 (SHARP)
93. SHARP 2 (EMPHASIS)

94. SLOW
95. SOME
96. STRUCTURE
97. SUBMISSION 1 (WEAK)
98. SUBMISSION 2
    (INFERIOR)
99. TIME 1 (PAST)
100. TIME 2 (PRESENT)
101. TIME 3 (FUTURE)
102. TIME 4 (GENERAL TIME)
103. TRANSPORTATION
104. TRIVIAL 1
    (UNIMPORTANCE)
105. TRIVIAL 2
    (DE-EMPHASIS)
106. TRUE
107. UNREAL
108. UP
109. UPSET
110. VEGETATION
111. WANT 1 (NEED)
112. WANT 2 (ABSENCE)
113. WORK
114. YOUNG

DEFINITIONS AND DESCRIPTIONS OF CATEGORIES

The listed categories are defined in detail below. In many of the examples, additional scoring may be possible, even though not indicated. The definitions and descriptions of the categories are designed to highlight the core concepts which are basic to each of the categories.

1. ABSURD: The category ABSURD includes two major notions: ridiculousness and incomprehensibility. In the area of ridiculousness come such words as *anomaly, stupid, farce*— "What a *grotesque* (ABSURD) hat she is wearing." In the area of incomprehensibility come such words as *ignorance, incomprehensible*—"She is a *dumb* (ABSURD) blonde."

   AGREE: This category is to be understood in part in conjunction with the category CONFLICT. There are three subdivisions which are scored separately.

2. AGREE 1 (SYMPATHY): Words having to do with loving, admiring, liking, cherishing, friendship, sympathy, and empathy are scored here. The opposite category is CONFLICT 2

(HATE). This category has to do with positive feeling. "She is my *dearest* (AGREE 1) *friend* (AGREE 1)."

3. AGREE 2 (AGREEMENT): Words having to do with agreeing, admitting, cooperating, approving, or consenting are scored here. In general, these words express concordance without the stronger affective overtones of AGREE 1 (SYMPATHY). This category has more to do with rational agreement. "He *consented* (AGREE 2) to the plan."

4. AGREE 3 (SIMILARITY): Words having to do with similarity, likeness, appropriateness, matching, comparison, equality, suitableness, and sameness. Essentially this category has to do with the comparisons and similarities of things. "The wheels were *aligned* (AGREE 3) and *balanced* (AGREE 3)."

ALL: This category is to be considered in conjunction with the category SOME. There are three subdivisions which are scored separately.

5. ALL 1 (WHOLE): References to all, totality, entirety, generality, and universality are scored here. "Pack *every* (ALL 1) piece of equipment in a wooden crate."

6. ALL 2 (MUCH): References to large amounts or parts, such as *innumerable, much, most, plenty, sufficient,* and *enough* are scored here. Plurals of numbers (*hundreds, dozens*), where great amounts are suggested, are scored here and may also have an additional score of NUMBER. *"Many* (ALL 2) people attended the lecture." *"Thousands* (ALL 2, NUMBER) came to see the show."

7. ALL 3 (FREQUENT): References to high likelihood, high probability, and commonness are scored here. An additional TIME scoring may also be appropriate. "He *often* (ALL 3, TIME 4) comes here."

8. ANIMAL: All animal life is scored here. A second scoring is often necessary to further characterize the word scored. All birds are scored UP in addition. All sea life is scored SEA in addition. "You may often see *birds* (ANIMAL, UP) and *fish* (ANIMAL, SEA) but rarely *lions* (ANIMAL) and *tigers* (ANIMAL)."

9. ART: This category applies to creative, artistically oriented activities in any media. It encompasses what we know in general to be the arts: painting, sculpturing, creative writing, music, architecture, artistic crafts, and ballet. Usually another

category scoring will accompany this one. Thus, *symphony* is scored ART, HEAR; *novel* is scored ART, LANGUAGE 2; a *painting* is scored ART, COLOR.

In some instances there may be doubt as to whether PLAY or ART might apply, since entertainment and recreational aspects of art are sometimes prominent. The distinction is made on the basis that ART refers to an esthetic activity where PLAY refers to a recreational activity. In many instances both scores are possible. "She attends the school of *drama* (ART, PLAY)."

ASTRONOMY: There are two subdivisions which are scored separately.

10. ASTRONOMY 1 (SPACE): Words referring to astronomical bodies, space, the ionosphere, and to superterrestrial phenomena are scored here: *moon, meteor, heaven, star, sun, planet,* and *air* (where the primary notion is spatial). The score UP will often also apply, although other scores may also apply. "The *sky* (ASTRONOMY 1, UP) was clear and blue." "The *sun* (ASTRONOMY 1, HOT) was blinding."

11. ASTRONOMY 2 (WEATHER): This subdivision includes words referring to weather, climate, and aspects of weather such as *rain, cloud, storm, lightning, wind,* and *air* (where the primary notion is pertinent to weather or climate). References to seasons are not scored here, but scored under TIME. "He lives in a *torrid* (ASTRONOMY 2, HOT) zone." "A *tornado* (ASTRONOMY 2, CONFLICT 1) struck the southwestern states."

12. BACK: This category is to be understood in conjunction with FORWARD. Basically it involves the physical location or direction back, rather than any temporal features. Any reference to a backward tendency, to a place behind, or to following behind something is given this score. "He lives at the *rear* (BACK) of the store."

In some instances there may be difficulty in choosing this scoring rather than the scoring TIME 1 (PAST). In general, where past time is involved, TIME 1 (PAST) is scored; but if there is an implication of being physically behind or after something, then BACK is scored. Words like *earlier* and *previous* are not scored BACK. Their emphasis is on past time.

13. BAD: This category may sometimes be confused with the

category FALSE. BAD is opposed to GOOD. FALSE is the opposite of TRUE. Depending on the implication of the context, words like *fault* and *wrong* are scored either BAD or FALSE. A moral or ethical judgment is often involved in the category BAD. "What you are doing is *wrong* (BAD) and *sinful* (BAD)." "That is the *wrong* (FALSE) answer."

14. BEGIN: The kinds of words under this category are:
   a. Procreation. These are words having to do with birth and creation. "She was *born* (BEGIN) of poor parents."
   b. Origination. These are words having to do with initiation, starting, commencing. "He was arrested for *instigating* (BEGIN) a riot."

15. BIG: All words indicating largeness, increase, thickness, and prolongation are scored here. The reference may be to size or to time. In addition, general words referring to size, amplitude, or extent are scored here, even if the reference to bigness is not explicit. "That tree is *huge* (BIG)." "How *tall* (BIG) is the boy?"

16. BLURRED: The essential characteristic of this category is the element of vagueness. The kinds of words scored here are:
   a. Words expressing doubt, obscurity, lack of clarity, and uncertainty. Included are words like *puzzle* and *confuse*. "I have a *question* (BLURRED) about it in my mind."
   b. Words referring to physical formlessness, as: *smear* and *shapeless*. "The amoeba is *amorphous* (BLURRED)."

17. CALM: The kinds of words which come under this heading are:
   a. Those having to do with ease, comfort, pacification, peace, and quiet. "It was a *serene* (CALM) setting."
   b. Those having to do with enjoyment, pleasure, and happiness. "The party was *gay* (CALM)."
   c. Those having to do with humor, joking, and laughter. "He told a *funny* (CALM) story." In some instances the context will also emphasize ridiculousness along with humor. The ABSURD scoring may be added in such cases. "As chairman, he is a *joke* (CALM, ABSURD)."

18. CHANGE: The kinds of words which are scored here are:
   a. Words which refer to deviation: *bent, crooked, jagged, tortuous, winding, derail, avoid, evade,* and *distract*. "He *turned* (GO, CHANGE) the corner."
   b. Words referring to alteration either of form or position:

convert, mutation, revise, transform, and shift. "The dress
was altered (CHANGE)."

c. Words referring to instability or to inconstancy. "His opinion *fluctuates* (CHANGE) from moment to moment."

d. Words referring to transience, temporariness, or momentari-
ness. FAST may be an additional scoring here in some
instances. "I caught a *fleeting* (CHANGE, FAST) glimpse
of him as he ran." "The country was ruled by a *provisional*
(CHANGE) government."

19. CLEAN: The types of words scored here are:

a. Words referring to personal cleanliness and grooming:
toothbrush, comb, wash, towel, and *soap. "Scrub* (CLEAN)
behind your ears."

b. Words which refer to elimination of dirt: *purification, cleanliness, dusting,* and *laundry.* "She finished *mopping*
(CLEAN) the floor."

20. CLOTHING: All references to wearing apparel and things
pertinent to being clothed or dressed are scored here. In addition, related activities or references, such as *sew* and *darn,*
are scored here. Some clothing is clearly male, female, or
infant. In such cases the additional scoring of MALE, FE-
MALE, or YOUNG is applied. "His *trousers* (CLOTHING,
MALE) had to be altered." "She *wore* (CLOTHING)
a beautiful *dress* (CLOTHING, FEMALE)." "She changed
the baby's *diaper* (CLOTHING, YOUNG)."

21. COLD: All words in which the idea of coolness or coldness
is of importance are scored here. "It's *freezing* (COLD) in
here."

22. COLOR: All references to color and shades of color are
scored here, including black and white. Words like *brightness,
shading,* and *darkness* are scored. Related references suggesting
color such as *paint, lipstick,* and *rouge* are scored. Words like
orange and *rose* are scored COLOR if they clearly refer to
colors. Where such words are used to refer to the fruit, orange,
or to the plant, rose, they do not receive the COLOR scoring
but do receive whatever other scoring is applied. Other examples are words such as *ruby* and *emerald* which may refer
either to colors or to precious stones.

23. COMMERCE: All words referring to the business world,
commercial activity, trade, industry, and investment are scored
here. All references to the organized modes of production of

commodities, exchange of goods, and general business activities come under this heading. Direct references to money or money equivalents are scored under MONEY. "She went to *market* (COMMERCE)."

24. CONFINE: The types of words scored under this heading are:

    a. Words referring to blocking, interfering, restraints, or confinement. Included are words having to do with physical as well as with more nebulous limitations. "He ran up against a stone *wall* (CONFINE)."

    b. Words referring to shutting, closing, and locking. "They *sealed* (CONFINE) the opening with cement."

CONFLICT: This category contains three subdivisions which are scored separately. The subdivisions reflect a continuum of intensity of aggression. A number of words may at times have a CONFLICT meaning and at times not. The context determines whether or not they are scored here. Such words are: *blood, blow, break, burn, chop, crack, hammer, hit, knock, scald,* and so on. The basic criterion for scoring in this category is the presence of aggression or conflict. In some instances a given word will have a meaning appropriate either to 1, 2, or 3. The context will generally show the appropriate scoring.

25. CONFLICT 1 (HARM): These are words having to do with harm and hurting. Words bearing on violence and physical destruction are scored here, such as *army, gun, weapon, hit, violence, harm, injure, bloody,* and the like. Words relating to hazards, dangers, misfortunes, emergencies, and accidents are also scored here. Where the aggression or conflict expressed by a word is comparable to physical harm or hurting, this score is applied. "He was *wounded* (CONFLICT 1) by a *bullet* (CONFLICT 1)."

26. CONFLICT 2 (HATE): These are words having to do with aggressive feelings, verbal hostility, and hostile attitudes, and in which disadvantages, detriment, and insult are implied. Basically the affects of hating and disliking are involved here. Some words like *aggression, abuse,* and *attack* are scored either CONFLICT 1 (HARM) or CONFLICT 2 (HATE), depending on the context. "I *detest* (CONFLICT 2) spinach."

27. CONFLICT 3 (DISAGREE): Words referring to dissimilarity, differences, exceptions, and contests are scored here. Note that words which entail blocking or confining are scored under

CONFINE, although joint scoring is not precluded. In a number of instances (*oppose, contest, repudiate*) there may be difficulty in choosing between CONFLICT 2 (HATE) and CONFLICT 3 (DISAGREE). If the affective hostility is prominent, CONFLICT 2 (HATE) is appropriate. If the primary notion is that of dissimilarity or opposition, CON-FLICT 3 (DISAGREE) is scored. The adjective and pronoun *other(s)* is scored here, when the notion of difference or opposition is involved. "I beg to *differ* (CONFLICT 3)." "We must also look at the *other* (CONFLICT 3) side."

28. CRIME: Words with implications of illicitness and law-breaking are scored here. "He *robbed* (CRIME) the jewelry store."

29. CURE: This includes words which have to do with health or the recovery of health. Matters and agencies which bear on health or the recovery of health are scored here. However, words which have only an indirect bearing on the notion of health are not included (*exercise, nutrition, cleanliness*). Some of the specific areas of reference are:

   a. Doctors and specialties within the medical and related fields. Thus, *physician, nurse, surgeon, psychiatry, Freud, Lister,* and *orthopedic.* "She went to the *doctor* (CURE)."

   b. Institutions and places related to care and treatment of the ill, such as *hospital, ward,* or *clinic.* "He was placed in an *asylum* (CURE, HOLLOW 1)."

   c. Terms relating to treatment, cure, or care of illness, including the names of drugs: *therapy, aspirin, thorazine,* and *remedy.* "The *doctor* (CURE) prescribed *penicillin* (CURE)."

   d. Terms relating to a state of health or matters conducive to health: *health, hygiene, sanitary,* or *cure.* "He got *well* (CURE, GOOD) as a result of the *treatment* (CURE)."

30. DEAD: All references to death, dying, and related matters are scored here. In some cases an additional CONFLICT 1 (HARM) score may be appropriate, as in *murder.* "He *perished* (DEAD) in the fire."

31. DIFFICULT: This category covers words having to do with physical heaviness or weightiness, as well as words having to do with complexity, intricacy, and the quality of being problematic and difficult of solution.

   a. Weightiness: *heavy, burden,* and words relating to carrying or bearing where weightiness or heaviness of burden is implied. "He finds his task *onerous* (DIFFICULT)."

    b. Problematic: *intricate, complicated, impossible.* "This is a *complex* (DIFFICULT) *problem* (DIFFICULT)."

32. DIRTY: This includes all words involving filth, trash, dirt, excrement, wastes associated with dirtiness, decay, deterioration, impurity, or uncleanliness. Such words are *deteriorate, ruin,* and *rot.* "Her dress was *stained* (DIRTY)."

DOMINANCE: This category includes two major subdivisions, one referring to achievement, strength, and fame; the other to leadership. The two subdivisions are scored separately. The active voice of some verbs like *defeat* and *beat* will receive the DOMINANCE score, whereas the passive voice will receive the SUBMISSION score.

33. DOMINANCE 1 (STRONG):

    a. Words referring to ability, strength, capability, agility, aptitude, brilliance, braveness, energy, and skill. "I am *able* (DOMINANCE 1) to do that."

    b. Words relating to accomplishment, achievement, success, attainment, victory, winning, or being unbeatable. "He was *outstanding* (DOMINANCE 1) in his class."

    c. Names of great or famous men, such as *Beethoven, Einstein,* and *Freud.* Great men may also be scored under DOMINANCE 2 (LEAD). There the primary characteristic is greatness as a leader. Great names, other than those of leaders of men, ordinarily receive the DOMINANCE 1 (STRONG) score as the equivalent of *famous* and some other scoring indicating the area of fame. "*Tolstoy* (DOMINANCE 1, LANGUAGE 2) was a *great* (DOMINANCE 1, GOOD) writer."

34. DOMINANCE 2 (LEAD): Words are scored here which have to do with being a leader, or leading. Names of leaders such as *Roosevelt, Hitler, Eisenhower,* and *Christ* are scored here but may also receive some other scoring to indicate the area of leadership. Words scored here are those referring to the act of leading, commanding, directing, being an authority, or being a leader, as well as those referring to an area of dominion, a dynasty, or the location or area of dominance of the leader, for example, *kingdom.* In some instances there will be difficulty in choosing between DOMINANCE 1 (STRONG) and DOMINANCE 2 (LEAD). Words referring

primarily to achievement, fame, strength, victory, and so on
are scored DOMINANCE 1 (STRONG). Words which imply
lead or control are scored DOMINANCE 2 (LEAD). "He is
the *captain* (DOMINANCE 2) of the ship."

35. DOWN: This category is to be understood in conjunction with
UP. In general, words which have some reference to "down-
ness" or "upness" are scored under one of these categories.
Words in which there is an implicit reference to up and down
are scored in whichever category is appropriate and may be
scored both categories. Thus, a word like *suspend* is scored
DOWN, as having the implicit notion of *hang down; elevator*
is scored UP and DOWN since both of these notions are implied. Ordinarily one extreme, UP or DOWN, will be clearly
dominant. "The is the *bottom* (DOWN) of the barrel."

36. DRINK: All words referring to the activity of drinking and to
potables, as well as to containers where the drink reference is
clear, are scored here. "He was addicted to the *bottle* (DRINK,
HOLLOW 2)." SEA will often be a second scoring. "They
had *soda* (DRINK, SEA) at the party."

37. DURABLE: The types of words scored here are:
    a. Words referring to continuity, persistence, a continuing
    stretch of time, stability, changelessness, continuous recur-
    rence, endurance, eternity, and long-lastingness. An addi-
    tional TIME scoring is often appropriate. "He *still*
    (DURABLE, TIME 4) lives here."
    b. Words referring to the usual, customary, or habitual. "I'm
    used to (DURABLE) doing it this way."

38. EARTH: All references to terra firma are scored here. Aspects
of the terrain other than waterways are scored under EARTH.
References to valleys, mountains, hills, land, fields, countryside,
gardens, clods, stones, and rocks are scored here. Size of the
reference to terra firma is not important. Thus, *continent* and
plot (of land) are both scored here, as references to the solid
part of our geography. "The *ground* (EARTH) is soft."

39. EASY: This category is to be considered in conjunction with
the category DIFFICULT. The types of words scored here are:
    a. Words referring to lightness of weight. *"Weightlessness*
    (EASY) is a strange experience."
    b. Words having to do with simplicity, easiness, lack of com-
    plexity, or lack of difficulty. Sometimes there is overlap
    with TRIVIAL. In the EASY category there need not be

an element of unimportance. "The problem was *readily* (EASY) solved."

c. Words referring to physical (not psychological) states of softness and smoothness. "The jolt was *cushioned* (EASY) by the rubber wheels."

40. EAT: All words having to do with meals, eating, places of eating, and utensils are scored here. Certain rules for double scoring are to be observed. Wherever there is reference to meat, the scoring is EAT, ANIMAL. Thus, *chops, spare ribs, hamburger,* and so on are scored this way. Wherever there are references to vegetables or fruits, the double scoring is EAT, VEGETATION. When there is reference to seafood, the scoring is EAT, SEA. The scoring of a word such as *lamb* depends on its context. It may be EAT, ANIMAL, if the reference is to lamb as a food, or ANIMAL, YOUNG, if reference is to lamb as an animal. In the case of sea animals the food scoring is EAT, SEA, whereas other references to them are scored SEA, ANIMAL. Some examples are: "A *chicken* (ANIMAL, UP) ran across the road." "They had *chicken* (ANIMAL, EAT) for *supper* (EAT)." "There are many *fish* (ANIMAL, SEA) in the sea." "They had *fish* (EAT, SEA) for *lunch* (EAT)." "He had an *orange* (EAT, VEGETA-TION)." FUNCTION is an additional scoring where there is a clear reference to the process of chewing, eating, swallowing, digesting, or tasting. Oral activities like smoking and sucking are scored here, and pertinent references like *pipe, cigar,* and *cigarette* are also scored here. "The children *munched* (EAT, FUNCTION) on *crackers* (EAT)."

41. END: The types of words scored here are:
a. Words referring to stopping, ceasing, halting, or finishing. "The game is *over* (END)."
b. Words pertaining to an end point, a result, a goal, an outcome, or a destination. END and CONFINE sometimes overlap. END carries no necessary implication of a forced halting as CONFINE does. "He *completed* (END) his training."

42. ESSENTIAL: The types of words scored here are:
a. Words pertaining to the basic, fundamental, vital, or essential. "It was one of the *principal* (ESSENTIAL) points of his discussion."

b. Words pertaining to importance, urgency, seriousness, worth, or value. "This is a *crucial* (ESSENTIAL) matter."

43. FALSE: FALSE is the opposite of TRUE. The types of words scored here are:
   a. Words relating to errors, mistakes, and fallacies. "That is *untrue* (FALSE)."
   b. Words relating to deception, fraud, misrepresentation, hypocrisy, fooling others, lying, and distorting. "He *tricked* (FALSE) me."

44. FAR: The types of words scored here are:
   a. Words relating to distance as opposed to nearness. Included here also are words relating to the foreign or alien, as opposed to native and local. "He went *abroad* (FAR) for the summer."
   b. Words relating to unfamiliarity, strangeness, unusualness, or the esoteric. "It had a *curious* (FAR) texture."
   c. Words referring to rareness, such as *rarely* or *seldom*. An additional TIME score may be appropriate here. "I *seldom* (FAR, TIME 4) see him."

45. FAST: The types of words scored here are:
   a. Words having to do with speed, suddenness, quickness, or rapidity. An additional TIME scoring may be appropriate here. "Come here *immediately* (FAST, TIME 4)."
   b. Words having to do with action where there is a basic notion of rapidity. "He *hastened* (FAST) his work."
   c. Words having to do with awaking or being alert are also scored here, as opposites to the kind of words scored under SLOW. "He was *aroused* (FAST) by the sounds of fighting."

   The scoring GO may also appear with such words as *dash, hurry, hasten,* and *rush,* where the notion of going from one place to another is involved. "He *hastened* (GO, FAST) home."

46. FEATURE (BODY): References to visible or external parts of living things are scored here, such as parts or aspects of plants, humans, and animals. Parts of living things that are internal and not visible and references to body or vegetative functions are scored under FUNCTION (BODY). A double scoring sometimes helps make the scoring more pertinent. *Eye* is scored FEATURE (BODY), SEE; *fur* is scored FEATURE (BODY), ANIMAL; *leaf* is scored FEATURE

(BODY), VEGETATION. "He held her *hand* (FEA-TURE)." "The dog's *fur* (FEATURE, ANIMAL) was wet." "The *trunk* (FEATURE, VEGETATION) of the tree was huge."

47. FEMALE: The scoring FEMALE is applied where there are clear and significant references to femininity. Where the language itself implies a distinction between male and female, the appropriate scoring is made, as in: *prince,* MALE, DOMI-NANCE 2 (LEAD); *princess,* FEMALE, DOMINANCE 2 (LEAD). "He took a *girl* (FEMALE, YOUNG) to the movies." "*Miss* (FEMALE) Jones has just left."

48. FORWARD: Words scored here are those indicating priority, precedence, before, in front of, primary; and words relating to series and sequences. "He went *ahead* (FORWARD)." "They stood in a *row* (FORWARD)." The scoring GO may sometimes accompany these words, where physical movement forward is emphasized.

49. FUNCTION (BODY): All words having to do with body functions and internal body parts or vegetative processes are scored here. Words like *smell, aroma, odor, breathe, eat,* and *taste* are also scored here as referring to basically physiological activities. "His *heart* (FUNCTION) beat rapidly." "He *sniffed* (FUNCTION) the fresh air."

50. GO: Words suggesting physical movement from or to some-where are scored here, no matter what the medium of move-ment. Thus, *walk, come, run, fly, swim, take to, bring to, drive,* and *throw* are all scored here. In addition, words relating to paths, routes, and direction are scored here. The category SEPARATE frequently comes into play when there is a notion of leaving someone or something. Other categories are often scored along with GO. "They *went* (GO) to a movie." "The *road* (GO) was crooked." "He *left* (GO, SEPARATE) the country." "*Pass* (GO) the sugar."

51. GOOD: The types of words scored here are:
   a. Words relating to morality, honor, propriety, and civility. "He is a man of *character* (GOOD)."
   b. Words relating to admirable or good qualities, such as *beauty, grace, marvelous, magnificent,* and *fine.* "That was an *excellent* (GOOD) performance."

52. GROUP: Often the words under this heading receive double

scorings. The words scored under GROUP involve reference to a group, gathering, or bunch of people or things. "A *committee* (GROUP) was formed for the dance." "There is a beautiful *cluster* (GROUP) of roses." References to political parties and organizations of people are scored here such as: the *Democrats,* the *Indians,* and the *French. "Liberals* (GROUP) would oppose this legislation."

53. HAPPENING: This category contains words, generally of a somewhat abstract nature, referring to events, behavior, and conditions. There are three subdivisions.

    a. Events: included would be words such as *incident, occurrence,* and *affair.* "A historic *event* (HAPPENING) has just *transpired* (HAPPENING)."

    b. Behavior: included would be words like *deed, do, bearing, manner,* and *reaction.* "His *conduct* (HAPPENING) leaves much to be desired." Note that special care must be exercised with the verb *to do.* Where it has a primarily grammatical function as an auxiliary verb, it is not scored. *"Did* (NO SCORE) you hear me?" However: "I *did* (HAPPENING) what I was supposed to."

    c. Condition: included would be words such as *situation, circumstances,* and *state.* "She was in a *state* (HAPPENING) of agitation."

54. HEAR: All words having some aural reference are scored here. Words having to do with music and musical instruments are also scored. Words like *quiet, silent,* and *still* are scored, even though there is an implication of absence of sound. "The *noise* (HEAR) was unbearable." "He is taking *piano* (HEAR, PLAY) lessons." "There was a momentary *hush* (HEAR)." Where the notion of hearing is not central, this scoring is not applied, as in many references to spoken language where the act of hearing is necessitated but is not a central reference. Thus, *speaking, saying, telling,* and *conversation* are not scored HEAR.

55. HELP: This category includes words which indicate assisting, nurturing, aiding, benefiting, coddling, reassuring, and protecting. The scoring applies to words which indicate giving or receiving gratification or benefit, providing or receiving protection, and giving or receiving assistance. A distinction from the category CALM is required. Words referring to emotions

such as *joy, delight,* and *happiness,* although the implication may be that the emotions are contingent on being helped or gratified, are scored under CALM.

Words like *give, present, offer, let, permit, provide,* and *allow* are scored HELP since they ordinarily have the implication of giving, permitting, or helping. "He *allowed* (HELP) me to enter the building." "He sought *asylum* (HELP) at the American Embassy."

There are some instances in which the HELP notion occurs without direct reference to another person, for example: "He was *helped* (HELP) by the turn of events." The category which stands in opposition to HELP is CONFLICT 1 (HARM).

56. HILL: The types of words scored here are:
   a. Words referring to fullness, turgidity, overloading, or surcharge. "A *pile* (HILL) of twigs accumulated."
   b. Words referring to protrusions, such as *hill, cliff, promontory, prominent,* or *salient.* "A huge rock *juts* (HILL) from the side of the *cliff* (HILL, EARTH)."

HOLLOW: Two scorings distinguish two types of words:

57. HOLLOW 1 (DWELLINGS): All words referring to rooms, offices, dwellings, caves, nests, and surroundings where men or animals live or work. "This is my *room* (HOLLOW 1)." "Bees live in a *hive* (HOLLOW 1, ANIMAL)."

58. HOLLOW 2 (OBJECTS):
   a. Words referring to hollow objects within which things are or may be put: *pot, mouth, womb, stomach, cup, bathtub,* or *pocket.* "Put the groceries in the *bag* (HOLLOW 2)."
   b. Words referring to emptiness: *blank, hollow, empty, vacuous,* and *gap.* "The town was *deserted* (HOLLOW 2)."
   c. Words with reference to surroundings or including other things: *circle* and *envelope.* "There was a *ring* (HOLLOW 2) of trees *around* (HOLLOW 2) the field."

59. HOT: All words referring to heat and warmth are scored here, such as *fire, boil,* and *burn.* Certain words that carry strong implications of heat, such as *sun* and *summer,* get this scoring even though they may have another scoring. "It was a *scorching* (HOT) day." "I hate to *cook* (HOT, EAT)." "*Summer* (HOT, TIME 4) is coming."

60. HOUSEHOLD: This refers to items typically furnishing a household such as *table, chair, lamp, couch,* and *furniture.*

The things referred to may often be found in other places as well as in households, but the basis of scoring is the reference to something typically found in a home. Words like *house, room,* and *home* are scored under HOLLOW 1 (DWELLINGS). "It was a bright colored *carpet* (HOUSEHOLD)."

61. ILLNESS: Words clearly referring to illness, infection, disease, and malady are scored here. Mental and physical illnesses are included, and disabilities such as blindness, deafness, and lameness are also scored. In general, all deviations from a state of health and normality are scored ILLNESS. "He suffered from a *neurosis* (ILLNESS)." "As a result of the accident, he was *crippled* (ILLNESS)."

62. IN: This category is limited to words indicating being physically in something, the act of entering, absorption, or being directed inward. The important feature of the category is the physical *in* and the physical orientation toward in. The preposition in gives the greatest difficulty in scoring under this heading. The preposition is scored only when there is a clear allusion to being inside something. The following are examples of uses of *in* which are not scored: *in case of, in respect to, in spite of, in my opinion,* and *in theory*. The following are examples of uses of *in* which are scored: "She is *in* (IN) the house." "The cake is *in* (IN) the oven."

63. INDIVIDUAL: The types of words scored here are:
   a. Reference to self, egocentricity, selfishness, subjectivity, aloneness, and singleness. All these are references to the state of being alone or single. "He led an *isolated* (INDIVIDUAL, SEPARATE) life."
   b. References to a single thing or individual where the quality of singleness is important as: *a character, a party, a person,* and *someone*. "He was the *sole* (INDIVIDUAL) inhabitant of the island."
   c. The word *one* presents special problems. Where *one* is used as a number it receives only the NUMBER scoring. "*One* (NUMBER) and *one* (NUMBER) are two." Where *one* is used as an indefinite pronoun or adjective it receives the INDIVIDUAL scoring as: "*One* (INDIVIDUAL) must go his own way." "*One* (INDIVIDUAL) man's meat is *another* (INDIVIDUAL) man's poison." Where *one* is used in a pronoun sense with a specifiable noun referent, it receives the scoring of the noun. In such cases *one* is scored

either as NUMBER or INDIVIDUAL as well as receiving the scores of the noun to which it refers. "The boy had two *apples* (VEGETATION, EAT) and gave *one* (NUMBER, VEGETATION, EAT) away." "I like this *painting* (COLOR, ART), but this *one* (INDIVIDUAL, COLOR, ART) is better." In some instances both the NUMBER and INDIVIDUAL scoring may be applied, where *one* as quantity is involved but the idea of singleness or individuality is also important. Thus, "They spoke as with *one* (INDIVIDUAL, NUMBER) voice."

64. JOIN: Types of words scored under this heading are:
   a. Words referring to coming together, meeting, visiting, joining, accompanying, marrying, associating, allying, becoming related, or uniting. The word *with* is often a key to this category. "They had a *rendezvous* (JOIN) at noon." "I went *with* (JOIN) him to the theatre." "We *met* (JOIN) briefly *with* (JOIN) them."
   b. Words referring to family relationships like *cousin, brother, sister,* and *uncle.* Some kinship words ordinarily do not include the JOIN scoring where certain other scoring features are more important. Thus, *father* is scored MALE, DOMINANCE 2 (LEAD); and *mother* is scored FEMALE, HELP. Ordinarily a MALE or FEMALE scoring accompanies the JOIN scoring where the sex of the kin is clearly indicated. Thus, *brother* is scored MALE, JOIN, but *cousin* is simply scored JOIN. "My *aunt* (FEMALE, JOIN) came to visit us with her *nephew* (MALE, JOIN)."
   c. Words referring to things bound, tied, hooked, stuck, and magnetized to each other. "He *glued* (JOIN) his model airplane *together* (JOIN)."
   d. Words referring to physical contact, such as *touch, pat,* or *shake* (hands). *"Tap* (JOIN) him on the shoulder."

LANGUAGE: This category includes all references to language communication and implements and to linguistic things. It is divided into two major categories which are to be scored separately; one having to do with spoken and the other with written language.

65. LANGUAGE 1 (SPEAK): Words scored here involve reference to use of the voice, animal or human. In many instances it may not be clear whether vocal or written language usage is being referred to; in these instances the scoring is LAN-

GUAGE 1 (SPEAK). Included in this scoring are all references to instruments and devices usually used for vocal communication, such as *microphone, intercom,* and *telephone.* In some instances there may be a choice between the scorings LANGUAGE 1 (SPEAK) and HEAR, and, in some cases, both are used. Where verbal communication is involved, the preferred scoring is LANGUAGE 1 (SPEAK). Where aural aspects of the reference are important, HEAR is scored. Thus *radio* is scored HEAR, since music as well as speech may be transmitted and since listening is an important feature of the reference. "He gave a *verbal* (LANGUAGE 1) *report* (LANGUAGE 1) to the chief." "They were awakened by the *barking* (LANGUAGE 1, HEAR) of a dog." Both LANGUAGE 1 (SPEAK) and LANGUAGE 2 (WRITE) may be scored in some instances: "The teacher *read* (LANGUAGE 1, LANGUAGE 2) to the class." "He *read* (LANGUAGE 2, SEE) a *book* (LANGUAGE 2)."

66. LANGUAGE 2 (WRITE): All references to written language, to instruments of writing, and to written or printed documents come under this heading. The reference must be clearly to writing or to something written. Many words are scored either LANGUAGE 1 (SPEAK) or LANGUAGE 2 (WRITE) depending on their context. Thus, "The *words* (LANGUAGE 2) were in bold *print* (LANGUAGE 2)." "He *enunciated* (LANGUAGE 1) his *words* (LANGUAGE 1) carefully." Some other examples of the scoring of LANGUAGE 2 (WRITE) are: "Here is a *pencil* (LANGUAGE 2) and a *pen* (LANGUAGE 2)." "The *book* (LANGUAGE 2) sold well."

67. LAW: The types of words included here are:
    a. Words referring to law, courts, suits, and legal action and related words. "He passed the *bar* (LAW) examination."
    b. Words referring to law enforcement, as *police, FBI, detective,* and *cop.* "Many *gendarmes* (LAW) were at the parade."
    c. Words referring to constitutional procedures and legislation, such as *constitution* and *charter.* "The *bill* (LAW, LANGUAGE 2) was signed into *law* (LAW)."

68. LITTLE: This category includes words referring to smallness, brevity, and diminution. In some instances there may be a problem of choice between LITTLE and SOME. The category LITTLE comes into play where the quality of being small or

less is important. "He was a *short* (LITTLE) fellow." "There was a *decrease* (LITTLE) in earnings for 1961."

69. LIVING: Words included here are:

a. References to life, mortality, immortality, and existence. "They believed in the *survival* (LIVING) of the fittest."

b. References to dwelling, inhabiting, residing, and subsisting. "He *lived* (LIVING) at a hotel."

70. MALE: The scoring of MALE is given only where there is a distinct and significant reference to maleness. In instances where maleness is present but not a significant feature of the references it is *not* scored as: "Roosevelt was president." While *Roosevelt* is obviously male, the MALE scoring is not applied. Where the language itself implies a distinction, MALE is scored, as: *prince,* MALE, DOMINANCE 2 (LEAD); *king,* MALE, DOMINANCE 2 (LEAD). "The *stallion* (MALE, ANIMAL) was kept in the barn."

71. MATERIAL: References to basic materials or simple materials out of which other products are made are scored here. In some instances there may be a second scoring. These are useful basic or raw materials, or simple products which in turn are useful in daily life. An additional scoring may be EARTH, ANIMAL, VEGETATION, or other, depending on the origins of the material. "*Iron* (MATERIAL, EARTH) is an important *metal* (MATERIAL)." "*Leather* (MATERIAL, ANIMAL) has many uses." "*Cotton* (MATERIAL, VEGETATION) comes from the South." "Many toys are made of *plastic* (MATERIAL)."

72. MECHANISM: Words scored here refer to mechanical devices, gadgets, and mechanized instruments. Since a large range of objects may be regarded as mechanisms, this scoring will usually be employed either as a second scoring or where no other scoring seems applicable. "The *motor* (MECHANISM) burned out." "The *machinery* (MECHANISM) is oiled every week." "She is skilled on the *typewriter* (MECHANISM, LANGUAGE 2)."

73. MEASUREMENT: Words scored here include measures of length, of weight, and of quantity, as well as references to instruments of measurement. Words in this category are usually specific dimensions of length, weight, and quantity. Numbers as such are scored under NUMBER and not under MEASUREMENT. "He walked a *mile* (MEASUREMENT)." "He

drank a *pint* (MEASUREMENT) of ale." "She handed the boy a *ruler* (MEASUREMENT)."

74. MONEY: All direct mentions of money or money equivalents and all references to activities directly involving money, such as buying and selling, are scored here. "He *paid* (MONEY) for whatever he *bought* (MONEY, POSSESS) in *cash* (MONEY)."

75. NEAR: The types of words under this heading are:

   a. Words having to do with nearness: *close by, in the presence of, in the vicinity of, almost,* and *nearly.* "He sat *by* (NEAR) the bed."

   b. Words having to do with familiarity, domesticity, being known, and being local (in the sense of familiar). The opposite notion is contained in the category FAR. "He lives in the *neighborhood* (NEAR)." "I am *acquainted* (NEAR) with him."

   c. Words having to do with imminence, the immediate future, or the immediate past. Such words usually receive an additional TIME scoring. "I *just* (NEAR, TIME 2) saw the article." "We expect him *soon* (NEAR, TIME 3)."

76. NEGATION: Words like *no* and *not* are scored here. The idea of negation is sometimes indistinguishable from the idea of opposition. It also often conveys the notion of absence of something. In the various uses of negation, there may be distinctly different references, as shown in these examples: "I do *not* know." "I have *nothing.*" "This is *not* like that." "Are you coming?" *"No."* The core idea in this category is that of negation, the opposite of *yes.* Some aspects of the scoring are described below.

   a. *No* and *not* must be examined in connection with the words they modify. The negative, the word modified, and the vector arising from the negation should all be scored. Thus, in "This is *not like* that," the scoring of *not like* would be NEGATION, AGREE 3 (SIMILARITY), CONFLICT 3 (DISAGREE). However, a scorable vector does not always arise out of the combination of a negative and another word. Thus, in "I am *not going,*" the idea of staying is not necessarily implied and *not going* would simply be scored NEGATION, GO. *Can't* and *not able,* in such uses as "He *can't* swim as far as I," and "I am *not able* to lift that weight," where there is clear indication of inability, are scored

NEGATION, SUBMISSION 1 (WEAK) without separating out the DOMINANCE 1 (STRONG) score which would ordinarily be given to *can* and *able.*

The pronoun *none* presents a problem like the pronoun *one* (see INDIVIDUAL). In this case the NEGATION scoring is given to the pronoun, plus the scoring of the nouns to which it refers.

b. The negative may convey absence. "I have *none* (NEGATION)." "There is *nothing* (NEGATION) in the refrigerator."

Words like *unlike, dislike, contraindicated,* which stress the opposition idea, are not scored NEGATION. The hallmark of NEGATION is the use of some variant of *no.* Such words are: *never, naught, neither, no, none, nothing, negative, negate,* and *deny.*

c. Where *no* is used alone as a response, it is scored only NEGATION and not CONFLICT 3 (DISAGREE), as: "Are you ready?" "*No* (NEGATION)."

77. NUMBER: Any reference to a number, big or small, is scored NUMBER. Thus, *two, 2, two hundred and ten,* and *210* all get the scoring NUMBER. In addition, references to numerical operations and numerical quantities where number is not definitely specified, as well as references to instruments related to numerical or mathematical matters, are scored here. Another scoring may sometimes be used. Thus, *subtraction* is scored NUMBER, SEPARATE; *addition* is scored NUMBER, BIG; *calculus* is scored NUMBER, REASON 3 (SCIENCE); and *computation* is scored NUMBER. "The *figures* (NUMBER) *6* (NUMBER) and *300* (NUMBER) are to be *squared* (NUMBER, BIG)."

78. OPEN: The types of words scored here are:

a. Those relating to discovering, finding, revealing, bringing to light, making public, being obvious, or being evident. "The *apparent* (OPEN) difference between them was dispelled by discussion."

b. Those relating to freedom, escape, and liberty. "When will he obtain his *release* (OPEN, SEPARATE)?"

c. A physical or metaphorical opening or being open. "The door was *ajar* (OPEN)."

79. OUT: The kinds of words under this category are:

a. Words having reference to out, exit, or external. These

words generally have the prefix *out-,* or *ex-.* "The *exterior* (OUT) was painted green."

b. Words referring to an emanation, exudation, or an issuance of something outward. Where the notion of something issuing from a container or a body is clear, the OUT scoring is appropriate. In some instances there may be doubt as to whether the SEPARATE scoring is more appropriate. OUT and SEPARATE may be applied together. "He was *ejected* (OUT, SEPARATE) by the guards."

80. PLACE: All place names of locations and references to geographical places or areas are scored here. Names of buildings or arenas are not scored here, even though they may be closely tied up with geographical places. Names of places which are phrases receive special consideration. The individual words are scored independently, and the phrase as a whole gets the score PLACE. Where one of the words in the phrase ordinarily gets the PLACE score, the over-all phrase is not scored PLACE in addition. "He lives in *France* (PLACE)." "The *French* (PLACE, GROUP) are a temperamental people." "What *city* (PLACE) do you come from?" "He lives on *Old* (TIME 1) *Green* (COLOR) *Street* (PLACE)." "They went to the *Canary* (ANIMAL, UP) *Islands* (EARTH, SEA, PLACE)."

In addition to place names, words such as *place* (verb and noun), *locate* (as in "He decided to *locate* his shop on a busy corner"), *location,* and *area* are scored here.

81. PLAY: All words are scored here which have to do with holidays, vacation, sports, parties, and entertainment. In general, the notion of recreation is involved, and any pertinent activities or media are scored. "Let's have a *game* (PLAY) of *baseball* (PLAY)." "They went to the *carnival* (PLAY)." "*Bing Crosby* (PLAY, DOMINANCE 1) is a well-known *actor* (PLAY, MALE)."

82. POSSESS: In this category the distinctive thing is having, gathering, holding, possessing, maintaining, or keeping something. The verbs *to have, to get,* and *to take* are to be scored with care. These verbs are scored POSSESS only where there is a reference to possession as: "I *have* (POSSESS) an idea." "I've *got* (POSSESS) two dollars." In addition there should be the notion that possession is by someone. Thus, in the example, "A pile of twigs *accumulated,*" *accumulated* would not

be scored POSSESS, but in "He *accumulated* (POSSESS) a fortune" it would.

REASON: This category is divided into three major headings. The appropriate subdivision is to be scored.

83. REASON 1 (COGNITION): Words suggesting rational cognitive processes, such as *thinking, knowing, analyzing, explaining, understanding,* or *remembering.* "They *considered* (REASON 1) the problem very carefully." Cognitive processes where wants or needs are involved are scored only under WANT.

84. REASON 2 (EDUCATION): Words pertaining to education, school, learning, training, and teaching. "He *taught* (REASON 2) the eighth *grade* (REASON 2)."

85. REASON 3 (SCIENCE): Words pertaining to organized bodies of knowledge and to activities and operations involving the organization of knowledge. Words like *mathematics, science, physics,* and *philosophy* are scored here. "He *studied* (REASON 2) *biology* (REASON 3, FUNCTION)." Words which refer to a body of skills rather than of knowledge (*carpentry, cooking*) are not scored here.

86. SACRED: The words scored here refer to religion, religious things, religious concepts, religious activity, and God or god figures in any religion whatever. "They *worshipped* (SACRED, AGREE 1) *Allah* (SACRED, DOMINANCE 2)." "He read his *Bible* (SACRED, LANGUAGE 2)."

87. SEA: The types of words scored here are:
a. Words referring to bodies of water and related things, such as *sea, ocean, ship, navy, beach, island,* and *harbor.* "This *stream* (SEA, GO) *flows* (SEA, GO) to the *ocean* (SEA)." "They took a *ferry* (TRANSPORTATION, SEA) to Staten *Island* (SEA, EARTH)."
b. Words referring to liquids as: *liquid, water, drop, rain, wet, damp, drizzle,* and *pour.* "He fell in a *puddle* (SEA)."

88. SEE: All words which have a visual implication are scored here. Words having to do with seeing, such as *sight, glasses, goggles, eyes, blindness,* and *pupils* (of eyes) are scored. Words having to do with being visible, such as *appearing, scene, view,* and *manifestation,* are scored where there is a definite visual suggestion. Words having to do with vanishing, disappearing, or being invisible are scored here also, in cases where visual implications are present. "He was frightened by an *apparition*

(SEE, UNREAL)." "The *lens* (SEE) of this *camera* (SEE) is broken." *"Look* (SEE) at these *photos* (SEE)." "An *unseen* (SEE) force works for our benefit."

89. SELF-REFERENCE: All uses of the first-person pronoun are scored here, whether singular or plural. An additional scoring is made if the self-reference pronoun has some other pertinent noun scoring. *"I* (SELF-REFERENCE) am going out." "They didn't invite *us* (SELF-REFERENCE)." Since this category inevitably appears with great frequency in autobiographical and personal accounts, and is usually totally absent in other-person and impersonal accounts, its general usefulness is dubious.

90. SEPARATE: The kinds of words which are scored here are:
   a. Words which have to do with splitting or cutting things apart: *split, fission, break, dissect,* and *sever.* "Cut (SEPARATE, SHARP 1) a piece of bread for me."
   b. Words having to do with someone or something being separate, being removed from, or leaving someone or something else: *deserted, left* (He *left* his wife), *forsake, apart, aloof,* or *isolated.* "He ran *from* (SEPARATE) the scene." "He fell *off* (SEPARATE) the horse."
      In this category the prepositions *from* and *off* are often the key to the separation idea.

91. SEX: All words with sexual implications are scored here, whether homosexual or heterosexual. Words having to do with sexually directed relationships between people are also scored here, such as *marriage, wife, husband, petting, kissing, love* (when there is a suggestion of sexual love), and *dating.* "His intentions were *amorous* (SEX, AGREE 1)."

SHARP: Two basic groups are to be differentiated and scored separately.

92. SHARP 1 (SHARP): Words having to do with:
   a. Sharp edges, points, and cutting, such as *knife, pierce,* and *needle.* In these words the suggestion of the point or cutting edge is prominent. "He *trimmed* (SHARP 1, CLEAN) the hedges with garden *shears* (SHARP 1)."
   b. Words having to do with precision, unequivocality, directness, accuracy, definiteness, or clarity. "His meaning was *clear* (SHARP 1, OPEN)." "This is an *exact* (SHARP 1) copy of the original chair."
   c. Words having to do with focusing, concentrating, or center-

ing upon some limited area or point. "He *aimed* (SHARP 1) at the *target* (SHARP 1)."

93. SHARP 2 (EMPHASIS): Words having to do with emphasis, either by referring to emphasis or accentuation or by providing, adverbially, an emphasis. Thus words like *accentuate* and *emphasis,* as well as words like *emphatically, absolutely,* and *downright,* are scored here. "He is *very* (SHARP 2) smart." "He *stressed* (SHARP 2) cooperation among all groups."

94. SLOW: The types of words scored here are:
   a. Words having to do with waiting, immobility, standing still, sitting, quiescence, slow motion, gradualness, hesitation, pausing, or laziness. "The boat *drifted* (SLOW, GO) aimlessly." "The children *squatted* (SLOW) on the ground." "They *posed* (SLOW) for pictures."
   b. Words having to do with sleeping, hibernation, resting, lying down, unconsciousness, or sedatives. "He *dozed* (SLOW) in the chair." "His *repose* (SLOW) was interrupted."

95. SOME: This category is to be considered in conjunction with the category ALL. Words scored here refer to:
   a. A part of a whole, a portion, a segment, or a phase in a larger process. "This is one *element* (SOME) in a larger picture."
   b. An unspecified quantity such as *several, some,* or *few.* "An *amount* (SOME) of money was due him." Words scored here sometimes get an additional NUMBER scoring. "Only a *fraction* (SOME, NUMBER) of the populace voted."
   c. Events that are not frequent or that are not highly probable. Such words as *occasional* and *sometimes* are scored here. The TIME scoring may be appropriate in some instances. Words referring to highly infrequent events are to be scored under FAR. "It is *possible* (SOME) but not likely."

96. STRUCTURE: Words scored under this heading have to do with structures, constructions, arranging, building, configurations, ordering, and organizing. Any words which suggest an organized, structured arrangement or configuration are scored here, such as *cross, circle, frame, outline, skeleton, organization, hierarchy,* or *architecture.* Since this is a category which may apply to a large number of different references, it should not be given preference where other meaningful scorings are available. "He works in an *orderly* (STRUCTURE) fashion." "He *arranged* (STRUCTURE) his material efficiently."

SUBMISSION: This major category is to be understood in conjunction with the category DOMINANCE. There are two subdivisions, paralleling those for DOMINANCE, which are scored separately. Note that the active voice of many verbs will be scored DOMINANCE, but the passive voice will receive the SUBMISSION score.

97. SUBMISSION 1 (WEAK): Words referring to defeat, failure, inability, incapacity, awkwardness and ineptness, delicacy, innocence, shyness, or humbleness. *"Faint* (SUBMISSION 1) heart never won fair lady." "He was *beaten* (SUBMISSION 1) in chess."

98. SUBMISSION 2 (INFERIOR): Words indicating subjection or inferior position, being controlled or manipulated, such as *slave, follower, subject, satellite, disciple,* or *puppet.* Note that words referring to physical following are scored BACK. "He had his *subordinate* (SUBMISSION 2) do the minor work."

TIME: This is a general heading including four types of words. The appropriate subheading is to be scored. Grammatical tense is not scored.

99. TIME 1 (PAST): The types of words scored here are:
   a. Those having to do with past time, either recent or distant. "In the *early* (TIME 1) *days* (TIME 4) of our country there was no established law." "He left a *minute* (TIME 4) *ago* (TIME 1)."
   b. Those having to do with oldness. "That is an *ancient* (TIME 1) story."
   c. Those having to do with history, for example, *Reformation, Renaissance,* and *Middle Ages. "Paleolithic* (TIME 1) man used stone implements."

100. TIME 2 (PRESENT): Two types of words are scored here.
   a. Words like *current, present, now,* and *today. "These* (TIME 2) *days* (TIME 4) we do it differently."
   b. Words having to do with freshness, novelty, newness, and modernity. "These are the *latest* (TIME 2) fashions."

101. TIME 3 (FUTURE): Words referring to future time are scored here. *"Tomorrow* (TIME 3) is another *day* (TIME 4)."

102. TIME 4 (GENERAL TIME): Any reference to time in general, periods of time, seasons, clock time, or time of day is scored here. "The *hour* (TIME 4) went quickly." "It took an

age (TIME 4) for him to go." "*Spring* (TIME 4) is here." "I will be here at *eight* (TIME 4, NUMBER)."

103. TRANSPORTATION: All words referring to vehicles of transportation are scored here as *car, train, airplane, bus, bicycle,* or *ship.* Animal words are not scored here even though the reference is to the animal as a means of transportation. Where parts or aspects of vehicles are referred to they are scored TRANSPORTATION only if used in a synecdochic (part-for-whole) manner. Thus, "They went by *rail* (TRANSPORTATION) to California." Words referring directly to parts of vehicles, and not in any metaphoric sense, either receive some other scoring appropriate to them, such as MECHANISM, or are not scored. Thus, "The *wing* (STRUCTURE, UP) of the *airplane* (TRANSPORTATION, UP) was covered with frost." "The *motor* (MECHANISM) of the *Buick* (TRANSPORTATION) was overhauled."

TRIVIAL: This category includes two types of words which are distinguished in the scoring.

104. TRIVIAL 1 (UNIMPORTANCE): Words having to do with triviality, cheapness, superficiality, insignificance, lack of value, or unimportance. In some instances NEGATION is also scored, as in "It is *nothing* (TRIVIAL 1, NEGATION)."

105. TRIVIAL 2 (DE-EMPHASIS): Words used to minimize or de-emphasize, such as *hardly, scarcely,* or *mere.* These are in contrast to emphatic words scored under SHARP 2 (EMPHASIS). "It is *only* (TRIVIAL 2) a scratch."

106. TRUE: The types of words which are scored here are:
   a. Words referring to truth, correctness, rightness, sincerity, and the quality of being bona fide. "The *authenticity* (TRUE) of the documents was *verified* (TRUE) by an expert."
   b. Words referring to proof, confirmation, validation, or verification. "This will be a *test* (TRUE) of endurance."

107. UNREAL: The kinds of words which are scored here are:
   a. Words referring to the supernatural, magic, fortune-telling, conjuring, and seers. "The *medium* (UNREAL) gazed into the crystal ball."
   b. Words referring to visions, hallucinations, dreams, fantasies, imagined events, and illusions. "He saw a *ghost* (UNREAL)."

108. UP: The types of references included here are:

a. All references to up, above, over, top, summit, height, tower, and in general all references to the direction "up" and to things which usually are associated with the direction "up." The word *up* is always scored here, even where its use does not seem primarily a reference to the direction "up." Thus, "They took *up* (UP) the matter at the conference." "They *climbed* (UP, GO) the mountain."

b. References to astronomical phenomena, such as *planet, stars, sky, space,* and *heavens,* where UP would not preclude some other significant score. "The *sky* (UP, ASTRONOMY 1) is blue today."

c. All references to flight, things flown, pilots, rockets, and birds. "He *soars* (UP, GO) through the *air* (UP, ASTRONOMY 1) with the greatest of ease."

109. UPSET: Words scored here refer to a state of disarray or an upset state of mind in which anxiety, guilt, or emotional upset in a broad sense is suggested. Words with primarily aggressive overtones are scored under CONFLICT. In addition, words like *trouble* are scored here. "He was *alarmed* (UPSET) over the state of affairs." "I'm *concerned* (UPSET) about his welfare."

110. VEGETATION: References to growing things other than animals are scored here. "There are many *trees* (VEGETATION) in the *forest* (VEGETATION)."

WANT: Two subdivisions are distinguished in the scoring, one of them relating to wishes, rights, preferences, and obligations, the second relating to being without something or not possessing something. The second subdivision is essentially the opposite of the category POSSESS.

111. WANT 1 (NEED): This subdivision refers to needs, wishes, choices, predilections, options, privileges, tendencies, and inclinations. The essential feature of the category is a will, a wish, an aspiration, a hope, an obligation, or a readiness for; any words indicating a choice or preference or feeling (inclination) would come under this heading. Emotions and feelings not scored under UPSET, CALM, or elsewhere may be scored here. "I *would like* (WANT 1, AGREE 1) to go." "I think I will *choose* (WANT 1) the blue hat." "He had difficulty in expressing *affect* (WANT 1)."

112. WANT 2 (ABSENCE): Words relating to a lack of something, such as *lose, missing, without, bereft,* and the like,

are scored under this subdivision. "This is a *homeless* (WANT 2, HOLLOW 1) man." "I *haven't* (POSSESS, NEGATION, WANT 2) any funds."

Words relating to physical and body needs receive a double scoring depending on the particular body need. Thus, *hunger* is scored WANT 1, EAT; *lust* is scored WANT 1, SEX.

113. WORK: All references to working and making things which involve work, labor, simple tools of labor, and types of work come under this heading. The paradigm activity is physical labor, and included are activities with marked expenditure of physical energy such as *exercise* and *exertion*. "He had a *job* (WORK) *shoveling* (WORK) snow."

114. YOUNG: Words suggesting youth, youthfulness, adolescence, infancy, and immaturity are scored here. "She is an attractive *girl* (FEMALE, YOUNG)." "The *children* (YOUNG) love to play."

GENERAL RULES AND CONSIDERATIONS IN SCORING

1. *Compound words.* Words like *nighttime* (TIME 4, TIME 4), *basketball* (HOLLOW 2, PLAY), and *sunrise* (ASTRONOMY 1, HOT, GO, UP) are broken apart into constituent words for scoring, with each constituent getting the scoring appropriate to it. An additional scoring applicable to the total compound may be appropriate if different from any of the subscorings. Some clarification is provided if compounds are regarded as occurring twice, once as made up of separate words, and once as a unitary word. If the scoring which would be appropriate to the unitary word has not occurred in any of the subdivisions, the unitary word is scored again with the additional categories. Thus, "It was a stout *merchantman* (COMMERCE, MALE and SEA, TRANSPORTATION)," and "There was a large *turnout* (GO, CHANGE, OUT and GROUP) for the game." "You are a *two-faced* (NUMBER, FEATURE and FALSE) liar."

Nida (1951) has given a discussion of combinations, describing, for example, *applesauce* and *blackbird* as structurally endocentric because the complex forms have substantially the same linguistic distribution as their head constituents, *-sauce* and *-bird;* and *upset* and *setup* as structurally exocentric because the distribution of these forms is different from that of the head constituent *-set*.

Applesauce, as the name of a food, is semantically endocentric, but as an exclamation of disbelief it is exocentric. In this latter case, *applesauce* has two macrosemes, endocentric and exocentric, and in the present system would be scored in the manner of *merchantman* and *turnout.* As a food, *applesauce* would be categorized VEGETATION, EAT, EAT. As an exclamation, it would be categorized VEGETATION, EAT, EAT, and ABSURD.

Words like *butterfly* and *sweetbread* cannot reasonably be broken into their constituent forms for separate assignment of meanings. Such words would be exocentric in Nida's description. Whether or not a word is broken into its components for purposes of categorization depends on a judgment of how intimately the components have become welded into a unit which no longer has the characteristics of the components as separate items. Usually, in a combination that can be broken apart, one of the words conveys the essential characteristic of the thing referred to and the second word provides some additional discriminative feature. In combinations that ought not to be broken apart, dividing the combination leaves one with words neither of which conveys an essential characteristic of the thing referred to.

Words which, by a prefix or suffix, convey an opposition to their head word, such as *blameless, unlike,* or *dislike,* are scored with regard to their total meaning rather than their component units, as if they were inseparable compounds like *butterfly* and *sweetbread.* Thus *blameless* would be given the category GOOD, *unlike* would be scored CONFLICT 3 (DISAGREE), and *dislike* would be scored CONFLICT 2 (HATE).

2. *Phrases and idiomatic expressions.* Such expressions as "hit the sack," "pass the buck," "kick the bucket," "cross the Rubicon," in which a distinct meaning over and above the ordinary reference of the individual words is conveyed, are usually still analyzable by individual word. Thus, in "hit the sack," *hit* may be seen as carrying the meaning GO, as in "We *hit* New York at midnight," and *sack* may be seen as an equivalent of *sleeping bag,* and accordingly scored SLOW, HOLLOW 2 (OBJECTS). Sometimes, such as in the phrase *"kick* (GO, DEAD) the *bucket* (HOLLOW 2)," an additional meaning (DEAD for *kick*) must be added to convey the idea of the phrase. Usually other expressions in which the same word has a similar meaning will come to mind. Thus, *kick* may have the DEAD meaning in such sentences as: "The old man was about to *kick off.*"

In instances where a meaning is implied but not explicitly stated, it is difficult to capture the meaning. Thus, in "Flags were flown at *half-mast*," the implication of mourning is implicit but must be lost in the scoring.

3. *Proper names and titles.* The use of ordinary words in proper names and titles presents a problem for categorizing as in: "He lives on *Big Oak Drive*," and *"War and Peace* is a great novel." *Big Oak Drive* may be regarded simply as a place name, or it may be regarded as a place name made of words with still significant reference in their own right; *War and Peace* could be identified as a title, or as a title with very specific content words. In other instances, the name has even less character as an independent reference. Thus, in *"Mr. Baker* will arrive shortly," and *"Mrs. Smith* is not at home," *baker* and *smith* have clearly lost most if not all of their ordinary reference as common nouns. Ullmann[1] (1962, pp. 72–73) prefers to regard proper names as identification labels otherwise devoid of reference, whose function it is to identify rather than to signify. However, since subjects asked to associate to *Big Oak Drive* might well produce associations to trees, vegetation, and bigness, as well as to places, an associationist viewpoint would hold that the ordinary references of the words in the name are still important. But it is also likely that subjects asked to associate to *Mrs. Smith* would only rarely give responses having to do with metalworking. In general it would seem that place names and titles do not completely vitiate the ordinary reference of their words, but that names of people do. Numerous exceptions to the rule will be obvious. Thus, *Mr. Brain* will never be able to avoid the ordinary reference of *brain,* and *New Haven* hardly carries any longer the meanings of *new* and *haven.* In the present approach, place names and titles, in addition to being classified as references to places and titles of things (books, paintings), also have their constituent words categorized insofar as possible. The ordinary reference of words in names of people is disregarded, and the name is scored as if it were a pronoun, taking the same scoring that a pronoun would receive.

---

[1] Ullmann (personal communication) feels that, since there is no element of choice in titles, phrases, and place names, it artificially increases particular category frequencies if the individual words themselves are categorized. The decision to accord recognition to the individual words in their own right stems from an effort to keep psychological aspects of language to the fore. If one takes the view that a stimulus word usually entails its relevant associations, then the particular setting, insofar as it does not obscure the independent configuration of the word, need not necessarily isolate the word from its ordinary associations and meanings.

This means that there must be available some scorable noun in the text with which the proper name can be identified. Thus, if the text says "brother Bill," *Bill* is scored MALE, JOIN as would be *brother*. "A writer named Smith," would give *Smith* a scoring of LANGUAGE 2 (WRITE). "A Frenchman named Dupré," would give *Dupré* the score PLACE, MALE. In certain instances proper names are scored MALE or FEMALE without the presence of other specifying features. Thus, "Every *Tom* (MALE), *Dick* (MALE), *Harry* (MALE), and *Sally* (FEMALE) was there."

Even though there may be two parts to a proper name, only a single scoring is applied. Where a person is given a title and the title can be categorized, then the name of the person is so categorized when it appears alone. *"Captain* (DOMINANCE 2) Jones was a brave man. *Jones* (DOMINANCE 2) was also a good man."

4. *Agent.* Words like *painter, writer, builder, worker,* and *scientist* do not take scores relating to person (for example, INDIVIDUAL or MALE) unless there is a special feature of the word calling for such scoring. Such words are ordinarily scored under the appropriate category as: COLOR; LANGUAGE 2 (WRITE); STRUCTURE; WORK; REASON 3 (SCIENCE).

5. *Scoring priorities.* Theoretically, there is no limit to the number of categories which may be applied to a single word. However, for the sake of expediency, a limit of two category scorings has been set for a single word. Word combinations and pronouns may, however, require more than two scorings. Certain priorities come into play in determining which scorings will be applied where more than two scorings are possible for a single word.

Usually one of the scorings will clearly be dominantly pertinent. Thus, in the case of the word *murder,* where it is possible to score DEAD, CRIME, CONFLICT 1 (HARM), the scoring DEAD has an intuitive priority. With respect to the other possible scorings, that scoring will be applied which is clearly more pertinent, applicable, or dominant. Where there is no distinct dominance, that scoring will be applied which tends to occur least frequently as a scored category. In the case of the word *murder,* where DEAD is selected as the primary score, the category CRIME could be chosen as the second scoring on the grounds that it is a less often applied category than CONFLICT 1 (HARM). The application of a less frequent scoring increases the possibility of discriminating between speech samples by bringing as many categories as possible into play. It is noteworthy that unreliability in scoring (differences between separate judges scoring new words) may reflect differences in choices of particular aspects of the meaning for scoring, rather than basic differences in interpretation of the meaning.

6. *Pronouns.* Pronouns present a special problem. In some instances they serve merely as formal elements with minimal independent reference, and in other instances they refer as distinctly as do their nouns to a content. The following rules have been adopted in categorizing pronouns.

   a. Relative pronouns are not categorized, since, as a rule, they serve only formalistic requirements of language and usually come in close conjunction with the nouns to which they refer. Thus, in the sentence, "The boy *who* threw the ball ran away," the relative pronoun *who* is not categorized since it would merely duplicate the categorization of the noun to which it referred.

   b. Other pronouns are scored with the categories of the noun to which they refer. Thus, in the sentence, "The small boy threw the ball, and he ran away," the pronoun *he* would get the same scoring as the noun *boy.* Sometimes it is difficult to identify a noun to which the pronoun refers. This is often true in the case of interrogative pronouns. In such instances the pronoun receives no score.

   c. The first-person pronoun (*I, we*) receives a special scoring of SELF-REFERENCE.

Application of the Scoring

As an illustration of the application of the system of categories, some pages from Swift's "Voyage to the Country of the Houyhnhnms," in *Gulliver's Travels,* have been scored below.

<pre>
                                                    Female
SR Durable   Hollow 1 Join SR Sex   Young   Near
   I   continued at home   with my wife   and children about
Number Time 4   Sharp 2 Calm Happening SR   Reason 2
five   months in a very   happy condition, if I could have learned
                                                    Go
   Reason 2 Reason 1 Time 4 SR   Good SR Separate SR Sub. 1
the lesson   of knowing   when I was well. I left   my poor
Female   Agree 2
Sex   Big Join Young   Possess   Help   Help   SR
wife, big with child, and accepted an advantageous offer made me to
</pre>

            Sea, Trans.   Sea, Trans.
    Dom. 2   Conflict 1   Dom. 1 Commerce Male   Number
be captain of the Adventure, a stout   merchantman   of 350
                            Go
Measurement SR Reason 1   Sea   Good   Happening
tons,   for I understood navigation well, and being grown
Upset   Cure   Work   Sea   Conflict 3 SR
weary of a surgeon's employment at sea, which, however,   I   could
            Time 4
Work   Some   SR Possess Dom. 1 Young Male   Work
exercise upon occasion, I   took   a skillful young man of that calling,
                            Sea   Go   Go
Indiv.   Young, Male   In SR Trans.   SR Begin Sea Separate
one   Robert Purefoy, into my ship.   We set   sail from
                                            Number   Number
Place   Number Time 4 Time 4   Time 4   Time 4
Portsmouth upon the 7th   day of September, 1710; on the 14th
SR Join Join Dom. 2   Place   Place   Go
we met with Captain Pocock of Bristol, at Teneriffe, who was going
        Sea   Mtl. Mtl.   Number
        Hollow 2 Place   Sharp 1 Veg. Veg.   Time 4
to the Bay   of Campechy to cut   logwood.   On the 16th
            Go   Astr. 2   Durable
Dom. 2   Separate Separate SR   Conflict 1 SR Hear Time 4 SR
he   was parted from   us by a storm; I   heard since   my
Go   Sea   Sub. 1   Neg. Go
Back   Dom. 2 Trans. Conflict 1   Indiv. Open   Conflict 3
return that his   ship foundered and none escaped but
            Sub. 2   Young
Number Hollow 1 Male Dom.2   Good Male   Good Sea
one   cabin   boy. He   was an honest man and a good sailor,
        Little Sharp 2 Sharp 1   Dom. 2 Possess Reason 1
but a little too   positive in his   own   opinions, which was
    Begin   Dom. 2 Conflict 1 Agree 3
the cause of his   destruction, as   it   had been of
        Indiv.   Reason 1
Some Conflict 3   Dom. 2   Sub. 2 SR Help Dom. 2
several others. For if he   had followed my advice he   might
                                        Group
        Help   Hollow 1 Join Dom. 2 Join   Time 2 Time 4
have been safe at home with his   family at this   time,

Agree 3   SR
as   well as myself.

                                                        Sea   Hot
    SR   Possess Some   Male Dead In SR Trans.   Illness
    I   had   several men   die   in   my   ship   of calentures,
           Conflict 1
         SR   Dom. 1   Possess Help   Out   Place
so that I   was forced to get   recruits out of Barbadoes and the
           Sea
Place   Earth   Place SR Join   Dom. 2   Commerce
Leeward Islands, where I   touched by the direction of the merchants
                          Time 3
     Work   SR   SR Possess Near Sharp 2 All 2 Reason 1
who employed me, which I   had   soon too   much cause   to
                          Time 3
Upset   SR   Open Back   All 2   Help
repent, for I   found afterwards that most of them had been
Sea   Help   Sea
Crime   SR Possess Number Feature   Trans.   SR Dom. 2
buccaneers. I   had   fifty   hands   on board, and my orders
           SR   Commerce Join   Group In   Place Sea
were that I   should trade   with the Indians in the South Sea,
              Open   SR Dom. 1   Bad   SR
and make what discoveries I   could.   These rogues who I   had
Possess Up Bad   SR   Conflict 3 Male   Male All 1 Structure
picked up debauched my other   men, and they all   formed
    Group   Confine   Sea
    Crime   Possess   Trans.   Confine SR   Male
a conspiracy to seize   the ship   and secure   me, which they   did
              Go
Indiv. Time 4 Fast   In SR Hollow 1   Confine SR Feature
one   morning, rushing into my cabin   and binding me hand
                      Go   Sea
    Feature Conflict 1   Conflict 1 SR Up Trans.   SR Want 1
and foot,   threatening to throw   me overboard if I   offered to
Change SR Lang. 1 Male SR   Male Confine   Sub. 1
stir.   I   told   them I   was their prisoner and would submit.
                      Sacred
    Male Dom. 1 SR Agree 2   Happening   Male Open
This they   made   me swear   to do,   and then they unbound

      Join   Number
SR Triv. 2 Confine Indiv.   SR Feature   Confine Near SR
me, only   fastening one   of my legs   with a chain   near my
Household   Help   Open   Help
Slow   Place   Conflict 1 Near SR Confine   Conflict 1
bed,   and placed a sentry   at   my door   with his
Mechanism   Lang. 1
Conflict 1 Hill   Dom. 2   Conflict 1 SR Dead SR
piece   charged, who was commanded to shoot   me dead if I
                                Sea
Want 1   SR Open Male Go SR Down Eat   Drink
attempted my liberty. They sent me down victuals and drink, and
                    Sea   Want 1
Possess   Dom. 2   Trans.   Male   Male Structure
took   the government of the ship   to themselves. Their design
           Sea   Conflict 1   Group
      Change Crime   Crime   Place   Male
was to turn   pirates and plunder   the Spaniards, which they could
           Time 4   Number
Neg. Happening Durable Male Possess All 2 Male   Forward
not do   till   they got   more men. But first
        Want 1   Sea
Male Reason 1   Money   Commerce In   Trans.   Go
they resolved to sell   the goods   in the ship, and then go to
                                      Time 4
Place   Help Some Join Male   Dead Durable SR
Madagascar for recruits, several among them having died since   my
           Go
Confine   Male Sea All 2 Time 4   Commerce Join
confinement. They sailed many weeks and traded   with the
                                  Confine
Group   SR Reason 1 Neg.   Go   Male Go   Durable
Indians, but I   know   not   what course they took, being kept
  Near
Confine Confine In SR Hollow 1   Want 1 Neg.   Little
a close   prisoner in my cabin,   and expecting nothing less than
     Dead
     Crime   Agree 3 Male All 3 Conflict 1 SR
to be murdered, as   they often threatened me.

In actual studies of samples of language, it will be desirable to work from a profile of categories, showing the frequency of occurrence of the various categories. Such a profile constructed from the sample of Swift's writing is shown below.

TABLE 22

CATEGORY PROFILE OF THE QUOTED SAMPLE FROM SWIFT'S
"VOYAGE TO THE COUNTRY OF THE HOUYHNHNMS," SHOWING
FREQUENCY OF OCCURRENCE OF EACH CATEGORY

1. ABSURD	0		38. EARTH	1
2. AGREE 1	0		39. EASY	0
3. AGREE 2	2		40. EAT	1
4. AGREE 3	3		41. END	0
5. ALL 1	1		42. ESSENTIAL	0
6. ALL 2	4		43. FALSE	0
7. ALL 3	1		44. FAR	0
8. ANIMAL	0		45. FAST	1
9. ART	0		46. FEATURE (BODY)	4
10. ASTRONOMY 1	0		47. FEMALE	2
11. ASTRONOMY 2	1		48. FORWARD	1
12. BACK	2		49. FUNCTION (BODY)	0
13. BAD	2		50. GO	15
14. BEGIN	2		51. GOOD	4
15. BIG	1		52. GROUP	5
16. BLURRED	0		53. HAPPENING	4
17. CALM	1		54. HEAR	1
18. CHANGE	2		55. HELP	10
19. CLEAN	0		56. HILL	1
20. CLOTHING	0		57. HOLLOW 1	5
21. COLD	0		58. HOLLOW 2	1
22. COLOR	0		59. HOT	1
23. COMMERCE	5		60. HOUSEHOLD	1
24. CONFINE	11		61. ILLNESS	1
25. CONFLICT 1	13		62. IN	6
26. CONFLICT 2	0		63. INDIVIDUAL	5
27. CONFLICT 3	4		64. JOIN	11
28. CRIME	5		65. LANGUAGE 1	2
29. CURE	1		66. LANGUAGE 2	0
30. DEAD	4		67. LAW	0
31. DIFFICULT	0		68. LITTLE	2
32. DIRTY	0		69. LIVING	0
33. DOMINANCE 1	5		70. MALE	24
34. DOMINANCE 2	14		71. MATERIAL	2
35. DOWN	1		72. MEASUREMENT	1
36. DRINK	1		73. MECHANISM	1
37. DURABLE	5		74. MONEY	1

75. NEAR	5	95. SOME		4
76. NEGATION	4	96. STRUCTURE		2
77. NUMBER	10	97. SUBMISSION 1	3	
78. OPEN	6	98. SUBMISSION 2		2
79. OUT	1	99. TIME 1		0
80. PLACE	11	100. TIME 2		1
81. PLAY	0	101. TIME 3		2
82. POSSESS	11	102. TIME 4		14
83. REASON 1	7	103. TRANSPORTATION		10
84. REASON 2	2	104. TRIVIAL 1		0
85. REASON 3	0	105. TRIVIAL 2		1
86. SACRED	1	106. TRUE		0
87. SEE	0	107. UNREAL		0
88. SEA	21	108. UP		2
89. SELF-REFERENCE	51	109. UPSET		2
90. SEPARATE	4	110. VEGETATION		2
91. SEX	2	111. WANT 1		5
92. SHARP 1	2	112. WANT 2		0
93. SHARP 2	3	113. WORK		4
94. SLOW	1	114. YOUNG		5

The reader should bear in mind that a much larger selection must be utilized to produce a reliable and meaningful profile. Nevertheless, in the small quoted selection the categories which stand out suggest some important themes in Swift's fantasy. The most prominent categories are: CONFLICT 1 (HARM), DOMINANCE 2 (LEAD), GO, MALE, SEA, SELF-REFERENCE, and TIME 4 (GENERAL TIME).

The large SELF-REFERENCE score is obviously an artifact of the first-person account, but its egocentric aspect is not to be overlooked. The GO and SEA scores mirror the theme in *Gulliver's Travels* of the voyage to distant lands, and we know from Swift's history how important separation from mother and home was for him (Greenacre, 1955). At the age of one he was taken secretly from his mother in Ireland and brought overseas to Whitehaven, England by his nurse. The mother, when she discovered what had happened, forebade the hazardous return across the Irish Sea, and as a result Swift lived with a foster mother for three years before rejoining his true mother. Only a few months after his return to Ireland and his mother, she herself departed for England, leaving him, and he lived apart from her until he was twenty-two.

The CONFLICT 1 (HARM), DOMINANCE 2 (LEAD), and MALE scores lend themselves to the interpretation that aggression, leadership, and masculinity were uppermost in Swift's thoughts. Such a configuration has many possible connections with Swift's life. The giant and dwarf fantasies in *Gulliver's Travels* may reflect on the one hand the wished-for magnification of power and masculine potency and, on the other, the fear of being overcome by other men and being impotent with women (Ferenczi, 1928). The stress on time may also have several interpretations, perhaps relating to a concern with illness and aging which were preoccupations of Swift's when he wrote *Gulliver* (Grant Duff, 1937).

In the present selection the NUMBER category is not quite as marked as some of the other categories. However, the segment from *Gulliver's Travels* quoted in Chapter 5 indicates that this was a significant category for Swift. It is not difficult to see in the heavy use of numbers the passion for exactitude which was part of Swift's obsessiveness.

These speculations do not have much substance in themselves because they are based on very little of Swift's writing. However, they do indicate how an author's choice of words might contribute to an understanding of the dominant themes of his life at the moment he creates his story.

Note—References to James Strachey (Ed.), *The Standard Edition of the Complete Psychological Works of Sigmund Freud,* 24 vols. (London: Hogarth Press, 1953–), will be listed as *Standard edition.* Works will be referred to by their dates of original publication.

References

Abraham, K. *Selected papers.* New York: Basic Books, 1953.

Allport, G. W., & Cantril, H. Judging personality from voice. *J. soc. Psychol.,* 1934, **5,** 39–56.

Arieti, S. *Interpretation of schizophrenia.* New York: Brunner, 1955.

Atkinson, J. W., & McClelland, D. C. The projective expression of needs. II. The effect of different intensities of the hunger drive on thematic apperception. *J. exp. Psychol.,* 1948, **38,** 643–658.

Basilius, H. Neo-Humboldtian ethnolinguistics. *Word,* 1952, **8,** 95–105.

Bentley, M. Oxygen-tension and the higher mental processes. *Amer. J. Psychol.,* 1939, **52,** 72–82.

Betz, W. Zur Überprüfung des Feldbegriffes. *Z. für vergl. Sprachforsch.,* 1954, **71,** 189–198.

Birdwhistell, R. *Introduction to kinesics.* Washington, D.C.: Foreign Service Institute, Department of State, 1952.

Bloch, B., & Trager, G. L. *Outline of linguistic analysis.* Baltimore:

Linguistic Society of America, 1942.

Bloomfield, L. *Language*. New York: Henry Holt, 1933.

Bousfield, W. A. The occurrence of clusters in the recall of randomly arranged associates. *J. gen. Psychol.*, 1953, **49**, 229–240.

Bousfield, W. A., & Barclay, W. D. The relationship between order and frequency of occurrence of restricted associative responses. *J. exp. Psychol.*, 1950, **40**, 643–547.

Bousfield, W. A., & Cohen, B. H. General review of a program of research on associative clustering. In J. J. Jenkins (Ed.), *Associative processes in verbal behavior: a report of the Minnesota Conference.* Dept. Psychol., Univer. Minn., 1955. (a)

Bousfield, W. A., & Cohen, B. H. The occurrence of clustering in the recall of randomly arranged words of different frequencies-of-usage. *J. gen. Psychol.*, 1955, **52**, 83–95. (b)

Bousfield, W. A., Cohen, B. H., & Whitmarsh, G. A. Verbal generalization: a theoretical rationale and an experimental technique. *Tech. Rep. No. 23*, ONR Contr. Nonr–631 (00), Univer. Connecticut, 1958. (a)

Bousfield, W. A., Cohen, B. H., & Whitmarsh, G. A. Associative clustering in the recall of words of different taxonomic frequencies of occurrence. *Psychol. Rep.*, 1958, **4**, 39–44. (b)

Bousfield, W. A., Cohen, B. H., Whitmarsh, G. A., & Kincaid, W. D., with Cowan, T. M., & Puff, C. R. *The Connecticut free associational norms.* Univer. Conn., Studies on the mediation of verbal behavior, *Tech. Rep.* **35**, Nov., 1961.

Bousfield, W. A., & Sedgewick, C. H. W. An analysis of sequences of restricted associative responses. *J. gen. Psychol.*, 1944, **30**, 149–165.

Bousfield, W. A., Whitmarsh, G. A., & Danick, J. J. Partial response identities in verbal generalization. *Psychol. Rep.*, 1958, **4**, 703–713.

Breuer, J., & Freud, S. On the psychical mechanism of hysterical phenomena: preliminary communication (1893). In S. Freud, Vol. II. *Standard edition.*

Brown, R., & Berko, J. Word association and the acquisition of grammar. *Child Develpm.*, 1960, **31**, 1–14.

Brown, R. W., & Lenneberg, E. H. A study in language and cognition. *J. abnorm. soc. Psychol.*, 1954, **49**, 454–462.

Brozek, J., Guetzkow, H., Vig Baldwin, M., & Cranston, R. A quantitative study of perception and association in experimental starvation. *J. Pers.*, 1951, **19**, 245–264.

Buck, C. D. Words for world, earth and land, sun. *Language*, 1929, **5**, 215–227.

Buck, C. D. *Dictionary of selected synonyms in the principal Indo-European languages.* Chicago: Univer. Chicago Press, 1949.

Cameron, N. Reasoning, regression, and communication in schizophrenics. *Psychol. Monogr.,* 1938, **50,** 1–33. (a)

Cameron, N. A study of thinking in senile deterioration and schizophrenic disorganization. *Amer. J. Psychol.,* 1938, **51,** 650–665. (b)

Carnap, R. *Introduction to semantics.* Cambridge: Harvard Univer. Press, 1942.

Carroll, J. B. *The study of language: survey of linguistics and related disciplines in America.* Cambridge: Harvard Univer. Press, 1953.

Carroll, J. B., & Casagrande, J. B. The function of language classifications in behavior. In E. E. Maccoby, T. M. Newcomb, & E. L. Hartley (Eds.), *Readings in social psychology.* New York: Henry Holt, 1958.

Cassirer, E. *Language and myth.* New York: Harper, 1946.

Chase, S. *The tyranny of words.* New York: Harcourt, Brace, 1938.

Clark, R. A. The projective measurement of experimentally induced levels of sexual motivation. *J. exp. Psychol.,* 1952, **44,** 391–399.

Cofer, C. N. A study of clustering in free recall based on synonyms. *J. gen. Psychol.,* 1959, **60,** 3–10.

Cofer, C. N., & Shevitz, R. Word-association as a function of word-frequency. *Amer. J. Psychol.,* 1952, **65,** 75–79.

Conklin, H. C. Haunoo color categories. *Southwest J. Anthrop.,* 1955, **11,** 339–344.

Crosland, H. R. The psychological methods of word-association and reaction-time as tests of deception. *Publ. Univer. Oregon Psychol. Series I,* 1929, 1–104.

Deese, J. The prediction of occurrence of particular verbal intrusions in immediate recall. *J. exp. Psychol.,* 1959, **58,** 17–22.

Deese, J. On the structure of associative meaning. *Psychol. Rev.,* 1962, **69,** 161–175.

DeLaguna, Grace A. *Speech, its function and development.* New Haven: Yale Univer. Press, 1927.

Diven, K. Certain determinants in the conditioning of anxiety reactions. *J. Psychol.,* 1937, **3,** 291–308.

Dulany, D. E., Jr. Hypotheses and habits in verbal "operant conditioning." *J. abnorm. soc. Psychol.,* 1961, **63,** 251–263.

Dulany, D. E., Jr. The place of hypotheses and intentions: an analysis of verbal control in verbal conditioning, *J. Pers.,* 1962, **30,** Suppl., 102–129.

Dunn, Sandra, Bliss, Joan, & Siipola, Elsa. Effects of impulsivity, introversion, and individual values upon association under free conditions. *J. Pers.*, 1958, **26**, 61–76.

Empson, W. *Seven types of ambiguity*. New York: New Directions, 1955.

Erikson, E. H. The problem of ego identity. *Psychol. Issues*, 1959, **1**, 101–171.

Esper, E. A. A contribution to the experimental study of analogy. *Psychol. Rev.*, 1918, **25**, 469–487.

Ferenczi, S. On obscene words (1911). In Vol. I, *The selected papers of Sandor Ferenczi*. New York: Basic Books, 1950.

Ferenczi, S. Stages in the development of the sense of reality (1913). In Vol. I, *The selected papers of Sandor Ferenczi*. New York: Basic Books, 1950.

Ferenczi, S. Gulliver phantasies. *Int. J. Psychoanal.*, 1928, **9**, 283–300.

Fermin, M. H. J. *Le vocabulaire de Bifrun dans sa traduction des quatre evangiles*. Amsterdam: L. J. Veen's Uitgevers Mij. N. V., 1954.

Fishman, J. A. A systematization of the Whorfian hypothesis. *Behav. Sci.*, 1960, **5**, 323–339.

Foakes, R. A. Suggestions for a new approach to Shakespeare's imagery. *Shakespeare Surv.*, 1952, **5**, 81–92.

Frazer, Sir J. G. *The golden bough* (1922). New York: Macmillan, 1951.

Freud, S. *On aphasia* (1891). New York: Int. Univer. Press, 1953.

Freud, S. Project for a scientific psychology (1895). In S. Freud, *The origins of psychoanalysis*. New York: Basic Books, 1954.

Freud, S. *The interpretation of dreams* (1900). Vols. IV–V. *Standard edition*.

Freud, S. *The psychopathology of everyday life* (1901). Vol. VI. *Standard edition*.

Freud, S. *Jokes and their relation to the unconscious* (1905). Vol. VIII. *Standard edition*.

Freud, S. Formulations on the two principles of mental functioning (1911). Vol. XII. *Standard edition*. (a)

Freud, S. Psycho-analytic notes upon an autobiographical account of a case of paranoia (dementia paranoides) (1911). Vol. XIII. *Standard edition*. (b)

Freud, S. Totem and taboo (1913). Vol. XIII. *Standard edition*.

Freud, S. The unconscious (1915). Vol. XIV. *Standard edition*.

Freud, S. Metapsychological supplement to the theory of dreams (1917). Vol. XIV. *Standard edition*.

Freud, S. Introductory lectures on psycho-analysis (1916–1917). Vols. XV–XVI. *Standard edition.*

Freud, S. The ego and the id (1923). Vol. XIX. *Standard edition.*

Freud, S. Negation (1925). Vol. XIX. *Standard edition.*

Freud, S. *An outline of psychoanalysis* (1940). New York: W. W. Norton, 1949.

Gellhorn, E., & Kraines, S. H. The influence of hyperpnea and of variations in the O_2 and CO_2 tension of the inspired air on word association. *Science,* 1936, **83,** 266–267.

Gill, M. M. Topography and systems in psychoanalytic theory. *Psychol. Issues,* 1963, **3,** No. 2 (Monogr. 10).

Goldstein, K. Methodological approach to the study of schizophrenic thought disorder. In J. Kasanin (Ed.), *Language and thought in schizophrenia.* Berkeley: Univer. California Press, 1944.

Goldstein, K. *Language and language disturbances.* New York: Grune & Stratton, 1948.

Gonzales, R. C., & Cofer, C. N. Exploratory studies of verbal context by means of clustering in free recall. *J. gen. Psychol.,* 1959, **95,** 293–320.

Goodenough, W. H. Componential analysis and the study of meaning. *Language,* 1956, **32,** 195–216.

Grant Duff, I. F. A one-sided sketch of Jonathan Swift. *Psychoanal. Quart.,* 1937, **6,** 238–259.

Gray, L. H. *Foundations of language.* New York: Macmillan, 1939.

Greenacre, Phyllis. The mutual adventures of Jonathan Swift and Lemuel Gulliver. *Psychoanal. Quart.,* 1955, **24,** 20–62.

Greenberg, J. H. The word as a linguistic unit. In C. E. Osgood & T. A. Sebeok (Eds.), Psycholinguistics, a survey of theory and research problems. *J. abnorm. soc. Psychol.,* 1954, **49,** No. 4, Part 2, Suppl.

Hall, R. S., Jr. Idiolect and linguistic super-ego. *Stud. Ling.* 1951, **5,** 21–27.

Hallig, R., & Wartburg, W. V. Begriffssystem als Grundlage für die Lexikographie. Versuch eines Ordnungsschemas. *Abh. der Dtsch. Akad. der Wiss. zu Berlin, Klasse für Sprachen, Literatur und Kunst,* 1952, No. 4.

Hallig, R., & Wartburg, W. V. Begriffssystem als Grundlage für die Lexikographie. Versuch eines Ordnungsschemas. (2nd ed.) Berlin: Akademie-Verlag, 1963.

Harmon, H. H. *Modern factor analysis.* Chicago: Univer. Chicago Press, 1960.

Harris, Z. S. *Methods in structural linguistics*. Chicago: Univer. Chicago Press, 1951.

Hassol, L., Magaret, A., & Cameron, N. The production of language disorganization through personalized distraction. *J. Psychol.*, 1952, **33**, 289–299.

Hayakawa, S. I. *Language in action*. New York: Harcourt, Brace, 1941.

Hiorth, F. On the relation between field research and lexicography. *Stud. Ling.*, 1956, **10**, 57–66.

Hoijer, H. (Ed.). *Language in culture*. Chicago: Univer. Chicago Press, 1954.

Holt, R. R. A critical examination of Freud's concept of bound vs. free cathexis. *J. Amer. Psychoanal. Assn.*, 1962, **10**, 475–525.

Horan, E. M. Word association frequency tables of mentally retarded children. *J. Consult. Psychol.*, 1956, **20**, 22.

Howes, D. On the relation between the probability of a word as an association and in general linguistic usage. *J. abnorm. soc. Psychol.*, 1957, **57**, 75–85.

Hull, C. L., & Lugoff, L. S. Complex signs in diagnostic free association. *J. exp. Psychol.*, 1921, **4**, 111–136.

Humphrey, G. There is no problem of meaning. *Brit. J. Psychol.*, 1951, **42**, 238–245.

Huston, P. E., Shakow, D., & Erickson, M. H. A study of hypnotically induced complexes by means of the Luria technique. *J. gen. Psychol.*, 1934, **11**, 65–97.

Jenkins, J. J. Effects on word-association of the set to give popular responses. *Psychol. Rep.*, 1959, **5**, 94.

Jenkins, P. M., & Cofer, C. N. An exploratory study of discrete free association to compound verbal stimuli. *Psychol. Rep.*, 1957, **3**, 599–602.

Johnson, P. O. *Statistical methods in research*. Englewood Cliffs, N.J.: Prentice-Hall, 1949.

Jones, E. The theory of symbolism. In *Papers on psycho-analysis*. New York: William Wood, 1923.

Joos, M. Description of language design. *J. accoust. Soc. Amer.*, 1950, **22**, 701–708.

Jung, C. G. *The psychology of dementia praecox*. New York: Journal of Nervous and Mental Diseases Publishing Co., 1909.

Jung, C. G. The association method. *Amer. J. Psychol.*, 1910, **21**, 219–269.

Jung, C. G. *Studies in word association*. London: William Heinemann, 1918.

Kantor, J. R. *An objective psychology of grammar*. Bloomington, Ind.: Indiana Univer. Press, 1936.

Kaplan, B. On the phenomena of "opposite speech." *J. abnorm. soc. Psychol.*, 1957, **55**, 389–393.

Kasanin, J. *Language and thought in schizophrenia*. Berkeley: Univer. California Press, 1944.

Keller, H. E. *Étude descriptive sur le vocabulaire de Wace*. Berlin: Akademie-Verlag, 1953.

Kent, G. H., & Rosanoff, A. J. A study of association in insanity. *Amer. J. Insan.*, 1910, **67**, 37–96, 317–390.

Kephart, N. C., & Houtchens, H. M. The effect of the stimulus word used upon scores in the association-motor test. *Amer. J. Psychiat.*, 1937, **94**, 393–399.

Kohs, S. C. The association method in its relation to the complex and complex indicators. *Amer. J. Psychol.*, 1914, **25**, 544–594.

Korzybski, A. *Science and sanity*. Lancaster, Pa.: Science Press, 1933.

Krasner, L. Studies of the conditioning of verbal behavior. *Psychol. Bull.*, 1958, **55**, 148–170.

Kris, E. On preconscious mental processes. *Psychoanal. Quart.*, 1950, **19**, 540–560.

Krout, M. H. A preliminary note on some obscure symbolic muscular responses of diagnostic value in the study of normal subjects. *Amer. J. Psychiat.*, 1931, **11**, 29–73.

Kubie, L. S. Body symbolization and the development of language. *Psychoanal. Quart.*, 1934, **3**, 430–444.

Laffal, J. The learning and retention of words with association disturbances. *J. abnorm. soc. Psychol.*, 1952, **47**, 454–462.

Laffal, J. Response faults in word association as a function of response entropy. *J. abnorm. soc. Psychol.*, 1955, **50**, 265–270.

Laffal, J. The contextual associates of sun and God in Schreber's autobiography. *J. abnorm. soc. Psychol.*, 1960, **61**, 474–479.

Laffal, J. Changes in the language of a schizophrenic patient during psychotherapy. *J. abnorm. soc. Psychol.*, 1961, **63**, 422–427.

Laffal, J. The use of contextual associates in the analysis of free speech. *J. gen. Psychol.*, 1963, **69**, 51–64.

Laffal, J. Freud's theory of language. *Psychoanal. Quart.*, 1964, **33**, 157–175. (a)

Laffal, J. Psycholinguistics and the psychology of language: Comments. *Amer. Psychol.*, 1964, **19**, 813–815. (b)

Laffal, J., & Ameen, L. Hypotheses of opposite speech. *J. abnorm. soc. Psychol.*, 1959, **58**, 267–269.

Laffal, J., & Feldman, S. The structure of single word and continuous word associations. *J. verb. Learn. and verb. Behav.*, 1962, **1**, 54–61.

Laffal, J., & Feldman, S. The structure of free speech. *J. verb. Learn. and verb. Behav.*, 1963, **2**, 498–503.

Laffal, J., Lenkoski, L. D., & Ameen, L. "Opposite speech" in a schizophrenic patient. *J. abnorm. soc. Psychol.*, 1956, **52**, 409–413.

Langer, Susanne K. On Cassirer's theory of language and myth. In P. A. Schilpp (Ed.), *The philosophy of Ernst Cassirer*. Evanston, Ill.: Library of Living Philosophers, 1949.

Latif, I. The physiological basis of linguistic development. *Psychol. Rev.*, 1934, **41**, 55–85, 153–176.

Lenneberg, E. H. Cognition in ethnolinguistics. *Language*, 1953, **29**, 463–471.

Longerich, M. C., & Bordeaux, J. *Aphasia therapeutics*. New York: Macmillan, 1954.

Lorenz, M. Language as expressive behavior. *Arch. Neurol. Psychiat.*, 1953, **70**, 277–285.

Lorenz, M., & Cobb, S. Language behavior in psychoneurotic patients. *Arch. Neurol. Psychiat.*, 1953, **69**, 684–694.

Lounsbury, F. G. Transitional probability, linguistic structure, and systems of habit-family hierarchies. In C. E. Osgood & T. A. Sebeok (Eds.), Psycho-linguistics: A survey of theory and research problems. *J. abnorm, soc. Psychol.*, 1954, **49**, No. 4, Part 2, Suppl.

Lounsbury, F. G. A semantic analysis of the Pawnee kinship usage. *Language*, 1956, **32**, 158–194.

Luria, A. R. *The nature of human conflicts*. New York: Liveright, 1932.

Macalpine, Ida, & Hunter, R. A. Discussion of the Schreber case. In Daniel Paul Schreber: *Memoirs of my nervous illness*. Cambridge, Mass.: Robert Bentley, 1955.

McCarthy, Dorothea. Language development in children. In L. Carmichael (Ed.), *Manual of child psychology*. New York: John Wiley & Sons, 1949.

McClelland, D. C., Clark, R. A., Roby, T. B., & Atkinson, J. W. The projective expression of needs. IV. The effect of the need for achievement on thematic apperception. *J. exp. Psychol.*, 1949, **39**, 242–255.

Maclay, H., & Osgood, C. E. Hesitation phenomena in spontaneous English speech. *Word*, 1959, **15**, 19–44.

McQuown, N. A. Linguistic transcription and specification of psychiatric interview materials. *Psychiatry,* 1957, **20,** 79–86.

Mahl, G. F. Disturbances and silences in the patient's speech in psychotherapy. *J. abnorm. soc. Psychol.,* 1956, **53,** 1–15.

Mahl, G. F. Measuring the patient's anxiety during interviews from "expressive" aspects of his speech. *Trans. N. Y. Acad. Sci.,* 1959, **21,** 249–257.

Mahl, G. F. Measures of two expressive aspects of a patient's speech in two psychotherapeutic interviews. In L. A. Gottschalk (Ed.), *Comparative psycholinguistic analysis of two psychotherapeutic interviews.* New York: Int. Univer. Press, 1961.

Mahl, G. F., & Schulze, G. Psychological research in the extralinguistic area. In T. A. Sebeok, A. S. Hayes, & Mary C. Bateson (Eds.), *Approaches to semiotics.* The Hague: Mouton & Co., 1964.

Matoré, G. *La méthode en lexicologie.* Paris: Marcel Didier, 1953.

Mezger, F. Systems of linguistic expression, conceptual dictionaries, and dictionaries of usage. *Proc. Seventh Int. Congr. Ling.* London: Titus Wilson & Son, 1956. Pp. 77–85.

Miller, G. A. *Language and communication.* New York: McGraw-Hill, 1951.

Miller, G. A. What is information measurement? *Amer. Psychol.,* 1953, **8,** 3–11.

Miller, G. A. Some psychological studies of grammar. *Amer. Psychol.,* 1962, **17,** 748–762.

Morris, C. Foundations of the theory of signs. *Int. Encycl. Unified Sci.,* 1938, 1.

Morris, C. *Signs, language and behavior.* Englewood Cliffs, N.J.: Prentice-Hall, 1946.

Mowrer, O. H. The psychologist looks at language. *Amer. Psychol.,* 1954, **9,** 660–694.

Murphy, G. Types of word-association in dementia praecox, manic-depressives, and normal persons. *Amer. J. Psychiat.,* 1923, **2,** 539–571.

Naess, A. Synonymity as revealed by intuition. *Phil. Rev.,* 1957, **66,** 87–93.

New Haven Register. Religious phenomenon upsets Yale as "Glossolalia" invades campus. March 11, 1963, p. 1.

Nida, E. A. A system for the description of semantic elements. *Word,* 1951, **7,** 1–14.

Nida, E. A. Analysis of meaning and dictionary making. *Int. J. Amer. Ling.,* 1958, **24,** 279–292.

Niederland, W. G. Three notes on the Schreber case. *Psychoanal. Quart.*, 1951, **20**, 579–591.

Niederland, W. G. Schreber: father and son. *Psychoanal. Quart.*, 1959, **27**, 151–169.

Noble, C. E. An analysis of meaning. *Psychol. Rev.*, 1952, **59**, 421–430.

O'Connor, J. *Born that way*. Baltimore: Williams & Wilkins, 1928.

Ogden, C. K. *Opposition, a linguistic and psychological analysis*. London: K. Paul, Trench, Trubner, 1932.

Ogden, C. K., & Richards, I. A. *The meaning of meaning* (1923). New York: Harcourt, Brace, 1956.

Öhman, S. Theories of the "linguistic field." *Word*, 1953, **9**, 123–134.

Olmsted, D. L., & Moore, O. K. Language, psychology, and linguistics. *Psychol. Rev.*, 1952, **59**, 414–420.

Osgood, C. E. Studies on the generality of affective meaning systems. *Amer. Psychol.*, 1962, **17**, 10–28.

Osgood, C. E. On understanding and creating sentences. *Amer. Psychol.*, 1963, **18**, 735–751.

Osgood, C. E., & Sebeok, T. A. Psycholinguistics: a survey of theory and research problems. *J. abnorm. soc. Psychol.*, 1954, **49**, No. 4, Part 2, Suppl.

Osgood, C. E., Suci, G. J., & Tannenbaum, P. H. *The measurement of meaning*. Urbana, Ill.: Univer. Illinois Press, 1957.

Piaget, J. *The language and thought of the child*. New York: Harcourt, Brace, 1926.

Piaget, J. *Judgment and reasoning in the child*. New York: Harcourt, Brace, 1928.

Piaget, J. *The child's conception of physical causality*. New York: Harcourt, Brace, 1930.

Piaget, J. Comments on Vygotsky's critical remarks concerning *The language and thought of the child,* and *Judgment and reasoning in the child*. Cambridge: M. I. T. Press, 1962.

Pittenger, R. E., & Smith, H. L., Jr. A basis for some contributions of linguistics to psychiatry. *Psychiatry*, 1957, **20**, 61–78.

Price, L. *Dialogues of Alfred North Whitehead*. Boston: Little, Brown, 1954.

Proc. Seventh Int. Congr. Ling. London: Titus Wilson & Son, 1956.

Pronko, N. H. Language and psycholinguistics. *Psychol. Bull.*, 1946, **43**, 189–239.

Quine, W. V. O. *From a logical point of view*. Cambridge: Harvard Univer. Press, 1953.

Rapaport, D. *Organization and pathology of thought.* New York: Columbia Univer. Press, 1951.

Rapaport, D., & Gill, M. The points of view and assumptions of metapsychology. *Int. J. Psychoanal.,* 1959, **40,** 153–162.

Rapaport, D., Gill, M., & Schafer, R. *Diagnostic psychological testing.* Chicago: Yearbook Publishers, 1946.

Reuning, K. *Joy and Freude: a comparative study of the linguistic field of pleasurable emotion in English and German.* Swarthmore, Penna.: Swarthmore, 1941.

Roget, P. M. *Roget's international thesaurus* (1852). New York: Thomas Y. Crowell, 1960.

Rosanoff, I. R., & Rosanoff, A. J. A study of association in children. *Psychol. Rev.,* 1913, **20,** 43–89.

Rosen, E., & Russell, W. A. Frequency-characteristics of successive word-association. *Amer. J. Psychol.,* 1957, **70,** 120–122.

Russell, W. A., & Jenkins, J. J. *The complete Minnesota norms for responses to 100 words from the Kent-Rosanoff association test.* Univer. Minnesota studies on the role of language in behavior, Tech. Rep. 11, August 1954.

Salzinger, K. Experimental manipulation of verbal behavior: a review. *J. gen. Psychol.,* 1959, **61,** 65–94.

Sanford, R. N. The effects of abstinence from food upon imaginal processes. *J. Psychol.,* 1936, **2,** 129–136.

Sanford, R. N. The effect of abstinence from food upon imaginal processes: a further experiment. *J. Psychol.,* 1937, **3,** 145–149.

Sapir, E. Speech as a personality trait. *Amer. J. Sociol.,* 1927, **32,** 892–905.

Saussure, F. de. *Course in general linguistics* (1915). New York: Philosophical Library, 1959.

Schafer, R. A study of thought processes in a word association test. *Char. and Pers.,* 1945, **13,** 212–227.

Schilder, P. Language and the constructive energies of the psyche. Part I. Psychology of language. Part II. The psychopathology of language. *Scientia,* 1936, **59,** 149–158, 205–211.

Schlosberg, H., & Heineman, C. The relation between two measures of response strength. *J. exp. Psychol.,* 1950, **40,** 235–247.

Schreber, D. P. *Denkwürdigkeiten eines Nervenkranken.* Leipzig: Oswald Mutze, 1903.

Schreber, D. P. *Memoirs of my nervous illness.* Cambridge, Mass.: Robert Bentley, 1955.

Schwarz, H. Leitmerkmale sprachlicher Felde. In H. Gipper (Ed.), *Sprache, Schlüssel zur Welt.* Düsseldorf: Schwann, 1959.

Shannon, C. E., & Weaver, W. *The mathematical theory of communication.* Urbana, Ill.: Univer. Illinois Press, 1949.

Silberer, H. On symbol-formation (1912). In D. Rapaport (Ed.), *Organization and pathology of thought.* New York: Columbia Univer. Press, 1951.

Siipola, Elsa, Walker, W. Nanette, & Kolb, Dorothy. Task attitudes in word association, projective and nonprojective. *J. Pers.,* 1955, **23,** 441–459.

Simonini, R. C., Jr. Phonemic and analogic lapses in radio and television speech. *Amer. Speech,* 1956, **31,** 252–263.

Skinner, B. F. *Verbal behavior.* New York: Appleton-Century-Crofts, 1957.

Spence, N. C. W. A hardy perennial: the problem of *la langue* and *la parole. Arch. Ling.,* 1957, **9,** 1–27.

Spitz, R. *No and yes: on the genesis of human communication.* New York: Int. Univer. Press, 1957.

Spurgeon, C. *Shakespeare's imagery and what it tells us* (1935). Cambridge, Eng.: Univer. Press, 1958.

Staats, A. W. Learning theory and "opposite speech." *J. abnorm. soc. Psychol.,* 1957, **45,** 268–269.

Tausk, V. On the origin of the "influencing machine" in schizophrenia (1919). In R. Fliess (Ed.), *The psychoanalytic reader.* New York: Int. Univer. Press, 1948.

Thomas, D. *The collected poems of Dylan Thomas.* New York: New Directions, 1953.

Thorndike, E. L., & Lorge, I. *The teacher's word book of 30,000 words.* New York: Teachers Coll., Columbia Univer., 1944.

Tinsley, Sister Lucy. *The French expressions for spirituality and devotion.* Washington, D.C.: Catholic Univer. of America Press, 1953.

Trier, J. Das sprachliche Feld. *Neue Jb. Wiss. Univer. Jugenbildung,* 1934, **10,** 428–449.

Ullmann, S. *The principles of semantics.* Glasgow: Jackson & Son, 1959.

Ullmann, S. *Semantics, an introduction to the science of meaning.* New York: Barnes & Noble, 1962.

Urban, W. M. Cassirer's philosophy of language. In P. A. Schilpp (Ed.), *The philosophy of Ernst Cassirer.* Evanston, Ill.: Library of Living Philosophers, 1949.

Von Domarus, E. The specific laws of logic in schizophrenia. In J.

Kasanin (Ed.), *Language and thought in schizophrenia.* Berkeley: Univer. California Press, 1944.

Vygotsky, L. *Thought and language* (1934). New York: John Wiley & Sons, 1962.

Warren, H. C. *A history of association psychology.* New York: Charles Scribner's Sons, 1921.

Wartburg, W. V. *Problèmes et méthodes de la linguistique.* Paris: Presses Univer. de France, 1946.

Watson, D. L., & Laffal, J. Sources of verbalizations of psychotherapists about patients. *J. gen. Psychol.,* 1963, **68,** 89–98.

Watson, J. B. *Behaviorism* (1924). New York: W. W. Norton. Revised 1930.

Weinreich, U. Travels through semantic space. *Word,* 1958, **14,** 346–366.

Weisgerber, L. Sprache und Begriffsbildung. *Actes du quatr. Congr. Int. Ling.* Copenhagen: Einar Munksgaard, 1938. Pp. 33–39.

Weisgerber, L. *Vom Weltbild der Deutschen Sprache.* Düsseldorf: Schwann, 1953.

Wepman, J. M. *Recovery from aphasia.* New York: Ronald Press, 1951.

Werner, H. *The comparative psychology of mental development* (1940). New York: Int. Univer. Press, 1957.

Werner, H. Microgenesis and aphasia. *J. abnorm. soc. Psychol.,* 1956, **52,** 347–353.

Werner, H., & Kaplan, B. *Symbol formation.* New York: John Wiley & Sons, 1963.

Werner, H., & Kaplan, Edith. The acquisition of word meanings: a developmental study. *Monogr. soc. for Res. in child develpm.,* 1950, **15,** No. 1. (a)

Werner, H., & Kaplan, Edith. Development of word meaning through verbal context: an experimental study. *J. Psychol.,* 1950, **29,** 251–257. (b)

Wheat, L. B. *Free associations to common words.* New York: Teachers Coll., Columbia Univer., 1931.

White, W. A. The language of schizophrenia. *Arch. Neurol. Psychiat.,* 1926, **16,** 395–413.

Whorf, B. L. *Language, thought and reality.* New York: John Wiley & Sons, 1956.

Wispé, L. G. Physiological need, verbal frequency, and word association. *J. abnorm. soc. Psychol.,* 1954, **49,** 229–234.

Woodrow, H., & Lowell, F. Children's association frequency table. *Psychol. Monogr.*, 1916, **22**, 1–110.

Woods, W. L. Language study in schizophrenia. *J. nerv. ment. Dis.*, 1938, **87**, 290–316.

Woodworth, R. S. *Experimental psychology.* New York: Henry Holt, 1938.

Zipf, G. K. *The psycho-biology of language.* Boston: Houghton-Mifflin, 1935.

A

ABRAHAM, K., 156, 227
Abreaction of affect, 160
Agent, category scoring of, 219
ALLPORT, G. W., 227
Ambisexuality, 149
AMEEN, L., 30, 35, 83, 103, 234
Animism, 102, 174
Antonym, 187
Aphasia, 3–4, 112, 157, 175
  asymbolic, 158
  expressive, 3, 167
  and psychoanalytic theory of language, 166–171
  psychotherapeutic treatment, 158, 167–171
  supportive treatment, 168
  verbal, 158
ARIETI, S., 83, 227
ARISTOTLE, 98
ASCHAFFENBURG, 55
Association, associative, 5, 10, 12–14, 16–19, 23–25, 35, 40–42, 125–127, 135, 147–149, 161, 167, 174, 178, 186, 218. *See also* Meaning
  centers, 7
  children's, 16–18, 48–55, 57–58
  clusters, 63–64, 71, 124
  contextual, 89, 101, 126–127
  coordinate, 100–101
  dementia praecox, 50–52
  diagnostic, 48, 55–57
  disturbance, 55–57
  fields, 10
  free, 55
  group and individual, 45, 47–55, 90, 97–98
  hierarchy, 1, 10, 12, 16–18, 24, 41–42, 45, 48, 62–63
  idiosyncratic and individual, 10, 13, 42, 50–55, 60–62, 75, 79
  instructions, change in, 62–63
  manic-depressive, 52
  and needs, 58–63
  norms, 48–55
  psychotic, 48–55, 182
  remote, 15, 23–24, 42, 45, 177
  similarity, 186–187
  structure, 41, 47, 62–72, 79
  subordinate and superordinate, 100–101
  verbal, 41, 79, 98, 126, 158
  weak, 13–15, 17, 23, 62, 81
  word, 10–11, 29, 31, 42–43, 47–72, 73–79, 90–91, 93–96, 103, 126–127, 145, 152, 155, 183

Index

ATKINSON, J. W., 62, 227, 234
Auditory
  modality, 160, 161
  verbal discharge, 159, 161
  verbal quality, 172
Autism, 27–28
Autoplastic operations, 176
Awareness in verbal reinforcement, 36–38

B

BACON, 118
BALDWIN, M. V., 59–62, 228
BALLY, 10
BARCLAY, W. D., 49, 228
BASILIUS, H., 71, 112, 227
BATESON, M. C., 235
BENTLEY, M., 62, 227
BERKO, J., 18, 228
BETZ, W., 113, 227
BIFRUN, 123
BIRDWHISTELL, R., 227
Black, 40, 42–45, 66–71, 98, 133, 193
BLISS, J., 229
BLOCH, B., 22, 227
BLOOMFIELD, L., 22, 228
Body, 81, 114, 118–119, 151
  categories, 188, 199–200, 224
  damage, 167, 168
  experience, 185
  and language, 173–177
  needs, 81, 173, 216
BORDEAUX, J., 168, 234
BOUSFIELD, W. A., 35, 40–41, 49, 63–67, 71, 124, 228
BREUER, J., 157, 160, 228
BROWN, R. W., 18, 112, 228
BROZEK, J., 59–62, 75, 228
BUCK, C.D., 114, 228–229

C

CAGNEY, J., 132, 146
CAMERON, N., 229, 232
CANTRIL, H., 227
CARMICHAEL, L., 234
CARNAP, R., 22, 229
CARROLL, J. B., 112, 229
CASAGRANDE, J. B., 112, 229
CASSIRER, E., 27, 29, 101–103, 109–112, 174–175, 229
Catastrophic reaction, 167, 171
Categories
  definitions and descriptions of, 189–216

Categories (*cont.*)
  dictionary of, 183
  and experience, 101–103, 112, 185, 186
  hierarchy, 73, 76, 81
  list of, 188–189
  and meaning, 184
  principles underlying, 183–188
  in Schreber's language, 149–152
  scoring, 216–225
  structure, 90, 91, 180, 182
  superordinate, 64–66, 72, 89, 186
  word, 63–74, 90–91, 94–97, 100, 103, 116, 120–124, 126, 148, 179–182, 184–185
Catharsis, 157, 160
Cathexis, 160, 164–166, 177, 178
CATTELL, 55
Censorship, 77–79, 150
CHASE, S., 42, 229
Child, 16–18, 27–28, 30, 119, 128, 140, 144–147, 151, 182, 185, 198, 212, 216, 220. *See also* Association, Language, Body, experience
CLARK, R. A., 62, 229, 234
COBB, S., 234
COFER, C. N., 41, 64, 98, 124, 229, 231–232
COHEN, B. H., 35, 40, 63–64, 71, 228
Communication, 3–4, 12–13, 15, 23–27, 80–81, 83–85, 87, 90, 100, 109, 111, 117, 130, 139, 143, 148, 157, 178–179, 205. *See also* Speech
Compleat Angler, 117
Complex, psychological, 55–57
Condensation, 29, 78, 177
Conditioning, 36, 39, 163
CONKLIN, H. C., 22, 229
Connotation, 19, 22–27, 38–40, 121, 184
Consciousness, 83–84, 111, 122, 172. *See also* Language
  and attention, 161, 172
  and memory, 161–162
  and pain, 172
  sense organ as, 159
Contextual analysis. *See* Association, Language, Government, *England* and *English*
Contiguity, 98–100, 126
Cora Indian, 102–103
COWAN, T. M., 228
CRANSTON, R., 59–62, 228
CROSLAND, H. R., 55, 229

Culture, 25, 28, 38, 48, 102, 112, 122, 124, 127, 145, 157, 176

D

DANICK, J. J., 41, 64–67, 228
Death, 29, 44, 45, 114, 118, 133, 135, 141
  as category, 188, 195, 217, 219, 222–224
DEESE, J., 35, 41, 47, 64–67, 71, 98, 124, 229
DELAGUNA, G. A., 26, 229
Dementia praecox. *See* Association
Denotation, 23–24, 27, 38–40, 42, 186
Dictionary, 9–10, 21, 185. *See also* Categories
  conceptual, 114–124
Displacement, 78, 177
DIVEN, K., 57, 229
DOLLARD and MILLER, 37
Donne, Life of, 117
Dream, 17, 27, 214. *See also* Language, Word, Speech
  distortions and primary process, 29, 78
  interpretation, 77–78, 125, 159, 164
  work, 109, 164
DULANY, D. E., JR., 37, 229
DUNN, S., 229

E

Ego, 159, 172
Ellipsis, 83
Emperor of Tartary, 5–6, 165
EMPSON, W., 24, 230
Energy, psychic, 158, 160–161, 163, 165–166, 173
England and *English,* contextual analysis, 132, 138–146
Entropy, 94–95, 180–181
Equivalence principle, 102
ERICKSON, M. H., 57, 232
ERIKSON, E. H., 176, 230
ESPER, E. A., 49, 230
Experience, 4–6, 10, 15, 18, 23, 27, 41–42, 186–187. *See also* Language, Thing
  communal, 48, 164–166
  dimensions of, 175–176
  epigenesis, 176
  and memory, 117
  and naming, 175
  structure of, 176, 182
  verbal component, 162

F

Fault, response. *See* Speech, Response
FELDMAN, S., 66–71, 90–95, 103, 234
FERENCZI, S., 173–174, 226, 230
FERMIN, M. H. J., 115, 123, 230
Field
  linguistic, 124
  reference, 158, 184
  semantic, 112
  theory, linguistic, 71, 112–115
FISHMAN, J. A., 112, 230
FLECHSIG, DR., 151–156
FLIESS, R., 238
FOAKES, R. A., 118, 230
Food, 11, 14, 16–17, 30, 72, 75, 114, 118–119, 198, 217
  responses, 58–62, 101
FRAZER, J. G., 29, 230
FREUD, S., 3–4, 17, 27, 29, 34, 55, 77–78, 83, 109, 111, 157–178, 195–196, 227–228, 230–231. *See also* Language, psychoanalytic theory of; Aphasia; Word, and thing; D. P. SCHREBER

G

GALTON, 55
GELLHORN, E., 62, 231
Gesture, 109, 173, 174
Gibberish, 84–87, 168
GILL, M. M., 49, 57, 75, 166, 231, 237
GIPPER, H., 238
Glossolalia, 87–88
God, 133, 140, 144, 150–156, 169–171, 210
GOLDSTEIN, K., 112, 167, 231
GONZALES, R. C., 64, 98, 231
GOODENOUGH, W. H., 22, 231
GOTTSCHALK, L. A., 235
Government, contextual analysis, 132–137, 140–147, 178
Grammar, 3, 9–10, 21, 38, 50, 55, 90, 132, 146, 184, 187, 201, 213
GRANT DUFF, I. F., 226, 231
GRAY, L. H., 25–26, 231
GREENACRE, P., 225, 231
GREENBERG, J. H., 20–21, 231
GUETZKOW, H., 59–62, 228
Gulliver's Travels, 120–121, 220–226
GUNTERT, H., 121

H

HALL, R. S., JR., 9, 231

HALLIG, R., 71, 112, 114, 184–185, 231
Hallig and Wartburg conceptual dictionary, 121–124
HARMON, H. H., 67, 231
HARRIS, Z. S., 21–22, 232
HARTLEY, E. L., 229
Harvard Society of Fellows, 42
HASSOL, L., 232
HAYAKAWA, S. I., 42, 232
HAYES, A. S., 235
HEBB, D., 63–64
HEINEMAN, C., 47, 49, 237
HERDER. *See* VON HERDER
HIORTH, F., 232
HOCKETT, CHARLES F., 20
HOIJER, H., 20, 232
HOLT, R. R., 159, 165–166, 232
Homonym, 78, 186
Homosexual, 13–14, 131, 149, 151, 211
HORAN, E. M., 53, 232
HOUTCHENS, H. M., 57, 233
HOWES, D., 90, 232
HULL, C. L., 56, 232
HUMBOLDT. *See* VON HUMBOLDT
HUMPHREY, G., 19, 232
Hunger, 75–76, 216
and association, 58–62
HUNTER, R. A., 234. *See also* D. P. SCHREBER
HUSTON, P. E., 57, 232
Hysteria, hysterical, 137, 142, 157, 160–161, 167, 173

I

Id, 159
Idiolect, 9, 11–12, 16, 47, 98
Idiomatic expressions and phrases, 217–218
Information, mathematical, 94–95, 180–182
Intention, 11, 37, 74–75, 79–83, 88, 90, 116, 184
Intrusion, 81–82, 89, 93
pathological, 31, 182
verbal, 64
IPSEN, GUNTHER, 112

J

JENKINS, J. J., 62, 228, 232, 237. *See also* Russell-Jenkins list
JENKINS, P. M., 41, 232
JOHNSON, P. O., 153, 232
JONES, E., 79, 232

JOOS, M., 22, 232
JUNG, C. G., 49, 55–57, 232–233

K

KANTOR, J. R., 25–26, 233
KAPLAN, A., 20–21
KAPLAN, B., 28, 34–35, 233, 239
KAPLAN, E., 53, 239
KASANIN, J., 231, 233, 239
KELLER, H. E., 115, 123, 233
KENT, G. H., 233
Kent-Rosanoff list, 17–18, 38, 43, 49–54, 57, 59–60, 90
KEPHART, N. C., 57, 233
KINCAID, W. D., 228
Kinesthetic modality, 4, 159–160, 165, 175
KOHS, S. C., 56, 233
KOLB, D., 62, 238
KORZYBSKI, A., 42, 233
KRAINES, S. H., 62, 231
KRASNER, L., 36, 233
KRIS, E., 159, 233
KROUT, M. H., 233
KUBIE, L. S., 173, 233

L

LAFFAL, J., 30, 35, 49, 66–71, 82–83, 90–95, 103, 148, 150, 153, 155, 158, 178–181, 233–234, 239
LANGER, S. K., 109, 234
Language. *See also* Body, Meaning
anthropological studies, 22
in the child, 27–29, 36, 109–111. *See also* Language, development
collective, 10–11
common, 7, 9
communal, 1, 3, 28, 113, 166, 178
community, 166
and consciousness, 157–167
consensual, 6–7, 9, 164, 166
contextual analysis of Schreber's, 149–156
contextual analysis of the word, 132, 137–148, 178
creative, 15
description and scoring of categories, 188, 191, 204–205, 206, 210, 219, 223–224
development, 157–158, 171–176
disturbance and distortion, 12–14, 23, 50, 83–88, 125–126, 147, 158
in dreams, 166
egocentric, 28

Language (*cont.*)
 energy discharge, 160–161
 evocative and emotive, 23, 25, 39
 and experience, 4–6, 97, 101–103, 112–124, 175, 177
 as expression, 24–25, 35
 failure, 167, 171
 free flowing, 182, 186
 idiosyncratic, 28, 152, 164, 166
 imitative tendency, 16, 171–172
 as interpersonal behavior, 24–27, 35
 and magic, 27–29, 35, 101–102, 177
 mentalistic view of, 25–27
 and mother, 145–148, 178
 and myth, 27, 101–102, 109, 111
 normal, 15
 and primary process, 164–166, 177
 psychoanalytic theory of, 157–178
 psychological study of, 1–2, 9, 18–19, 22, 24–25, 124, 185–186
 rational functions of, 24–27
 response, 1, 9–10, 15
 sample, 183–185, 224
 in schizophrenia and psychosis, 15, 27–35, 42, 83–87, 124–127, 131–132, 157–158, 166, 176–182, 184
 science of. *See* Semiotic
 and secondary process, 164, 166, 177
 stimulus, 1, 9–10, 13, 42
 structure, 21, 96, 113, 157–158, 176, 178, 182
 theory, 19, 20, 24
 and thought, 109–113, 157, 160, 162
 and unconscious, 158–167
 Watson's theory of, 162–163
 written, 30, 184, 204–205
Langue, la, 6–12, 14, 42, 47–48, 97–98, 111, 157, 164, 166, 177, 184
Latent content, 78, 125–127
LATIF, I., 173, 234
LENKOSKI, L. D., 30, 83, 103, 234
LENNEBERG, E. H., 112, 228, 234
Lexicology, 22, 114
Linguist, 6, 9, 20–22, 112, 115, 121
Linguistic, 12, 20–22, 28, 114–115, 124, 157. *See also* Field theory
LONGERICH, M. C., 168, 234
LORENZ, M., 234
LORGE, I., 90, 238. *See also* Thorndike-Lorge list
LOUNSBURY, F. G., 22, 234
LOWELL, F., 54, 240. *See also* Woodrow-Lowell list

LUGOFF, L. S., 56, 232
LURIA, A. R., 57, 234

M

MACALPINE, I., 234. *See also* D. P. SCHREBER
MACCOBY, E. E., 229
MACLAY, H., 234
Macroseme, 217
MAGARET, A., 232
Magic, 44, 173–175, 214. *See also* Language, Word
MAHL, G. F., 235
Manic-depressive. *See* Association
Manifest content, 78, 125
MARBE, K., 48, 49
MARLOWE, 118
MATORE, G., 114, 235
MCCARTHY, D., 234
MCCLELLAND, D. C., 62, 227, 234
MCQUOWN, N. A., 235
Meaning, 1–2, 13–14, 19–45, 99, 109, 111–112, 114, 121, 139, 142, 147, 177, 186–188, 211, 217–218, 220
 associative, 65–66, 103, 126, 148, 168
 communal, 88
 and essence, 101–102
 field of, 112–113
 idiosyncratic, 177
 and linguistics, 20–22
 and mediational process, 35, 38–40
 and predication, 38, 40
 psychological views of, 20, 35
 and verbal association, 35, 40–42, 45
 and verbal reinforcement, 35–38
 and work of language, 19–20, 24
Mediational theory. *See* Meaning
Mentalistic view. *See* Language
Metaphor, 23, 43, 102–103, 109, 117, 208, 214
Metonymy, 23
MEZGER, F., 114–115, 235
MILLER, G. A., 35, 235
Mnemic residues, 159–160. *See also* Speech
Moon, 103, 118, 156, 191
MOORE, O. K., 236
MORRIS, C., 19, 22, 235
Motivation, 11, 15, 18, 36, 62, 75, 77, 79, 83, 111, 117, 157–158, 167
MOWRER, O. H., 38, 40, 235
MURPHY, G., 52, 235

Myth, 101–103, 109, 156. *See also* Language

N

NAESS, A., 99–101, 235
Name and essence, 101–109
Names, proper, and titles, 218–219
Nature, 26, 102, 114–115, 118, 122, 123, 185
Need, 5, 12–18, 26, 28–29, 72, 76–77, 79, 81, 83, 88–89, 112, 173, 176–177, 182. *See also* Association
  description and scoring of category, 189, 215–216
Negation, 16, 34, 187
  description and scoring of category, 83, 189, 207–208, 214, 221, 223, 225
Neologism, 84, 132
NEWCOMB, T. M., 229
New Haven Register, 87–88, 235
Nicholas Nickleby, 5, 165
NIDA, E. A., 216–217, 235
NIEDERLAND, W. G., 151, 154, 236
NOBLE, C. E., 35, 41, 236
Normal individuals, 14, 17–18, 147

O

Object concept, 158. *See also* Thing
O'CONNOR, J., 60, 236
OGDEN, C. K., 2–3, 25–26, 39, 187, 236
ÖHMAN, S., 71, 236
OLMSTED, D. L., 236
Operant behavior, 36, 43
Opposite speech, 16, 30–35, 83–84, 103
Opposition, 10, 14–15, 38, 74, 122, 132, 146, 187, 195, 199, 202, 207–208, 215, 217
OSGOOD, C. E., 35, 38–40, 231, 234, 236
Overlap coefficient, 65–71, 91

P

Parapraxes, 77, 158
Parole, la, 6–12, 164
Phenomenological world view, 122–124
Phonetics, 114
PIAGET, J., 27–29, 109–111, 174, 185, 236
PITTENGER, R. E., 236
Poet, poetry, 23–25, 45, 117, 120

Polyseme, 187
Pragmatics, 22–24
Preconscious, 158–160, 164–165. *See also* Language, and consciousness
PREUSS, 102
PRICE, L., 44, 236
Primary process, 29, 77–79, 83, 109, 111, 166, 175, 182. *See also* Language
Primitive, 28, 101–103, 109–110, 175
PRONKO, N. H., 26, 236
Pronoun, scoring of, 140, 203–204, 208, 211, 218–220
Psychoanalysis. *See* Language, Freud, Primary process, Dream
Psychosis, psychotic, 5–6, 12–13, 23, 30–31, 35, 108, 125, 148–149, 178–179, 182. *See also* Language
PUFF, C. R., 228

Q

QUINE, W. V. O., 236

R

RAPAPORT, D., 49, 57, 75, 79, 159, 237–238
Reality, 5–6, 9, 12–13, 15, 87, 110, 121, 160, 166, 172, 176–178. *See also* Word
Regression, 176
Reinforcement, 16, 43, 81, 173
Religion, 31, 87, 88, 115, 117, 119, 131, 138, 144–145, 148, 210
Repression, 34, 83, 162, 172
  in aphasia, 167
Response
  category of, 81
  fault, 49–50, 77, 83, 89
  frequency, 48–49
  hierarchy, 12–13, 19, 41–42, 76, 81–83, 94–95
  idiosyncratic, 12. *See also* Association, idiosyncratic and individual
  latency, 49–50
  strength, 12, 41, 49, 64, 72–73, 81–82
REUNING, K., 112, 114, 237
RICHARDS, I. A., 2–3, 25–26, 39, 236
ROBY, T. B., 62, 234
ROGET, P. M., 121, 186, 237
Roget's thesaurus, 38, 115–117
ROSANOFF, A. J., 52–54, 233, 237. *See also* Kent-Rosanoff list
ROSANOFF, I. R., 52–54, 237

Rosen, E., 47, 237
Russell, W. A., 47, 237
Russell-Jenkins list, 11, 17, 42–43, 65–66, 73–74

S

Salzinger, K., 36, 237
Sanford, R. N., 58–62, 237
Sapir, E., 237
Sartre, 117
Saussure, F. De, 7–11, 63, 113, 164, 237
Schafer, R., 49, 57, 75, 237
Schilder, P., 159, 237
Schilpp, P. A., 234, 238
Schizophrenia, 4, 83–84, 166. *See also* Language
  case history, 30–31, 34–35, 127–131
  psychotherapeutic interview, 103–109
  psychotherapeutic treatment of, 14–15, 34–35, 84–87, 131–132, 148, 178–182
Schlosberg, H., 47, 49, 237
Schreber, D. P., 148–156, 179, 180, 186, 234, 237
Schulze, G., 235
Schwarz, H., 238
Sebeok, T. A., 231, 234–236
Secondary process, 78, 166. *See also* Language
Sedgewick, C. H. W., 228
Selfridge's, 45
Semantic differential, 38–40
Semantics, 20–24, 112, 114, 137, 143, 217
Semiotic, 22–24
Set, psychological, 73–77, 80–81, 90
Sex, 14–15, 31, 62, 84, 87, 204
  description and scoring of category, 189, 211, 216, 220, 225
Shakespeare, W., 117–120, 124
Shakow, D., 57, 232
Shannon, C. E., 94, 180, 238
Shevitz, R., 229
Sign, 4, 7, 10, 22, 24, 102, 159
  sign test, empirical, 153–154
Shpola, E., 62, 229, 238
Silberer, H., 79, 238
Simonini, R. C., Jr., 81, 238
Skinner, B. F., 19, 26, 35, 42–45, 238
Slip of the tongue, 78–79, 81
Smith, H. L., Jr., 236

Sound, 7, 16, 20–21, 25, 36, 75, 109, 116, 143, 172, 186, 201
  image, 7–8
Speaker, 1–3, 7, 9, 11, 16, 24–25, 36, 42, 45, 93–94, 185–186. *See also* Speech, free
  average, 122, 184
  native, 21
Speaking, 2–3, 7, 9–10, 140, 143, 178, 201
  circuit, 7
  cycle, 11
  in tongues. *See* Glossolalia
Speech, 9, 18, 20, 25–26, 139, 148–149, 159, 169, 179, 182, 185, 219. *See also* Catharsis, Opposite speech
  category of, 204–205
  as communication, 172–173
  development, 172, 174
  as discharge, 162, 172–173
  disturbance and distortion, 73, 79–88, 125
  in dreams, 164
  egocentric, 109–111
  faults, 79
  free, 73–96, 103, 145, 183
  inner, 109, 111
  and mnemic residue, 159
  motor aspect, 162
  normal, 88
  organ, 177
  psychology of, 7, 26
  schizophrenic, 29, 177
  stereotypy, 129
  structure, 73, 88–96
  and thought, 160–162
Spence, N. C. W., 238
Spider and *scorpion,* responses to, 43–45
Spitz, R., 83, 173, 238
Spurgeon, C., 117–121, 123–124, 238
Staats, A. W., 35, 238
Stimulus
  intrusive, 12–13
  irrelevant, 13, 79, 80
Strachey, J., 227
Suci, G. J., 35, 38, 236
Sun, 103, 118, 191, 202, 216
  symbolism, 149–156
Swift, J., 120–121, 220–226
Symbol, symbolism, 1–3, 17, 25, 27, 35, 77–79, 109–110, 125, 182. *See also* Sun, God, Verbal
  body, 174
  psychoanalytic definition, 78–79

Syncretism, 28–29, 109–111
Synecdochy, 214
Synonymy, 75, 97–101, 126, 177, 184, 187
Syntactic, 18, 22, 114
Syntagm, 9–10

T

Table, 11, 16–18, 42–43, 48, 64, 72–75, 98, 100–101, 202
Tannenbaum, P. H., 35, 38, 236
Tausk, V., 176–177, 238
Thesaurus, 114. *See also* Roget's thesaurus
Thing. *See also* Word
  concept, 3
  idea of, 158, 166
  presentation, 41, 158, 162, 164–165
  representation, 3–7, 9, 29, 41
Thomas, D., 23, 238
Thorndike, E. L., 238
Thorndike-Lorge list, 49, 63, 90
Thought, in psychoanalytic theory, 160–163
Thumb, A., 48
Tinsley, Sister L., 114, 238
Trager, G. L., 22, 227
Trier, J., 71, 112–113, 238

U

Ullmann, S., 9–10, 21, 112–113, 117, 156, 187, 218, 238
Unconscious, 4, 29, 56–57, 78, 212. *See also* Language
Urban, W. M., 238

V

Verbal. *See also* Association, Aphasia, Auditory, Experience, Meaning
  behavior, 15, 36–37, 42–43
  communication, 205
  habit, 163
  modality, 160, 165
  motor aspect, 161
  operant conditioning, 37
  organization, 163
  reasoning and thought, 109, 111
  reinforcement, 36–37
  residue, 160
  response, 1, 10–16, 24, 36–37, 40, 42, 45, 93–96
  stimulus, 1, 10–14, 19, 23, 90
  structure, 11
  symbolic function, 173

Verbalization, 4, 14, 16, 23, 36, 43, 45, 125, 163, 171, 185
  and pain, 172
  and quality, 160, 172
Visceral organization, 163
Visual modality, 159, 160, 165, 210
Vocabulary, 18, 88–89, 123–124, 176, 178, 180, 185, 187
  and culture, 112, 115
  free flowing, 178
  patterns, 89, 182
  sample, 185
  structure, 66, 72, 113, 121–122, 182
  total analysis, 183
Voice, 30, 204
  active and passive, 213
Von Domarus, E., 83, 238
Von Herder, J. G., 112
Von Humboldt, W., 112
Vygotsky, L., 28, 110–112, 239

W

Wage, 123
Walker, W. N., 62, 238
Walton, I., 117
Warren, H. C., 98, 100, 239
Wartburg, W. V., 71, 112, 114–115, 121–124, 184–185, 231, 239. *See also* Hallig
Watson, D. L., 239
Watson, J. B., 162–163, 239. *See also* Language
Weaver, W., 94, 180, 238
Weinreich, U., 40, 239
Weisgerber, L., 112, 239
Wepman, J. M., 167, 239
Werner, H., 28, 34–35, 53, 175, 239
Wertheimer, 55
Wheat, L. B., 54, 239
White, W. A., 83, 239
White, 40, 42–43, 66–71, 193
Whitehead, A. N., 42–45
Whitmarsh, G. A., 35, 40–41, 64–67, 228
Whorf, B. L., 25, 112, 239
Wispe, L. G., 61–62, 239
Woodrow, H., 54, 240
Woodrow-Lowell list, 17–18, 52, 54
Woods, W. L., 83, 240
Woodworth, R. S., 48–49, 55, 240
Word. *See also* Categories, Association
  category scoring of, 189–216
  commonality, 126
  compound and combinations, 216–217, 219

Word (*cont.*)
concept, 3, 158
context, 89, 97, 103. *See also* Association, Language
in dreams, 164, 177
endocentric and exocentric combinations, 216–217
grouping, 184
idea of, 158, 166–167
image, 7
magic, 174–175
meaning, 113–114, 121–122, 184
obscene, 130, 138, 141
presentation, 158, 160, 162, 164, 166, 177–178

Word (*cont.*)
and reality, 27–29, 177–178
representation, 4–7, 41
in schizophrenia, 177–178
similarity, 78, 97–102, 124, 126, 186
stimulus, 11, 13–14, 17–18, 39, 41, 91–96, 98, 218
substitute, 41, 145, 162, 177
and thing, 1–6, 16, 24, 27, 29, 41–42, 178
WUNDT, 55

Z

ZIPF, G. K., 240
Zwischenwelt, 112, 115, 124